WILDLIFE IN EDUCATION:

A Guide for the Care and Use of Program Animals

Compiled and
edited by
Gail Buhl
and
Lisa Borgia

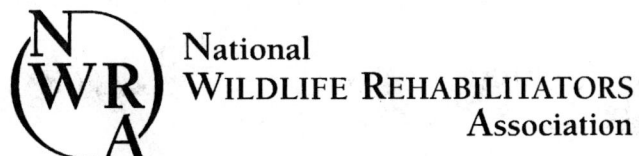

National WILDLIFE REHABILITATORS Association

Copyright © 2006 By National Wildlife Rehabilitators Association

About the Organization

The National Wildlife Rehabilitators Association (NWRA) was created in 1982 at the first national wildlife rehabilitation symposium held in Naperville, IL. The consensus at the symposium was that wildlife rehabilitation had evolved to a level demanding the establishment of a communication network, general operating procedures, standards, ethics and professional consultation.

The NWRA is incorporated for the support of the science and profession of wildlife rehabilitation and its practitioners. Wildlife rehabilitation is the treatment and temporary care of injured, diseased and displaced indigenous wildlife and the subsequent return of healthy animals to appropriate habitats in the wild. The NWRA's purposes are:

1. To foster continued improvement of the profession of wildlife rehabilitation through the development of high standards of practice, ethics and conduct;
2. To encourage networking and disseminate knowledge;
3. To engender cooperation among public and private agencies and individuals in support of its mission, and;
4. To foster respect for wildlife and natural ecosystems.

All Rights Reserved

Copyright © 2004, by the National Wildlife Rehabilitators Association. All rights reserved. Individual pages or sections, not to exceed five pages, of this work may be quoted or copied for purposes of research, rehabilitation, or education as long as attribution is displayed, clearly showing footers and page numbers.

Opinions expressed by the authors do not necessarily imply endorsement by the National Wildlife Rehabilitators Association. Although every step is taken to assure quality, publishing an author's works in no way guarantees accuracy, reliability or completeness of any of the facts, opinions, recommendations, information, statements, or data contained therein by the NWRA, its editors, reviewers, publishers and/or any other official representatives of the organization.

Preferred Citation:

Buhl, Gail and Lisa Borgia, Editors. 2004. *Wildlife in Education: A guide for the care and use of program animals.* National Wildlife Rehabilitators Association, St Cloud, MN. 162 pages.

First Edition published 2004
Second Printing 2006
Third Printing 2008

ISBN 1-931439-14-1

National Wildlife Rehabilitators Association
2625 Clearwater Road, Suite 110
St. Cloud, MN 56301-4539 USA
320-230-9920
nwra@nwrawildlife.org
www.nwrawildlife.org

TABLE OF CONTENTS

TABLE OF CONTENTS iii
LIST OF TABLES iv
ACKNOWLEDGEMENTS vi
CODE OF ETHICS vii
MESSAGE FROM EDUCATION COMMITTEE viii
STATEMENT OF PURPOSE ix
INTRODUCTION x

Chapter 1 ~ BASIC GUIDELINES FOR THE CARE OF EDUCATION ANIMALS 1
   Facilities 1
   General Management 2
   Training 2
   Shows and Programs 3
   Medical Care 3
   Staffing 3

Chapter 2 ~ RECORDKEEPING 5
   Required Recordkeeping for Permits 5
   Suggested Recordkeeping 5

Chapter 3 ~ GENERAL CARE 7
   Caging and Enclosures 7
      Design Considerations 7
      Construction 9
   Flooring 10
   Flooring Substrate 12
   Walls and Rooftop 14
   Cage Furniture 16
      Perches 16
      Hutches 17
      Water and Food Containers 17
      Plants 17
      Other Cage Furniture 17
   Water and Food 18
   Grooming and Bathing 19
      Bathing Water 19
      Sand and Dust Baths 20

Chapter 4 ~ CLEANING AND DISINFECTION 23
   Types of Cleaning Agents 23
   Properties of Disinfectants 26

Chapter 5 ~ REPTILES AND AMPHIBIANS 29
   Housing 29
   Feeding of Reptiles and Amphibians 32
      Live Food 32
      Non-Live Foods 34
      Vitamins and Minerals 34
      Water 34
   Using the Education Animal 35
      Amphibians 36
      Snakes 36
      Turtles 37
      Lizards 37
      Transport of Reptiles and Amphibians 37
   Species Choice and Suitability 38
      Turtles 38

	Snakes	39
	Lizards	40
	Amphibians	41
	Not Recommended for Education Programs	42

Chapter 6 ~ BIRDS 43
- Suitability of Species 43
- Raptors 45
  - Housing 45
  - Feeding 51
  - Cleaning 51
  - Handling and Transport of Birds for Programs 52
- Waterbirds 54
- Passerines and Miscellaneous Avian Families 59

Chapter 7 ~ MAMMALS 67
- Overview 67
- Housing 70
- Feeding 72
- Cleaning 72
- Handling and Transport 72

Chapter 8 ~ TRANSPORTATION 75
- Overview 75
- Special Requirements 76

Chapter 9 ~ LEGALITIES AND LIABILITIES 79
- Permits, Ordinances, and Courtesies 79

Chapter 10 ~ ANIMAL HEALTH 83
- Mental Health 83
- Physical Health 88

Chapter 11 ~ ANIMAL SELECTION 91
- Animal Criteria 91
- Handler Requirements 92

Chapter 12 ~ TRAINING 93

Chapter 13 ~ SAFETY 95
- Physical Safety 95
- Zoonotic Disease Control 96
- Zoonotic Diseases 97

Chapter 14 ~ PRESENTATION THEORY AND DESIGN 105
- Some Techniques to use in Educational Programs 107
- Presenter Etiquette 108

Chapter 15 ~ DISPOSAL OF CARCASSES AND WASTE PRODUCTS 111

APPENDICES 113
- **Appendix A** ~ Association Contact Information 113
- **Appendix B** ~ Federal, Provincial, State, Airline and Other Contact Information ... 119
- **Appendix C** ~ Forms 127
- **Appendix D** ~ Manufacturer's Information 147
- **Appendix E** ~ Example of Education Animal Record Set 149
- **Appendix F** ~ Zoonoses 157

List of Tables

Table 1 – Enclosure Construction *9*

Table 2 – Outdoor Cage Floors *10*

Table 3 – Indoor Flooring *11*

Table 4 – Outdoor Caging Substrate *12*

Table 5 – Indoor Caging Substrate *13*

Table 6 – Outdoor Roof and Wall Construction *15*

Table 7 – Cleaning and Disinfection Common Terms *23*

Table 8 – Properties of Disinfectants *26*

Table 9 – General Raptor Categories *45*

Table 10– Opening Sizes for Mesh or Bars on a Raptor Cage *46*

Table 11– Minimum Enclosure Sizes for Raptors in Captivity *47*

Table 12 – Recommended Perch Sizes for Captive Raptors *48*

Table 13– Recommended Minimum Shelter Box/Hutch Sizes

    for Captive Raptors *49*

Table 14– Recommended Outdoor Perch Design and Size

    for Tethering a Bird *50*

Table 15– General Nutrition for Raptors *51*

Table 16– General Descriptions of Common Equipment *52*

Table 17– Minimum Size Recommendations for Several

    Types of Raptor Transport Carriers *53*

Table 18– Minimum Housing Guidelines for Waterbirds used in Education *56*

Table 19– General Housing Requirements for Passerines used in Education *60*

Table 20– Injuries and Considerations *69*

Table 21– Minimum Housing Guidelines for Education Mammals *71*

Table 22– Enrichment Activities *84*

Editor's note: *This publication addresses those animals used in on-site and off-site education programming. Any cage sizes noted are a minimum size to be used when animals are not in transport carriers. This publication does not address animals used in static displays, which have much different requirements for permanent caging.*

Acknowledgements

There are so many people who helped on this project that I would like to acknowledge and thank. First, I would like to thank Ignacio Alonso, former NWRA board member and the author of the original draft of this book. I would also like to thank Diane Nickerson, chair of the NWRA Education Committee, who guided me throughout this process. She helped me with resources and provided encouragement to see this project to completion. Thanks to Bill Boesenberg, whose expertise in native reptiles and amphibians was invaluable. He graciously agreed to write the entire section on amphibians and reptiles for this book. I am indebted to Erica Miller, DVM, editor of the *Minimum Standards for Wildlife Rehabilitation, 3rd Edition*. The *Minimum Standards for Wildlife Rehabilitation* was the source of information on caging, disinfectants, disposal, and disease control included in this book.

A special thank you goes to all of the people that contributed many hours and expertise editing and reviewing this publication: Wendy Aeschliman, Carla Bascom, Lisa Borgia, Marlys Bulander, Sue Coulson, Mike Cox, Walter Crawford, Joanna Eckles, Harriet Forrester, Jaquie Genovesi, Kevin Hogan, Melissa Horton, Bea Orendorff, Stuart Porter, VMD, Amber Santangelo, Barbara Suto, Elaine Thrune, Florina S. Tseng, DVM, Linda Wolf, DVM, and Sandy Woltman.

I cannot express my gratitude enough to Jane Goggin, Brigid Pajunen, and Brad Johnson for their unending support in this project and help in organizing, researching, and editing. Many thanks to Kris MacPherson, whose expertise as a reference librarian was invaluable to the completion of this project.

Organizations that assisted in this project by giving permission to use their information or documents included: The Raptor Center at the University of Minnesota, Oregon Zoo's Discover Birds Show, The Minnesota Zoological Gardens Bird Show, Wolf Ridge Environmental Learning Center Raptor Program, The International Association of Avian Trainers and Educators, and the Minnesota Wildlife Assistance Cooperative.

A special thanks to the United States Fish and Wildlife Service, the United States Department of Agriculture, and the many state conservation agencies that shared information with us for the completion of this project.

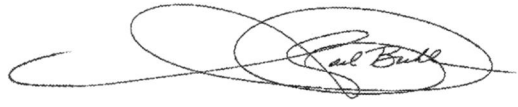

Layout and typesetting by Marc Daniloff and John Frink.

Editing and copyediting by Lisa Borgia and Diane Nickerson.

Funding for this book was made possible through the generous support of The Summerlee Foundation and the Kenneth A. Scott Charitable Trust, a KeyBank Trust.

A Wildlife Educator's Code of Ethics

- 1. A wildlife educator should strive to achieve high standards of animal care and programming through knowledge and training.

- 2. A wildlife educator should acknowledge limitations and enlist the assistance of a veterinarian or other trained professionals when appropriate.

- 3. A wildlife educator should respect other educators and persons in related fields, sharing skills and knowledge in the spirit of cooperation for the welfare of the animals.

- 4. The physical and mental well-being of each animal should be a primary consideration in management and presentation.

- 5. A wildlife educator should strive to provide professional and humane care for the animals in their care, respecting the wildness and maintaining the dignity of each animal in life and in death.

- 6. Non-releasable animals, which are inappropriate for education, foster parenting, or captive breeding have a right to euthanasia.

- 7. A wildlife educator must abide by local, state, provincial, and federal laws concerning wildlife and associated activities. Animals must be legally acquired with proper documentation. Animals transferred must go to legal and reputable facilities or individuals.

- 8. A wildlife educator should establish safe work habits and conditions, abiding by current health and safety practices at all times.

- 9. A wildlife educator should encourage community support and involvement through public education. The common goal should be to promote a responsible concern for living beings and the welfare of the environment.

- 10. A wildlife educator should work on the basis of sound ecological principles, incorporating appropriate conservation ethics and an attitude of stewardship.

- 11. A wildlife educator should conduct all business and activities in a professional manner, with honesty, integrity, compassion, and commitment; realizing that an individual's conduct reflects on the entire field of wildlife and environmental education.

Message from the NWRA Education Committee

WILDLIFE IN EDUCATION: *A Guide for the Care and Use of Program Animals* was born from the idea that *Minimum Standards for Wildlife Rehabilitation* was not intended to address those animals that were held beyond the normal scope of wildlife rehabilitation. Those animals needed special consideration and have unique husbandry requirements. Many years and many different drafts have evolved into this product.

This publication has been developed to assist the educator, who uses non-releasable animals in outreach education programming, to provide suitable habitats, appropriate living facilities, proper diets, and acceptable handling techniques for the animals in their care. This publication is not intended to address those animals on permanent display. Those animals have a different set of requirements based on individual need.

As is the case with *Minimum Standards*, this is not intended to be an enforcement program. Each state or province may or may not have their own requirements. Permit requirements vary widely. It is advised that anyone who intends to use live animals in outreach education programs, check with local, state, and federal agencies for appropriate permits and applicable regulations.

Wildlife in Education is also a complimentary publication to Introduction to Wildlife in Education Programming: *Tips and Techniques for a Better Presentation*. By using these together, it is hoped that wildlife rehabilitators will be assisted and guided in their educational endeavors.

We look forward to your comments and suggestions to improve both of these publications.

Diane Nickerson
Chair, NWRA Education Committee

Statement of Purpose

This book, *Wildlife in Education: A Guide for the Care and Use of Program Animals*, contains information for those rehabilitators and educators that would like to use permanently injured or otherwise non-releasable wildlife as a tool for their teaching efforts. This handbook to the minimum requirements on housing, feeding, training, and safety of these animals is designed to help answer questions about using wildlife for education. This information is to be used in conjunction with other research tools; specifically, books, articles, and the advice of experts in the field. Recognizing that these are minimum requirements, you are encouraged to build larger cages, and to ask others in the field for additional assistance and collaboration. Modifications to caging described in this book to accommodate the special needs of a new resident may be necessary. The authors stress that the comfort and safety of the animal, handler, and bystanders should be the first consideration in designing housing, handling techniques, and educational programs.

Most permanently injured wildlife cannot adapt to the stress associated with life in captivity, including the noises and smells associated with human activity and education programs. However, those animals that can adapt to life as an educator become ambassadors for the ecosystems from which they came. Their job becomes not only to "speak" for their species, but to act as a tangible connection to the natural world. That fragile connection may translate into political action, physical action, as in environmental protection, or it may encourage someone to slow down and enjoy the birds singing in their backyard. If the educational animal can help accomplish any, or even a part, of these things, then the animal's efforts have been successful.

While addressing housing, feeding, training, and safety for animals that are used in on-site and off-site educational programs, this text does not address using animals in any static display environments such as one would see at a zoo facility. The information in this book applies to animals either handled directly by a handler in front of a group or shown in a smaller container in a program setting. As we learn more about how to use wildlife in education, this book will change and expand to contain that new knowledge. We encourage feedback from the users of this book.

Wildlife in Education: *A Guide for the Care and Use of Program Animals* is not a tool for enforcement or any enforcement program. Each state, provincial, and federal agency may or may not have requirements regarding animals held for educational purposes, and what facilities or qualifications are needed to hold these animals for educational use.

Information about using wildlife in education programs is always changing. NWRA invites you to make suggestions for the improvement of this publication. Please use the enclosed reader evaluation form, or contact us at NWRA Central Office, 2625 Clearwater Road, Suite 110, St Cloud, MN 56301, or email nwra@nwrawildlife.org.

INTRODUCTION

"We will only conserve what we love, love what we understand, and understand what we are taught" –Baba Dioum

Many people educate others of all ages about our natural world and ways to conserve it for future generations. One way educators teach about the world, both locally and globally, is through the use of live animals in classrooms and presentations. Correctly used, live animals may make an important ecological point—or better yet—spark wonder about the world beyond the backyard in the hearts of youngsters.

While mammals, birds, reptiles, or amphibians may be effective tools for education, they are but one among many. Live animals come with many more responsibilities than nonliving tools like bone, skin, or a skull will ever entail. Anytime a naturalist, wildlife rehabilitator, or school teacher decides to keep and use live animals as part of their teaching repertoire, an unwritten "contract" with that animal is made. This "contract" extends to students that are to be taught using live animal presentations as well.

Unspoken but required by the contract is that the animal "ambassador" should be cared for and presented with respect. This implied business arrangement requires that the safety of the audience and the animal be assured. Live animal presentations should be done ethically, compassionately, and truthfully. Proper care on and off stage, proper training, and correct conditioning will assure success for this ambassador for wildlife and conservation of wilderness. Even a small thing like taking an overnight trip becomes complicated when you have to find "wildlife babysitters" for your education animals.

Keeping your part of this contract is no small task, and should not be entered into lightly without thought or research. The authors designed this text to help you with that research. There is information to assist you in management, legalities, and species selection. There are references for endemic non-releasable wildlife for use in educational programming in public presentations. Specifically not covered is the use of animals in static display environments.

Step one is to decide whether having a live animal(s) for a program is appropriate. Artifacts, storytelling, slides, games, and hiking outside are examples of other effective tools for teaching about the environment. Live animals require specific care, regardless of what other tasks you may face each and every day. You will need to consider the following questions when deciding how appropriate a live animal is for your needs:

- Will this species enhance my programming on a particular subject?
- How much will it cost to maintain (cage, food, staff time, vet care, etc)?
- Does this animal potentially carry any zoonoses of which to be aware?
- Who will train and/or condition this animal?
- Who can I network with regarding the care and presentation of this species?
- Are permits required to have the animal?
- Who will care for the animal when I am not able?

Some animals simply are not appropriate educational animals. Particular species and occasional individual animals never adjust to a life in captivity. Some animals or species are dangerous in all but the most expert hands. Wildlife harbor diseases that can infect other animals and humans. Some of these zoonoses can be annoying at the very least, life threatening or fatal at the very worst.

Wildlife in Education: *A Guide for the Care and Use of Program Animals* should be used in conjunction with other resources regarding caring for and using wildlife in educational programs. Some sources of information are listed in the Appendices. Careful and thoughtful decisions need to be made before you receive an animal to use. This thoughtful consideration before committing to the responsibility of having a wild animal will help you wisely decide to enter into the unwritten contract that may last a very long time.

Chapter 1
BASIC GUIDELINES FOR THE CARE OF EDUCATION ANIMALS

These suggested guidelines were created to provide assistance for wildlife educators who manage and present animals in public programs. Because it is virtually impossible to make specific suggestions that can be applied to all of the animal species used in education programs, these guidelines are general in nature.

FACILITIES (MILLER 2000)

- **Comfort and health:** Both the physical and mental health of the animal should be taken into consideration when designing housing areas. Animals should be housed in facilities that are comfortable for the individual. What is comfortable for one animal (or species) may not be comfortable for another. Consider carefully what the natural history of the species and preferences of the individual are when determining appropriate housing.
- **Cleanliness:** A regular cleaning program that utilizes appropriate disinfectants should be established to keep the housing area free of unhealthy levels of fecal matter, bacteria, fungus, etc.
- **Predators and vermin:** Animals should be housed in facilities that provide protection from predators and vermin. Predators and vermin include any animal that may cause death, injury, stress, or risk of disease.
- **Feathers:** Birds should be housed in facilities that are designed to maintain the good condition of the bird's feathers. Bent, broken, frayed, or soiled feathers are often signs of inadequate housing conditions. Various bird species are more inclined to experience feather damage from contact with wire mesh enclosures. Vertical bar construction techniques are suggested as an option for these species.
- **Protection from the elements:** Animals should be housed in facilities that provide protection from direct sunlight, heat, cold, rain, snow, and other potentially harmful weather conditions. Check the animal's natural history information for what temperature ranges and humidity levels the animal can comfortably tolerate.
- **Enclosure size:** Free-lofted birds should be able to freely fly and move about to their individual ability within the enclosure. Mammals, reptiles, and amphibians should also be able to freely navigate throughout the enclosure and have enough room to stretch and move about in a normal fashion.
- **Tethered birds:** Tethered birds (raptors) should be kept in a space designed to allow for movement without physical damage.
- **Ventilation:** Indoor housing facilities should have good air circulation and ventilation to protect against the spread of disease.
- **Perches and cage furniture:** Animals should be provided with different types and sizes of perches and other cage furniture to help prevent foot problems, provide comfortable perching options, and mentally stimulate the animal.
- **Floors:** Housing areas should have floors that drain well and are easily disinfected. Animals should not come into contact with hard flooring surfaces if there is a possibility of such contact being detrimental to their feet or physical health. Substrates and floor coverings should be safe, appropriate for the species, and not promote unwanted growth of bacteria, fungus, or other organisms.
- **Security:** All housing should be designed to protect animals from theft, attack, and accidental escape. Double door construction and locks are recommended.

GENERAL MANAGEMENT (MILLER 2000)

- **Water:** All animals should have access to clean fresh water as needed in appropriate containers that facilitate drinking and bathing.
- **Diets:** Diets should be fresh, nutritional, and appropriate for the intended species.
- **Enrichment:** Animals should be provided with some form of enrichment on a regular basis. Enrichment is anything that enhances the environment and promotes physical or mental health. The natural history of the species and preferences of the individual should be studied when determining the appropriateness of the enrichment strategy. Enrichment is generally something that is positive for the animal to experience. Handling and human interaction may be considered enrichment. Enrichment items should be selected for safe use, designed carefully, and routinely inspected to prevent injury to the animal.
- **Equipment:** All equipment should be routinely inspected and kept in good condition to avoid injury or the opportunity for accidental escape. Only the safest, most reliable, and completely humane equipment should be used.
- **Transport containers:** Transport and temporary holding containers should be large enough to allow the animal to turn around comfortably. All containers should be well ventilated, routinely cleaned, and regularly disinfected. While in any container, animals should be protected from potentially harmful temperature extremes, escape, harassment, and theft. The animal should be trained to quietly remain in the container. Transportation using containers should be done in a manner that reduces stress, prevents physical damage, and minimizes anxiety for the animal. Temporary or transport containers are not acceptable as long-term housing.
- **Recordkeeping:** General recordkeeping, including information on husbandry, health, life history, and identification should be maintained for each animal.

TRAINING (IAATE)

- **Records:** Weights, observations, and training progress should be recorded for each animal on a regular basis.
- **Equipment:** All equipment should be monitored and maintained in good working condition. Scales should be kept clean and maintained in accurate working condition.
- **Feeding:** To avoid anxious behavior, animals should be fed out of sight of other animals whose weight is being managed. Food should be presented in a way that avoids contamination.
- **Weight:** Weight management should be done with great care and under the guidance of an experienced animal trainer. Animals should be treated as individuals; weights should be reevaluated and possibly adjusted according to age, climate, season, and other factors. Protocols should be established for weighing and recording the animal's weight at approximately the same time every day. After appropriate weighing behavior is learned, the animal's weight should be maintained at the highest level practical. The animal's weight should never be reduced to a level that compromises its health or welfare. Signs of low weight level in an animal include excessive vocalizing, mantling (raptors), aggression, lethargy, and other behaviors indicating discomfort.
- **Mental welfare:** Extreme care should be taken to avoid putting animals in situations that cause them prolonged anxiety, stress, or fear.
- **Methods:** Training should be based on positive reinforcement techniques.
- **Telemetry:** Devices that incorporate telemetry tracking are recommended when free-flying birds.
- **Fly-off and escape protocol:** A plan should be in place for the location and recovery of missing animals.
- **Jesses:** Jesses are used for raptor training. To avoid the possibility of becoming tangled on tree branches or other hazards, it is recommended that birds should not be flown with slits in jesses. Aylmeri jesses are recommended over traditional jesses (Arent and Martell 1996).

Chapter 1: Basic Guidelines for the Care of Education Animals

SHOWS AND PROGRAMS *(IAATE)*
- **Daily workload:** The number of programs each animal participates in should not compromise the health or welfare of an animal. The animal's behavior and/or weight can be used to indicate how many programs can be tolerated by that individual. Check with federal or state regulations on any limits regarding the number of programs in which an individual may or is required to participate.
- **Aggression:** Only experienced trainers should handle aggressive animals. Animals that exhibit aggressive tendencies towards humans should not be presented in close proximity to the audience. Animals should not be put in any situations where aggressive interactions with other animals may occur.
- **Content:** All public programs and appearances should have an educational intent or purpose. Presenters should not encourage people to obtain any wild animal as a pet, and should indicate when it is not legal or ethical to do so. Presenters should promote conservation of wildlife and protection of natural habitats.

MEDICAL CARE *(MILLER 2000)*
- **Veterinarian:** The people who are managing education animals should have access to a veterinarian who has agreed to assist in emergency situations, examinations, and periodic consultations prior to obtaining any education animal.
- **First Aid:** Staff should have a basic understanding of first aid. First aid kits for people and animals both should be available at all times and supplied with current materials.
- **Quarantine:** Quarantine procedures should be in place and practiced.
- **Emergency plan:** An emergency plan should be in place to deal with any disaster; including flood, fire, hurricane, and other events. This plan should detail information on care of your animals, safety of staff, and instructions to the public.
- **Prevention:** A preventative health care program for your animals should be in place.
- **Necropsies:** Necropsies are recommended for all animal fatalities.

STAFFING *(IAATE)*
- **Experience:** Only experienced handlers and trainers should be allowed to handle sensitive, aggressive, or difficult to handle animals.
- **Qualification:** All handlers and trainers will be completely trained by experienced staff before they handle and train animals.
- **Education:** All staff should stay current on the latest, safest, and the most effective training and husbandry practices applicable to all species in the collection.
- **Training protocol:** A written training protocol should be in place and utilized to train new staff.
- **Volunteers:** Volunteers should be fully trained by experienced staff before handling any education animal and should be monitored and evaluated by experienced staff. The safety of the volunteer should be considered, and the health and welfare of the animal assessed before allowing a new or untrained volunteer to work with the animals. Use your best judgment when allowing others to handle your animals.

Literature Cited

Arent, L., and M. Martell. 1996. *Care and Management of Captive Raptors.* St. Paul, MN: The Raptor Center

International Association for Avian Trainers and Educators (IAATE) 350 St. Andrews Fairway, Memphis, TN 38111. email: secretary@iaate.org   website: www.iaate.org

Miller, E. A., Ed. 2000. *Minimum Standards for Wildlife Rehabilitation, 3rd Edition.* St. Cloud, MN: National Wildlife Rehabilitators Association

Chapter 2

RECORDKEEPING

It is important to keep various records on individual animals when using wildlife in educational programs. Some documentation of activity, medical care, husbandry, and other types of records are required for permits. This ensures your ability to track an individual animal's health, training, and maintenance. Keeping good records, while time consuming, is a very important activity in the proper care an education animal.

"Currently, there are no actual federal migratory bird educational use permit regulations. The United States Fish and Wildlife Service (USFWS) presently issues these permits under 50 CFR 21.27, which provides for permits for purposes not otherwise provided for specifically in other permit regulations. This is the same miscellaneous permit category under which the USFWS issued rehabilitation permits before the creation of a separate regulation. For eagles, there are other regulations addressing collection of eagles from the wild for both scientific research purposes and for exhibition by museums and zoos. These regulations do not say anything in terms of required conditions for keeping and actually exhibiting captive eagles. That section is: 50 CFR 22.21. The USFWS intends on creating a new section of regulations for permits for migratory bird educational use in the same way the agency did for wildlife rehabilitation. The section we have tentatively reserved for the educational use regulations is 50 CFR 21.32, but it is not finalized" (Savage, Eliza, USFWS pers com).

REQUIRED RECORDKEEPING FOR PERMITS

The USFWS requires a yearly report on any programming activities for each bird under your Special Purpose Possession-Live 50 CFR 21.29 permit. The information required includes the number of programs, type of programs, number of people attending the programs, and who presented the programs using the bird(s). A separate form asking similar information is used in reporting activities involving bald or golden eagles (*Haliaeettus leucocephalus* and *Aquila chrysaetos*). No permits are required for exotic species.

Various states' wildlife and natural resources departments require similar information provided yearly to fulfill reporting requirements for their permits. Many times, the same information required by the USFWS permit is also required at the state level. Reporting may be as easy as providing the same information to both agencies, but confirm the specific requirements with your state permitting officer before the report(s) are sent.

Suggested Recordkeeping

It is recommended that at least a minimum amount of recordkeeping be done for each animal in your educational collection. This information should include where, when, and how you received the animal, from whom you received the animal, and why it is not releasable into the wild. Keeping background information on each animal is vital to the maintenance of the animal in captivity as well as the educational message for the audience (see Appendix C for sample forms).

The documentation of information required for permits can also be of benefit to your facility. For example, the data gathered on how many program attendees you educated in a year may increase your fundraising and grant writing success rate (see Appendix C for sample form).

Literature Cited

Savage, Eliza, USWFS Washington DC Migratory Bird Management Office, personal communication, January 2004.

Chapter 3

GENERAL CARE

Every living thing on this planet requires certain basic resources in order to survive, and all wild animals have specific fundamental needs. Shelter, food, water, space for nesting and resting, and access to conspecifics are ubiquitous requirements. Of course, different species require different amounts and types of these resources, but all animals require some amount in order to thrive. So regardless of the species chosen for your educational programming, the general care requirements for all captive animals will be similar. How these specific needs vary is addressed more closely in the specific care chapters for the different types of animals (NIH 1985).

CAGING AND ENCLOSURES

All education animals need a cage or enclosure that will be their "home" while not actively in a program or class. This space is usually not their transport enclosure (see Chapter 8, Transportation, for more detail on transportation enclosures) but a larger or different area where the individuals spend the majority of their time. This space may differ in size and shape depending on the species or individual housed, but will share some similar basic characteristics *(Miller 2000)*.

All enclosures will have sides, a top and a floor. The enclosure should have easy access for handling, cleaning, and feeding. The construction design and material selection depends on whether the enclosure is outside or inside, and what species of animal is confined. One of the best general sources of information for designing a cage is the animal's natural history. Compiling natural history information from several sources, such as books, publications, and direct communication with people that work or study the species, will give you a complete picture of that particular species' needs. Using natural history information during enclosure design will help to ensure a more comfortable new home for the individual.

This information will help you decide on what materials you should use, but more importantly should not use, for a particular species. For example, building a cage primarily out of wood for a rodent such as a squirrel, woodchuck, or beaver would be a mistake. It will not take long for those animals to gnaw their way right out of the enclosure!

DESIGN CONSIDERATIONS BASED ON NATURAL HISTORY

Where does the animal prefer to reside? For example, does the animal in nature choose a high, medium, or low place to construct a nest or lair? Perhaps it even burrows underground. The enclosure design must accommodate the animal's preference, if possible.

- What time of day is the animal active? Is the animal nocturnal, diurnal or crepuscular? This behavioral factor may influence design or placement of the enclosure.
- What types of perching substrate are preferred in the wild? Does the animal use ledges, tree branches, tree trunks, rocks, burrows, water, sand or some other perching substrate? Many animals, especially raptors, are sensitive to perching material and placement.
- What type of habitat does the animal use in the wild? Specifically, does it require a specialized habitat or is it adaptive to many types of habitat? Specialized caging requirements need to be identified as quickly as possible in the design process.
- How large is the home range for this animal in the wild? Does it require a large enclosure, and does the animal need to be in contact with conspecifics, or is solitary in the wild? Determine the proper enclosure size early in the design progression.

- How do the temperature and/or season affect the animal's behavior in the wild? For example, does this animal migrate, or possibly hibernate in the winter? Knowing this information will help you determine if you can have the enclosure entirely outside, or if you have to provide complete shelter during winter months.
- Are activity levels of the animal high, medium, or low? What is the general activity level of the animal's wild counterpart during different times of the day, season and year? You may possibly need two enclosures to accommodate your animal during different seasons.
- How do the different sexes of a species vary in activity level or habitat requirement? Is this a seasonal effect? The enclosure design for a male may be very different than the design for a female of the same species.

Understanding the physical and mental limitations of an individual animal is another useful guideline for enclosure design. Specifically, you need to assess the animals' capacity for the following characteristics:

- How does the animal normally move, and what limitations does it now have on locomotion? Specifically, does it fly, walk, or run normally, or is it impaired in one or more of these areas?
- Can the animal see? Vision impairments are important considerations of enclosure design. If the animal is blind in one or both eyes, or has limited vision in one or both eyes, the enclosure may need modifications.
- Has the animal been imprinted on humans or another species? Animals imprinted on humans may have special enclosure needs.

This type of information will guide modifications for the enclosure. Once the degree of impairment is understood, enclosure adjustments may include:

- How high the perches should/can be for animal safety,
- How much exposure the individual that is vision impaired should have to noise or human activity, and
- How large or small the cage should be. For example, if the animal is unable to fly, it may not be necessary to design a cage for full flight.

CAGING AND ENCLOSURES–SPECIFIC DESIGN CRITERIA

When doing any construction on your property, always consult the local zoning and building authorities. You may have to take out a building permit, conform to building codes, or accommodate other restrictions on your enclosure project. You should consult with an architect for permanent structures. For example, snow load, weather extremes, and soil conditions may all determine requirements needed to safely construct an enclosure.

People who are experienced with the species to be housed can suggest cage sizes, materials, and cage furnishings. Having the help of someone who has done a similar project before can be invaluable. There are many design considerations that require insight into long-term housing requirements. An experienced person has probably solved many of the problems found below. Each of these items is related to enclosure design at a different level, and many are addressed in more detail later in this chapter. The table below is offered as a starting point when considering specific enclosure design.

TABLE 1 – ENCLOSURE CONSTRUCTION

Design Element	Criteria
Cleaning	Enclosures should be easily cleaned on a routine schedule.
Maintenance	Enclosures should be constructed so they are structurally sound and can be maintained to contain the animal and protect from injury or escape.
Ventilation	Ventilation must be designed so the enclosure does not become too warm or conversely, too cold. Indoor and outdoor enclosures will have different construction requirements. Proper ventilation will minimize drafts, reduce odors, and reduce moisture condensation.
Water/electricity	Outdoor caging design must consider electricity or water service sources for the enclosure. service. If the service hookup is outside the cage, how will you bring it into the cage (i.e., water hose)? If the hookup is inside the cage, how will you protect the animal, or prevent the animal from using fixtures in a dangerous manner?
Water	Clean drinking water must be available in adequate amounts at all times. Containers may vary (shallow to deep containers; extra traction in dish, other variations) to accommodate the animal's disability. Special consideration for water is needed for cold climates, including heating, or modified consumption based on natural history information. Enclosure design must accommodate all water requirements.
Climate	The weather will affect outdoor structure design. For example, the direction of the prevailing winds will determine what direction the cage faces and what walls need to be solid to protect the animal from the elements.
Humidity and temperature	An animal that needs extra humidity or lower humidity may require indoor housing for at least part of the year. The temperature of indoor facilities should be regulated so it is compatible with the health and comfort requirements of the animal. Auxiliary ventilation should be used when the air temperature within the animal holding facilities is 75 degrees F or higher. The air temperature in an indoor animal holding area should never fall below 45 degrees F nor exceed 85 degrees F. Outdoor enclosures require the ability to provide adequate protection during temperature extremes.
Shelter	The enclosure must provide sufficient shelter for security, protection from stress and the elements (wind, cold, rain, snow, sun, heat), and include the following:
Secure doors	Enclosures must prevent escapes, prevent predators from entering, and prevent unwanted humans from entering the enclosure.
Shift areas	A shift area where the animals can be trained to enter and closed off from the main area can be constructed for human safety and security for the animal.
Floor	The floor must be of material that is easy to clean and appropriate for the species.
Roof	The roof must be constructed to withstand snow loads, slanted to shed snow, or slotted (1 x 2 in. [2.54 x 5.08 cm] openings) to allow snow to pass through. Do not shovel or blow snow from a roof that is not constructed to safely handle the additional weight.
Walls	The enclosure mesh size or spacing of bars must prevent escape or access by predators. Special attention is needed where the walls intersect the floor for escape prevention and predator protection design.
Natural light	The enclosure must provide an adequate amount of natural light. Full spectrum (UVB, UVA, visible light and infrared) lighting can be used. The need for full spectrum lighting varies for species, so research the natural history information carefully.
Doors	A double door system will prevent escapes or make escaping difficult. A door that opens out will allow for snow removal and easy entry into an outdoor enclosure after a heavy snowfall. A low doorway may help prevent escapes by birds trying to fly out over your head.
Pools	Semi-aquatic and aquatic animals must be provided with a pool (or equivalent) of sufficient depth for the animal to completely submerge, dive, and feed, unless a disability prevents such activity.
Multi-animal housings	Make sure animals housed in the same enclosure are compatible. The enclosure should be of a sufficient size to allow animals to exercise natural behavior, avoid animals within herds or groups being unduly dominated by individuals, and avoid the risk of persistent and unresolved conflict. Pregnant animals or animals with young should have separate accommodations.
Metal and birds	Birds should not be housed where their feathers, beaks, or feet can come in contact with metal caging materials like chain link, hardware cloth, or any type of wire mesh.
Hide box	The enclosure should be provided with an area or shelter where the animals are able to retreat.
Stress	Animals must not be housed near other animals that cause them distress, and must be housed a sufficient distance from the public to prevent physical or psychological stress.
Perimeter fence	A perimeter fence around outdoor enclosures may provide predator protection and prevent unwanted human attention. The fence should be at least 6 feet high and may be electrified. There should be warning signs up on the fence, and electric fencing should not be used if children are present.

CONSTRUCTION OF CAGING AND ENCLOSURE ELEMENTS

Proper construction of different elements of the enclosure will provide the animal with a safe environment well suited to its needs. Material selection is a critical component in the proper design of an enclosure. Materials must be easily cleaned and disinfected, suited to the animal's behavior, and durable. The following section examines different materials and substrates used in different elements and then assesses the different characteristics of the materials. We will start with base flooring and subflooring, and then move through the other components of an enclosure. Each element will be considered in detail.

FLOORING

Flooring in an enclosure is very important for many reasons. First of all, the animal may spend part or all of its time on the floor of the enclosure. The floor must provide suitable perching or walking surfaces. Secondly, the feces and other "mess" accumulates on the floor, making cleaning and disinfecting important criteria. The base flooring can range from dirt in outdoor enclosures, to glass of an aquarium bottom. Because the flooring must have specific characteristics, choosing the best material is very important.

TABLE 2 – OUTDOOR CAGE FLOORS

Material	Criteria
Cement	Cement floors are easily cleaned, especially if a floor drain is installed; generally a substrate is used on top of the cement to prevent injuries to the animal such as pressure sores on feet, keels, and joint areas. If the floor is cement, ensure a slope of 1 in. (2.54 cm) for each 12 in. (30.48 cm) in the same direction to allow for water drainage.
Soil	Clay, soil, or dirt floors may cause problems, especially when it is wet, as the surface can become muddy and/or slippery. These surfaces can be difficult to clean. A natural substrate can benefit the animal because it can provide natural cushion for the animal's locomotion; but it can also harbor many types of bacteria or parasites. If the cage is large enough, grasses and other native plants can grow to help control erosion and mud problems. With this type of flooring you must have effective predator protection on the walls, roof, and under the cage perimeter.
Sand	Unless the animal uses sand in the wild, sand generally is not recommended as a base. Sand can become hot in the summer and can coat food, causing bowel impaction. If you can control these factors, sand can provide a soft surface for the animal to move on and through. Sand must be turned frequently and replaced at least every two years for most animals.
Water	Water flooring requires a pond liner of heavy gauge plastic to prevent leakage; or a pond or pool container that may be above ground, with either plastic or cement as a base. Using heavy liners allows for the installation of plants, hiding places, and filtration systems. A pump in a desired location or a filtration system similar to a swimming pool's with an overflow pipe will keep the water clean by skimming the surface. Test the water for harmful elements or contamination before using.
Mesh	A layer of chain link or 1 x 2 metal mesh can be laid down before you place another type of substrate on the cage floor. Metal mesh can provide predator protection and prevent escapes by digging. The substrate placed on top of the mesh must be deep enough to prevent injuries to the animal from the mesh itself.

Chapter 3: General Care

TABLE 3 – INDOOR FLOORING

Material	Criteria
Cement	A cement floor indoors can be very easy to keep clean and to disinfect, especially if painted with a high quality epoxy paint product for waterproofing. A drain will help facilitate cleaning and should be considered during the design process. This type of surface can cause pressure sores and other related problems. In birds, look for feet or keel sores, on mammals look for feet and joint sores. A frame could be built around the cement and a loose substrate (sand, pea gravel) or mats of different material could be placed on top.
Wood	A solid wood floor may be used in cage floors, and is softer than cement for the animal to walk on. Unless the wood is coated with a waterproofing chemical (like polyurethane), the wood will soon start to rot and harbor many types of unhealthy mold and bacteria. Wood flooring must be recoated periodically. "Treated" wood is not recommended for use in a cage as it is pressure treated with arsenic to preserve and waterproof the wood. Wood floors are not suitable for chewing animals like rodents.
Glass	Glass is found mostly in aquariums and terrariums. Glass can be perfect flooring for small mammals, reptiles, and amphibians if the proper substrate is placed over it. Without a substrate, glass is too slippery and unyielding. Glass can be easy to clean and disinfect but is breakable and silicone seals may have to be redone occasionally.
Mesh	Mesh is common in birdcages, dog and cat kennels, and ferret and small pet mammal cages. This type of flooring is satisfactory if the animal does not spend much time standing on the metal mesh or if the cage is not suspended from the ground. Mesh flooring can cause pressure-point sores and discomfort if too large. Birds raised in captivity (like parrots) can and do adapt to metal bottomed and sided cages. Birds that have not been raised in captivity should never be housed long-term on metal mesh floors.

FLOORING SUBSTRATE

Materials used to improve or augment the flooring for the ease of cleaning or the comfort/health of the animal are considered substrate in this section. Substrate is not used in some enclosures, such as a pool, but is often found over the base flooring in several types of enclosures. In the next section, different types and uses (both indoor and outdoor) for substrate are examined and the effectiveness of each discussed.

It may be advantageous to use a mixture of flooring substrates over the base floor. For example, part of the flooring surface could be rock, another part soil, and yet another part water (a pool). This approach provides a richer environment for any animal in long-term captivity.

TABLE 4 – OUTDOOR CAGING SUBSTRATE

Material	Criteria
Rock	Rocks should be rounded and irregular in shape, and roughly the size of pea gravel for best drainage. A layer 3 to 4 in. (7.62 to 10.16 cm) is placed over the base flooring, which can then be raked when cleaned. This substrate must be replaced occasionally when too contaminated, but it can be routinely cleaned with a water hose. Raptors are often kept on this substrate outdoors as it provides a surface that prevents pressure points and the unevenness of the rock itself can maintain feet and talons.
Plants	Grasses/plants grown in dirt/soil flooring cut down on erosion and mud in an enclosure. Plants in an enclosure can make the animal feel more secure by providing hiding areas and comfort for their feet. Plants can possibly provide some additional food or enrichment. Cleaning is difficult for all types of dirt flooring, especially if the cage is small. The plants may make monitoring food intake difficult. Grasses and plants need replanting and periodic maintenance.
Mats	Examples of commercially-made mats are Astroturf™, Dri-Dek™, and horse/cow rubber mats. Mats can be easily removed, cleaned, and replaced. Mats supply a good surface for the animal to stand on and are especially useful in very cold climates. When freezing temperatures make cleaning difficult, temporarily placed mats can be removed, cleaned, and replaced as necessary.
Hay/straw	Hay or straw holds moisture and can harbor mold or even Aspergillous spp., a type of fungus which is especially detrimental to birds. Thus, hay or straw is not recommended as a substrate outdoors for birds. Small amounts used in a hutch or box for a mammal enclosure is acceptable, but must be changed regularly.
Wood chips	Wood chips will make a poor substrate for any outdoor enclosure, as they hold moisture and can harbor mold.
Sand	A layer 2 to 4 in. (5.08 to 10.16 cm) in depth is best for drainage. Sand can cause impaction problems, but is soft and malleable for the animal to move and rest on. Sand can become uncomfortably warm in the summer for some species, and must be turned on a regular basis. Sand should be replaced every two years.

Chapter 3: General Care

TABLE 5 – INDOOR CAGING SUBSTRATE

Material	Criteria
Rock	Rocks should be rounded and irregular in shape, and roughly the size of pea gravel. Rock can make a wonderful substrate for many applications, especially for aquatic species. The rock can help in filtering out nitrates and ammonia and in breaking down organic matter with the help of an under-gravel filter and beneficial bacteria. Any rock placed in an aquarium should be non-porous. Rock used in any application in an enclosure (especially small amounts used inside) should be rinsed thoroughly and soaked in a container for 24 hours with a small amount of bleach. The rock should be thoroughly rinsed again with water and allowed to off-gas any remaining bleach for 24 to 48 hours. The application of bleach will destroy any bacteria.
Soil	Soil may make a good substrate for amphibians housed in aquaria. Make sure the soil is of good quality and is replaced regularly. Use pots when planting foliage in the soil. Use a layer of aquarium gravel or pea gravel 1 to 2 in. (2.54 to 5.08 cm) thick under the soil (2 to 4 in. [5.08 to 10.16 cm]), and top with sandy soil (2 to 4 in. [5.08 to 10.16 cm]) for best drainage.
Mats	Examples of commercially made mats are Astroturf™, Dry-Dek™, and horse/cow rubber mats. Mats can be easily cut to size, removed, cleaned, and replaced. Animals may chew or ingest any of this material. If ingestion is suspected, the animal may need medical treatment. The mat should be removed immediately and any other substrate replacing it should be monitored closely.
Hay/straw	Hay or straw holds moisture and can harbor mold or even *Aspergillous* spp., a type of fungus which is especially detrimental to birds. Do not house birds indoors near hay or straw.
Wood shavings or needles	Cedar shavings are not recommended for any reptile, amphibian or small mammal enclosure. Cedar shavings can cause respiratory difficulty and contain volatile oils. Pine shavings are not recommended for snake or turtle enclosures, and can be very dusty. When used for small mammals, pine shavings can cause respiratory difficulties. Aspen shavings have low dust and if shredded are absorbent. Aspen shavings can be used for reptile and small mammal enclosures. Pine needles are suitable for animals that do not ingest the needles. They are not suitable for ground foraging animals like doves and pigeons.
Paper	Newspaper or paper toweling can make a most effective substrate for some small mammals, birds, and reptiles. It is easily replaced, and feces and food consumption can be visually checked. Do not use glossy pages with colored inks, as the dyes and chemicals leach out when soiled. Soiled newspaper cannot be recycled and must be disposed of like contaminated waste.
Cat litter	Cat litter is not recommended for any application as a substrate.
Sand	Sand can cause impaction problems, and in large indoor cages can be difficult to clean. Sand tracked outside caging can easily get washed down floor drains and cause problems. In an aquarium situation, sand is more easily controlled, but may be ingested along with food. Before sand is used, especially in aquaria, it should be rinsed with running water until the effluent is clear.

WALLS AND ROOFTOP

Enclosure walls and roofs must be designed and built soundly to ensure the safety of the animal being housed. The largest elements in a cage or enclosure are the walls and the roof, and the materials selected to construct these elements are important. Walls and rooftops work in conjunction with one another to maintain the integrity of the enclosure. Outdoor caging must provide shelter from the elements, predator protection, and prevent escape. Indoor caging must be escape-proof while providing proper ventilation and light. All caging must be large enough to properly accommodate the animal.

As in the earlier sections of this chapter, different types of materials are assessed for use in different situations for both indoor and outdoor enclosures.

General design considerations for walls and roofs used in outdoor enclosures. Choosing the best material for enclosure construction is based on the natural history information specific to the animals being housed. Walls can be made from fiberglass, wood, cement block, metal mesh, or even a combination of materials. The walls need to protect the animal from predators and from injury. At least one wall should be of solid material, although sometimes two adjacent solid walls work best. Solid walls can provide a feeling of security as well as protection from prevailing winds.

Walls and roofs must provide protection from predators and prevent escape. Furthermore, the materials and construction techniques must not harm the animal. Protruding nails, rough or sharp edges, poor construction, or poor maintenance can all cause injuries such as broken feathers, abraded joints, abrasions on other body parts, and broken bones. Many of these materials have already been examined in previous sections for use in floor construction. While some material attributes remain the same regardless of where the material is used, others are more suited for wall and roof construction.

TABLE 6 – OUTDOOR ROOF AND WALL CONSTRUCTION

Material	Criteria
Cement	Cement can be an indispensable wall material in housing large mammals, such as bears, that may otherwise be able to escape.
Wood	Wood must be painted or treated with a polyurethane or similar product, and recoated on a regular basis. Arsenic treated (pressure treated) lumber should not be used if it will come in contact with the animal. Treated wood can be used as a base for the walls to prevent rot, but must be covered or somehow separated from the animal (especially chewing animals). If housing chewing animals like rodents, wood must be covered on the inside with metal mesh of small diameter to prevent escape and chewing. Wood can form the framework of the cage, while metal or fiberglass mesh, dowels, lath, or PVC pipe can form the actual wall or roof. Wood can be especially good in solid sheets or lath strips for most bird enclosures, but is not appropriate for woodpeckers. Wood lath spaced from 0.50 to 1.50 in. (1.27 to 3.81 cm) apart vertically (depending on the size of the species) is suitable for birds. Wood allows for ventilation and exposure to the sun. Wooden cages can be built in same-size sections and then easily put together.
Metal Sheeting	Metal sheeting, like pole building material, can be used for one or two walls to offer protection from the elements and security. Metal sheeting becomes too warm in warm climates or even in the summer sun in a moderate climate. If smooth, metal sheeting can be used for mammal and some avian enclosures.
Fiberglass	Fiberglass can be a very good material to use for walls and partial or total roof systems, although UV sensitive fiberglass will break down and become brittle over time. Fiberglass can be used for the solid walls in an enclosure, while another material is used for the other walls. Fiberglass must be used in conjunction with another material on the outside for predator protection. For instance, fiberglass walls are not strong enough to prevent black bears from entering an outdoor enclosure. If used as roofing in an area that has snow, fiberglass must have to be reinforced as it may not be strong enough to support a person shoveling snow off.
Dowels	Wooden dowels work very well vertically spaced 0.50 to 1.50 in. (1.27 to 3.81 cm) apart to act as a window in a door or wall for ventilation, and visual stimuli in avian enclosures.
PVC, mesh, wire and chain link	PVC pipes are used in a similar fashion as wooden dowels for window construction in a wall or door in avian enclosures. Heavy-duty plastic mesh may be suitable for some birds and mammals. Plastic does not offer much predator or escape protection, and birds can cause damage to feet or feathers by pushing them through the mesh. Welded wire is suitable for mammals in general. Welded wire can be buried in the ground next to outside walls, either straight down or at a 45-degree angle from the wall for predator protection. Welded wire can be placed on the outer side of wood avian enclosure walls to deter predators, provided the bird cannot come in contact with it. Smaller cages can be fitted with 1 to 2 in. (2.54 to 5.08 cm) wire on the roof to prevent too much snow load. Chicken wire is not a good material for an outdoor enclosure as it will rust quickly and break. Chain link provides predator protection for a single cage or as a fence around several cages. Chain link can create a double door passage way to prevent escapes. Chain link can be used for walls and roof for larger mammal enclosures and can be buried for predator protection, much like welded wire. Anchor enclosure made entirely of chain link firmly into the ground so the animal inside or a large predator outside cannot move or tip the cage.

CAGE FURNITURE
Cage furniture refers to any items added to the enclosure or cage for the animal's maintenance, behavior, or comfort. Items include water and food containers, perches, plants, hutches, hide boxes, or anything else similar in function. The cage should be designed so that furniture can be moved or removed easily. Flexibility in arranging furniture will increase enrichment options, and accommodate the individual animal's preferences. Food and water (drinking and bathing) containers, perches, hide boxes, hutches, and plants can be used in various combinations with one another to keep the animal healthy, stimulated, and comfortable.

PERCHES
Perches can be rounded, beveled, or flat surfaces, usually above the floor of the cage upon which the animal can perch, rest, and feed. The type of perch will depend on the type of animal being housed and type of permanent disability the animal has. The perch should encourage foot health (Gaunt and Oring 1997).

Specifically, the perch should not injure the feet over time because was it was too large or too small, or the wrong type. Perches can be made out of many different types of material. The most common are natural branches. Perches can be made from dimensioned wood (2 x 4 in. [5.08 x 10.16 cm], 2 x 2 in. [5.08 x 5.08 cm] for example) by beveling one side and wrapping rope around it. Perches can be wrapped with natural sisal rope of different diameters, Astroturf ®, coco mat, or other types of turf. These products can provide extra grip for the animal and change where the pressure points occur.

Platform perches are flat perches that are used for sitting, basking, and resting. Platform perches need to be "fitted" to the species and individual animal.

General consideration about perches
- Every cage should have at least a few perching options for the animal whether it is a ledge, a handmade hammock, natural branches, or a length of wrapped 2 x 4 in. (5.08 x 10.16 cm) piece of beveled wood.
- Natural branches need to be changed on a regular basis to avoid wear and smoothness.
- Natural sisal should be used on natural branches and other wood perches that are roped. Sisal rope needs to be replaced on a regular schedule or when it begins to get smooth to the touch.
- Perches that are covered with Astroturf®, coco mat, grass turf, or even Vetwrap™ need to be changed on a regular basis and cleaned daily. They need to be removed and replaced if worn, chewed on, or otherwise damaged.
- Natural perches should be from trees and plants that are non-poisonous to the animal that is using it.
- Animals generally will "perch" where they want to and not necessarily on perches. This means if wear areas begin to show on the animal's feet, it is because of where they are perching. Perch locations need to be altered so that the animal is perching where it would like, and on a perch that is better for its feet.
- Perches can be attached to the walls, to the floor, or suspended from the roof of the cage. Make sure that if the perches are in any of these places in an outdoor cage, that a predator will not be able to reach in and grab the animal while it is on the perch. Extra precautions need to be taken in outdoor cages because of the danger of predators. Putting perches on solid walls only, and low enough from the roof that a predator's foot cannot reach a perched animal will help protect the animal.
- Platform perches can be used for birds, mammals, and reptiles. Unless an animal is exclusively a platform (or flat) perching bird, reptile, or mammal, a platform perch should not be the only option in the enclosure.

HUTCHES
Hutches are usually three-sided structures, with a roof that helps to protect an animal from the elements. These simple additions can provide a feeling of security for the animal. The hutch should be large enough to accommodate the animal comfortably. "Comfortable" means the structure is well constructed and does not injure the animal, is large enough not to break feathers, and allows the animal to turn around easily. The optimal size hutch assists in retaining the animal's body heat, and is small enough to supply security and protection from the elements. If your hutch is too large, you will lose many of these attributes. A hutch can have perching options inside as well as on top of it. The animal should also be introduced to a hutch using food or by being placed in it physically. This introduction activity assures the animal recognizes that the hutch is a safe shelter.

HIDE BOXES
Hide boxes are usually fully-enclosed structures, with sides, roof and a bottom. A variation for bats can also be made without a bottom. These boxes are used by the animal mainly for security but may be designed to provide shelter from the elements as well

Additional construction tips for hide boxes
- Hide boxes should be ventilated, usually near the top on the sides.
- If nesting material is provided, it should be a nontoxic substance that is easily changed.
- Hide boxes should have a convenient entrance for the animal, and a hinged and latched door for easy handler access to allow for cleaning and handling.
- If a hide box is mounted off the ground, a perch, branch, or some other "roadway" to the box should be provided for the animal.

WATER AND FOOD CONTAINERS
Food and water containers have to be the right size for the animal using them. Too big, and the animal may not be able to access the water, or may get injured or even die by drowning in the water container. Too small, and the animal may not be able to use the container to access water effectively. All water containers should be constructed to prevent tipping, and be made of material easily cleaned and disinfected. Containers can be placed on the ground or mounted on the wall of the cage. Consulting the natural history information specific to each animal and accommodating its particular disability will help you correctly choose where to place the containers.

PLANTS
Plants can be a great addition to any enclosure. It is imperative that the plants are non-poisonous to the animal. Trees, grasses, and other plants can be planted in outdoor enclosures. You may consider building cages around large trees or similar vegetation. Discarded Christmas trees or cut branches with leaves may serve as a hideout or source of enrichment. Indoor caging can benefit from potted plants. Of course, plants need to have regular maintenance, watering, trimming, and replacement.

OTHER CAGE FURNITURE
Other cage furniture items include rocks, stumps, logs, pools, and hammocks, for example. Any item used for furniture should never pose a danger to or harm the animal. The size of furniture items should not make the enclosure too crowded for normal movement and should be appropriate for the animal's normal behaviors.

WATER AND FOOD

Water and food are two of the most basic requirements for animals in captive care. However, the type, amount, and timing of food and water can differ greatly between species. Again, researching the natural history information specific to the animal and talking to experienced people will help guide you to the correct foods and amounts to feed. Below you will find very general guidelines for the feeding and watering of the animals in your care (Abate 2000).

WATER

Water refers to the water ingested or absorbed by the animal for normal functioning on a cellular level. Not all animals need a direct water source like a water bowl. Some animals get most or all of the water necessary for survival from the food items consumed. In these cases, the appropriate food items and how these items are prepared and presented is critical in order to ensure the animal gets an appropriate amount of fluid. In other instances, animals receive water from dew or mist droplets on leaves and other plant matter. Misting daily in these enclosures is important for the health of these types of animals.

Other specific tips on water and water containers include–
- Containers should be clean and sanitary at all times, and water should be changed on a schedule that keeps it clean and fresh, usually at least daily. Water containers should be disinfected on a regular schedule; for example, once or twice per week. Be sure to completely rinse and dry the container after disinfection and before replacing in the enclosure.
- The depth and type of water container will vary depending on the type of animal you are using it for. If you are caring for an animal that spends a lot of time in the water in the wild, you will want to try to duplicate that in captivity for drinking and bathing (see bathing below). However, you may need to modify the water container(s) depending on the animal's disability. For small animals you can easily modify a water container to allow access to the water and prevent the animal from falling in and drowning by placing rocks or placing a cut detergent-free sponge inside the dish.
- Water containers should not tip over if the animal uses the edge to perch on or to put a paw on while drinking. You can reduce the tendency to tip by using a heavy container or by putting a large heavy rock inside the container.

Suggestions for water containers include, but are not limited to: bottoms (water-catchers) of plastic potting containers for plants; dog and cat dishes; tops of plastic food containers (e.g., plastic jar lids); gallon ice cream buckets with the handles removed; new oil changing pans; or plastic cement mixer pans of different sizes. Whatever the container, inspect it carefully for sharp edges. Again, make sure the animal can easily use it as a water source and is not in danger of drowning, and that it is easily cleaned and durable.

- The tool you use to clean the water container is important! If you use something rough, you will scratch the interior of the dish. These scratches will provide surfaces for hard-to-remove algal growth.
- In a cold climate, outside animals may be exposed to a possible danger from water containers. If the temperatures are very low, any water the animal is exposed to externally can cause frostbite very quickly.

FOOD

Captive animals must be provided with a diet appropriate to the species, age, size, and condition of the animal. Not all animals need to be fed daily. Each animal needs to be fed the appropriate amount that promotes normal healthy weight and body condition. These amounts may vary depending on the animal's age, gender, or annual cycle. You would not feed an animal during hibernation periods, veterinary treatment, normal fast, or during other professionally accepted times; for example, during the time when a snake is shedding its skin.

Specific tips for food and containers–
Food receptacles should be clean and sanitary at all times. Remove uneaten food within a reasonable time. This routine will help deter predators, parasites, spoilage, and odor.

Feed the freshest food possible to provide vitamins and other nutrients from the food at their highest level.

- If you raise food items (plants or animals), make sure you feed the food items a high quality diet and house them appropriately. Proper care of food items will ensure a healthier more nutritional food for the education animal you are feeding.
- If you are thawing frozen food, it is best to thaw it in the refrigerator overnight, not on a counter at room temperature. If you need to thaw food quickly, use cool or tepid water. Hot water will often thaw the outside of the food item quickly (and maybe cook it slightly) while leaving the internal part often still frozen. The food item is then open to bacterial contamination, as well as possibly destroying beneficial nutrients.
- Food items should be easily recognized by the animal as food, and is best presented as it would be in the wild (present the whole prey animal, for example). Presenting the food in a natural setting is also important; for example, place food into the water for some turtle species. Of course, there are exceptions to every rule. If the animal cannot eat normally because of a disability, or if the animal is being trained using part or all of its diet as motivation, you will need to change the food presentation.

GROOMING AND BATHING

Animals generally do not actively groom or bathe unless the surroundings are comfortable and they are experiencing minimal stress. If an animal is engaging in this type of behavior in a normal fashion, it indicates that they feel secure and relaxed. Most animals spend a great deal of energy in these activities.

Grooming, including preening and bathing, is done in many ways and for many different reasons. Obviously, this activity dislodges and removes dirt, parasites, and possibly harmful bacteria. Bathing and grooming keeps feathers, fur, and scales in top condition. Animals need to spend energy grooming for optimal waterproofing, insulation, and mate attraction. Bathing and grooming can be considered as an enrichment activity for the animal.

Bathing can take many forms. Some baths are paradoxically waterless. Many animals use dirt, fine gravel, or sand to "bathe", sometimes of out necessity, but many times out of choice. Many birds, mammals, and reptiles use dirt baths to remove soil and ectoparasites. To assist snakes in shedding their scales, a container with sphagnum moss moistened with water can be provided. Snakes enjoy moving through this "bath" freely (Conant and Collins 1991).

BATHING WATER

The presentation (or withholding) of water for bathing depends on the natural history information for that specific animal and the individual animal's personality. Sometimes the water used for bathing is also used as drinking water, other times it is a different source of water; and sometimes you do not need it at all. In another variation, some raptors would prefer a mist bath from a bottle or hose rather than jumping into a bath pan.

Optimally, water for bathing is available at all times for appropriate species, like most birds and some mammals. Alternatively, a mist bath or water pan should be offered on a regular schedule of a few to several times per week.

Before you allow your animals "into the pool"
- Change the water on a regular basis. Animals use a water bath to clean themselves, so the water must be free of dirt, body oils (from the last bath), and fecal matter.
- The animal must be able to easily and comfortably enter and exit the container without the chance of drowning or getting stuck in the container. Ramps to assist entering and exiting can easily be built of different materials. Unless the animal is semi-aquatic or aquatic, the container should be shallow enough so that the

animal can stand or easily touch the bottom of the container. If the container is too deep or too shallow, the animal will not feel comfortable enough to go into the bath container at all.
- The bottom surface of the bath container must provide traction so that the animal can comfortably stand or move without slipping. A textured surface will provide "grip" to move around in or get out of the container.
- The container should be large enough to allow the animal to really get a good bath. Watch how they take a bath—do they flap their wings? Do they roll over? Can they get their entire bodies (or as much as they want) wet? Can they curl up in the container without having to hang part of their body out to get the rest wet?
- In regions that experience below freezing temperatures, offering water baths can be dangerous. Most experienced wildlife rehabilitators withhold water baths in freezing weather conditions. You may be able to bring the animal in and offer it a mist bath or water pan in a different enclosure. The animal must be completely dry before being placed outside.
- Freezing weather and bathing can be hazardous for animals that have any type of equipment on them. For example, raptors often have bracelets and jesses on their legs. This equipment must remain dry under freezing conditions. If the animal or the equipment is even slightly damp frostbite can result. Frostbite under the equipment may remain undetected causing much damage to the tissue.

SAND AND DUST BATHS

For many desert species of lizards, birds, and mammals this is the only type of bath they would normally get in the wild. This type of bath can be beneficial to most wild animals that are kept in captivity, including those that do take water baths. Clean sand can make a fine dust bath for birds of all sizes. Sand or dust baths are an enrichment activity in the same way as water baths, and can serve many functions (Coborn 1992).

Before you let your animal into "the sandbox"
- The sand you use should be clean with no foreign objects in it. If possible, autoclave the material to kill any possibly harmful bacteria. Purchased commercial children's sandbox sand can work very well.
- As with water baths, the container must be large enough for the animal to be comfortable using it, and that they can get a satisfying bath with their entire bodies, not just one part at a time.
- The container has to be of sufficient depth, length, or width for the "splashed" sand not to go out of the container. If the container is not that large, easier cleanup of spilled sand can be accomplished by placing something under the container to catch some of the spillage. Large indoor cages with water drains on the floor or just outside the cage can have blocked pipes if you allow sand to flow into the drains.
- If the sandbox is in a cage outdoors, you can construct it level with the ground in some circumstances.
- The sand should be checked regularly, added to, replaced, and raked into place.
- Sandboxes can be great places to hide toys and some types of food items (ones that are not wet, or spoil quickly) for enrichment. This will encourage the animal to use and dig in the area.
- Sand bath areas might be used as basking areas for some reptiles.
- Consuming the sand is dangerous to the animal, and should be prevented. For example, if an animal consumes too much sand it can easily become impacted and create a medical emergency. Supervise any animal using sand baths if you know or think it may consume the sand. Keep the sand bath in the enclosure for limited amounts of time if you are concerned.
- Grit is important for some bird species, but sand baths should not be the source of this material.

Literature Cited

Conant, R., and J. T. Collins. 1991. *Peterson Field Guides: Reptiles and Amphibians: Eastern/Central North America. 3rd ed.* Boston, MA: Houghton Mifflin.

Miller, E. A., Ed. 2000. *Minimum Standards for Wildlife Rehabilitation, 3rd Edition.* St. Cloud, MN: National Wildlife Rehabilitators Association.

US Department of Heath and Human Services. 1985. *Guide for the Care and Use of Laboratory Animals.* 1985. NIH Publication No. 85-23.

Additional Reading

Abate, A. 2000. *Thoughts for Food: A step by step manual for providing healthy, nutritious and varied live food to insectivorous reptiles, amphibians, birds, mammals and other creatures.* San Diego, CA: Chameleon Information Network.

Coborn, J. 1992. *The Proper Care of Amphibians.* Neptune City, NJ: T.F.H. Publication

Gaunt, A. S., and L. W. Oring, eds. 1997. *Guidelines to the Use of Wild Birds in Research.* Washington, DC. The Ornithological Council.

Chapter 4

CLEANING AND DISINFECTION

The information found in this chapter is drawn from Minimum Standards for Wildlife Rehabilitation, 3rd Edition (Miller 2000). It is reprinted here with permission.

Disease control and prevention are the obvious "whys" of facility cleanliness. The following information pertains to the "hows" of creating and maintaining a clean facility.

TABLE 7 – CLEANING AND DISINFECTION COMMON TERMS

Term	Definition
Antiseptic	A substance capable of preventing infection by inhibiting growth of infectious agents.
Bacterial spores	The resting or vegetative stage of certain bacteria (especially of Bacillus and Clostridium) characteristically very resistant to environmental changes.
Cytoxic	Having the characteristic of killing cells.
Diluent	Substance used to make a concentrated solution more dilute. Sterile water and saline are common diluents for wound treatment, and tap water is a common diluent for general disinfection.
Disinfectant	A substance that destroys microbial organisms or inhibits their activity.
Disinfection	Destruction of vegetative forms of microorganisms.
Sterilization	The destruction of all microorganisms in or about an object (term is only used with inanimate objects). Note: "cold sterilization" refers to the specific method of using a disinfectant solution to soak objects, rather than applying heat, pressure, or gas as used in other methods of sterilization.
Volatiles	Agents that evaporate rapidly and pass readily in the form of a vapor. Toxic components within these vapors can be dangerous.

TYPES OF CLEANING AGENTS

There are types of various disinfecting agents that should be used after regular cleaning to properly sanitize. Suggested uses are listed under each category of cleaning agent, and some products work better against specific disease entities. The animal keeper, however, should be aware that none of these products is designed for any specific target or single use. In addition, none of these products is specifically effective against nematode eggs or larvae (intestinal worms). Most parasites are best removed from the environment by simple mechanical means (i.e., removal of feces and physical scrubbing of cages and cage contents), while other parasites, such as *Baylisascaris*, may be very difficult to completely remove from the environment. Many disinfectants emit potentially harmful volatiles; therefore, when disinfectants are used in cages, the cages should be allowed to dry thoroughly before placing animals into the cages. Some of the more common agents and methods are discussed here; additional information can be found in the additional reading section below.

Detergents

Detergents are cleaning compounds and include both soaps (anionic – alkali salts; negatively charged) and synthetic detergents (cationic – colloidal in solution; used as antiseptics, wetting agents, and emulsifiers; positively charged). While soaps are non-antibacterial, the physical scrubbing action of cleaning removes many of the microorganisms. Detergents alone do have minor disinfectant action against vegetative bacteria; however, they are not effective against fungi or viruses. Additionally, they lose their effectiveness in the presence of blood or tissue debris.

    Examples: dish detergents and laundry detergents.
    Uses: initial washing of cages, food bowls, etc., to remove organic matter.

Alcohols
Solutions of 50 to 70 percent isopropyl alcohol or 70 percent ethyl alcohol are commonly used alone or combined with other disinfectants. Isopropyl has a wider range of antibacterial action and is less corrosive than ethyl alcohol. Alcohols act by denaturing soluble proteins, interrupting metabolism, depressing surface tension and lysing (breaking open) cells.
- Because it is cytotoxic, alcohol should not be used in open wounds.
- Alcohols inactivate phenols, so the two should not be combined.
- Alcohols are not effective for cold sterilization, and may damage rubber, plastic and other synthetic materials.

    Example: rubbing alcohol.
    Uses: surgical preparation, antiseptic, instruments.
    Recommended dilution ratio: Use undiluted (i.e., 50 to 70%).

Aldehydes
The two most common disinfectants in this group are gluteraldehydes and formaldehyde. Gluteraldehydes are often combined with a synthetic detergent. These substances are irritating and cytotoxic, so their use is limited to disinfection, and instruments should be rinsed well before use. Exposure of three hours is required to kill bacteria spores. Formaldehyde is considered a carcinogen.

    Examples: Wavicide ™, Cidex ™.
    Uses: Gluteraldehydes may be used for cold pack sterilization, disinfection; formalin (40% formaldehyde in water) may be used to fumigate premises.
    Recommended dilution ratio: Use gluteraldehydes undiluted (i.e., 2.0%) for disinfection; use formalin at 1 to 10 percent for fumigation.

Chlorhexidine
This bisbiguanide compound acts on bacterial cell membranes, precipitates intracellular contents, and inhibits ATP (adenosine triphosphate, an energy source for cells—in this case the energy source for the bacteria). The cell membrane damage causes leakage of potassium and pentoses, which kill the bacteria, but also harms the host cells. These can be diluted in water or saline. The brand name Virosan ™ contains alcohol, making it effective against pseudomonads; however, once mixed with water this solution is only effective for 3 to 4 days.

    Example: Nolvasan ™ (2%), Virosan ™.
    Uses: Surgical preparation, wound treatment, disinfection.
    Recommended dilution ratio: 1ml chlorhexidine + 39 ml diluent (0.5%) for wounds, and 1 ml chlorhexidine + 19 ml diluent (1.0%) for disinfection.

Chlorine
Chlorine-based products are oxidizers, releasing free radicals that destroy cells. These compounds attack microorganisms, organic matter and living tissue. Chlorine decomposes in the presence of light and has toxic fumes that can lead to chemical pneumonia and skin and eye burns. Good ventilation, eye protection, and gloves are recommended when using chlorines.

    Examples: Clorox Bleach ™, Purex ™ (should be 5.25% sodium hypochlorite).
    Recommended dilution ratio: 1:32 (0.50 cup of 5.25% bleach per gallon diluent).

Stabilized Chlorine Dioxides
Stabilized chlorine dioxide is an inorganic compound of oxygen and chlorine and is a powerful oxidizing agent. Chlorine dioxides stimulate an oxidation process that safely breaks and eliminates sulfur bonds responsible for organic odor. These compounds can be safely used around birds. It will clean and provide disinfectant protection and is not harmful.

For hard surfaces, the solution is sprayed on and then wiped off after a five minute exposure. Rinsing is not necessary. Oxyfresh Dent-a-gene ™ is a full strength stabilized chlorine dioxide disinfectant that is a two-part product. The two parts are mixed (at this stage it does have toxic fumes) but once stabilized it is safe for use. A mixed solution can be used for seven days if sealed tightly and kept out of light.

    Examples: Bio-Rite ™, DioxiCare ™, Oxyfresh Dent-a-gene ™, Oxyfresh Cleansing Gele ™.
    Uses: Washing/soaking solutions for syringes, food dishes, feeders and water containers, general disinfection of premises.
    Recommended dilution ratio: Varies with product, follow label directions.

Chapter 4: Cleaning and Disinfection

Cresols
Cresols are wood tar distillates that have solvent and antibacterial properties. Commercial cresols available as disinfectants usually consist of pine oils combined with soap. These substances are often difficult to remove from surfaces and may leave a slick coating to floors and other surfaces.
> **Examples:** Hexol ™, Pine-Sol ™.
> **Uses:** Disinfection of premises.
> **Recommended dilution ratio:** none listed in literature.

Iodophores
These compounds consist of iodine complexed with surfactants or polymers. The most common compound is povidone iodine (iodine + polyvinylpyrrolidone), available as a solution and as a scrub. The detergent used in the scrub form is cytotoxic and should not be used in open wounds. The polyvinylpyrrolidone has a high affinity for cell membranes, delivering the iodine more directly to the target cells (i.e., bacteria), but it is the free iodine that contains the disinfectant action; therefore, dilutions of providone iodine actually disinfect or kill infectious agents better than more concentrated solutions. Iodine kills bacterial spores if contact time is greater than 15 minutes.
> **Example:** Betadine ™ Solution and Betadine ™ Scrub (10%).
> **Uses:** Surgical preparation, wound treatment, hand cleansers, foot baths, disinfection.
> **Recommended dilution ratio:** 1 ml povidone-iodine + 99 ml diluent (0.1%) for surgical preparation and 1 ml povidone-iodine + 9 ml diluent (1.0%) for wound treatment.

Phenols
Phenols are cytotoxic by disrupting cell walls and precipitating cellular proteins. Some phenols have been shown to cause neurotoxicity and teratogenicity (birth defects) after long dermal exposure, so animals should be removed from the quarters during cleaning; the use of goggles and gloves is recommended. Phenols are extremely toxic to cats and may be toxic to reptiles.
> **Examples:** Avinol-3 ™, Lysol ™, One Stroke Environ ™.
> **Uses:** General disinfection, foot baths.
> **Recommended dilution ratio:** 0.50 oz. of One Stroke per gallon diluent.

Quaternary Ammonium Compounds (QACs)
QACs are a form of cationic detergent, but they are not compatible with other soaps or detergents; even the residues of these substances and/or organic matter will inactivate QACs. Activity is increased, however, by the addition of ethanol. These compounds act by direct denaturation of bacterial enzyme systems and neutralization of acidic elements in the bacterial cell walls.
> **Examples:** Roccal D ™, Parvosol ™, Quintacide ™.
> **Uses:** Some wound treatment, general disinfection.
> **Recommended dilution ratio:** 1 part QAC to 2,500 parts diluent for wounds; 1 part QAC to 200 parts diluent for disinfection.

General Comment on Potential Environmental Toxins

Many disinfectants and their fumes, especially at full strength, may cause skin, eye, and lung irritation, and may be toxic if ingested. Care should be taken to wear gloves while using these products, and to work in a well-ventilated area. Most chemical compounds, including disinfectants, some cleansers and even some drugs, must be accompanied by a material safety data sheet (MSDS) explaining the potential health hazards and how to prevent or treat exposure. These information sheets are usually packaged with the products, or can be obtained from the manufacturer. The Occupational Safety and Health Administration (OSHA), as well as most insurance companies, require that a complete file of appropriate MSDSs be kept on scene and readily available/accessible to all employees and volunteers.

In addition to human safety, care must be taken to prevent chemical exposure to wildlife. Animals should be kept away from all volatile chemicals at all times. This includes phenols, ammonia, bleach, and most common household cleansers. If these cleansers must be used, the animals must be removed from the room they are being used in until it has thoroughly aired. If any of these chemicals are used to disinfect cages, they must be thoroughly rinsed and air-dried to prevent toxin accumulation. Cigarette smokers should not smoke near animals, particularly amphibians. Note that many pesticides will cause severe illness or even death in many birds, reptiles, and nearly all amphibians.

TABLE 8 – PROPERTIES OF DISINFECTANTS

Property or spectrum of action	Phenol	QAC	Cresol	Alcohol	Iodophore	Chlorine	Aldehyde	Chlorhexidine	Chlorine dioxide
GM+ Bacteria	High	High	High	High	High	High	High	High	High
GM– Bacteria	High	High	High	High	High	High	High	Mod*	High
Bacterial spore	None	None	None	None	Mod	None	Mod	None	Mod
Chlamydia	None	High	None	None	?	Low	?	None	?
Fungi and yeasts	Low	Mod	Mod	Mod	High	High	High	Mod	High
Viruses	Mod	Var	Mod	Mod	Mod	High	High	Mod	High
Protozoa	Low	Mod	?	Mod	High	None	?	Low	High
Effectiveness with organic matter	Mod	Low	Mod	None	Mod	None	Var	Mod	Low
Residual action	High	High	High	None	Low	None	Low	High	Low
Effectiveness in hard water	Var	Low	Var	NA	High	High	High	None	?
Most effective pH range	Acid	Alk	Acid	NA	Acid/Alk	Acid	Acid	Alk	?
Corrosiveness	High	None	Mod	Low	Mod	High	None	None	Low
Toxicity	High	Low	Mod	Low	Low	Low	Var	Mod	Low
Biodegradable	?	No	Yes	Yes	Yes	Yes	No#	No	Yes

KEY:

Mod ~ moderate

Var ~ variable with formulation

? ~ unknown or conflicting data published

NA ~ not applicable

Alk ~ alkaline

* ~ Virosan ™ brand is effective against pseudomonads; other chlorhexidines are not effective against pseudomonads

\# ~ Wavicide ™ brand product is biodegradable.

Other disinfectant notes

- Phenols and aldehydes perform better at warmer temperatures.

- Iodophores are only stable as long as dark color is maintained and may stain.

- QAC destroys chlamydia but is usually expensive.

- Alcohols evaporate rapidly and may require reapplication.

- Chlorines break down in light and solutions must be fresh. Chlorines are usually inexpensive.

Literature Cited

Miller, E. A., Ed. 2000. *Minimum Standards for Wildlife Rehabilitation, 3rd Edition.* St. Cloud, MN: National Wildlife Rehabilitators Association.

Additional Reading

Accrocco, J.O. 1998. *The MSDS Pocket Dictionary, 3rd ed.* Amsterdam, NY: Genium Publishing.

Clipsam, R. 1990. Environmental Preventive Medicine: Food and Water Management for Reinfection Control. Proceedings of the Association of Avian Veterinarians. Pp 87-105.

Davis, L. 1998. *Do you know how to disinfect?* The NWRA Quarterly. 16(3):10-12.

Gaunt, A. S. and L. W. Oring, eds. 1999. *Guidelines to the Use of Birds in Research.* Washington, D.C. The Ornithological Council.

Haufler, J. 1985. *Habitat Selection of Release Sites of Rehabilitated or Orphaned Wildlife.* P. Beaver, ed. Wildlife Rehabilitation. 3:139-143.

Laux, G. 1997. *Winter Care and Housing of Educational Animals.* The Ohio Rehabilitator. Page 3.

Lemarje, R. J., and G. Hosgood. 1995. *Antiseptics and Disinfectants in Small Animal Practice.* Compendium on Continuing Education. 17(11):1339-1351.

Standard Conditions, Special Purpose-Rehabilitation, 50 CFR 21.27, Washington, DC: United States Fish and Wildlife Service.

Stokhaug, C. 1988. *Selecting Release Sites for Raccoons (Procyon lotor).* Wildlife Rehabilitation. 7:151-156.

Chapter 5

REPTILES AND AMPHIBIANS

Reptiles and amphibians are very different from birds and mammals in many ways. These creatures lived on Earth long before birds or mammals, and adapted to the environment using very different strategies than the more "familiar" animals (Conant and Collins 1991). Their bodies are adapted to small and specific ranges of light, temperature, and humidity with a sensitivity not seen in mammals and birds. Some are so specific in dietary requirements that they would rather starve than eat any substitution. As cold-blooded creatures, they require temperature within close tolerances to be active, hunt, mate, digest food, or pump blood (Abate 2000).

Play and affection are virtually unknown behaviors in reptiles and amphibians. Often, they are solemn loners who do not look for solace from others, nor do they seek company of any kind. Family life is experienced by a few species and usually only for a short time (Oldfield and Moriarty 1994). As mammals, we can only guess at their motivations. In many instances, humans either do not understand the silent intricate ways of reptiles and amphibians, or fear their stony subtleness or unemotional ferocity.

These prejudices about reptiles and amphibians encompass biological reasons, to social and psychological behaviors in humans. Reptiles and amphibians populate our nightmares and superstitions, beginning early in the evolution of man. Movie monsters such as Godzilla and many other stories with snakes, crocodiles, alligators, and dinosaurs as "killers" proliferate this now irrational fear.

Using these animals in education programs successfully demands expert handling and presentation skills. The handler must be aware of what the animal is doing, and understand that particular species and individual so well as to nearly read its thoughts. The animal should be in excellent physical and psychological condition, ensuring the stress of doing programs will not be detrimental to the animal. Accomplishing these goals requires that the animal be chosen, housed, fed, and handled with intelligence and expert care (Coborn 1992).

Information to make intelligent decisions about how to care for this strange and special group of animals is needed to accomplish these goals. While this is not a comprehensive collection of all information available on reptiles and amphibians, this chapter provides carefully selected facts and information. Further reading is not just encouraged but necessary, as new information is constantly being added to our understanding of these unique creatures.

HOUSING
The housing discussed here is a starting point – basic, practical and easy to maintain while providing the animal with proper conditions (Miller 2000). However, since these enclosures will be the animals' homes for their entire lives, every attempt should be made to enrich the enclosures with plants, different substrates, hide boxes, varied terrain, logs, and other items. Do your homework, use your imagination, and create a wonderful home for the animals that do so much for us.

If same-species animals are kept together, it does not guarantee peace. Also, disease is often passed easily between same-species individuals and cannibalism is common in many animals. Multi-species enclosures are usually difficult to maintain at best and can be disastrous at worst. Same sex animals may compete for resources and opposite sex animals may breed. Keeping most species as lone animals is very often the safest course and it will not affect them psychologically.

BASIC ENCLOSURES
Aquariums or plastic sweater boxes are the best choices for reptile enclosures, with the exception being box turtles, which should not be kept long-term in either one. Aquariums can be found in various sizes, and tight fitting mesh lids and locking clips are easily purchased. Glass is easy to clean and disinfect and filters and lights

can be easily affixed. The disadvantage of glass aquariums is that they are heavy, unwieldy to move, and relatively easy to crack or break.

Plastic storage boxes are also available in a variety of sizes with lids made to fit, and are easily cleaned and disinfected. Plastic storage boxes are light, easier to move, and generally harder to break than glass aquariums. One disadvantage of plastic is that the lids require holes to be melted using a heated nail or wood-burning tool or the lid replaced with a tight fitting mesh screen for better airflow. Other disadvantages include the flexibility of plastic, which makes the container unstable when filled with water, and its unsuitability for use with lighting fixtures.

Specific enclosure requirements for various animals are listed by specific species later in this chapter. Substrates vary with species, but pine shavings should never be used because the oils are toxic to all reptiles and amphibians.

LIGHTING

Lights should be on timers set for 10 to 12 hours a day, then turned off at night to recreate a natural light/dark cycle. One of the generally accepted principles regarding lighting is that UV-B (ultra-violet B) lighting is required for long-term health of most reptiles and amphibians. It is highly beneficial for water turtles and most herbivorous lizards. It appears to be a much lesser factor for snakes, frogs, toads and salamanders. Be cautious of lights labeled "full spectrum" since many of these emit no UV light at all. The spectrum in this case is the visible spectrum, not the invisible ultra-violet spectrum.

There are two basic choices for UV lighting. The first are the UV-B light tubes (made by Zoo Med® and Vita-Lite®) with an effective range of about 18 in. (45.72 cm). These lights provide UV-B for about six months, although they will produce non UV-B light for much longer. They give off little heat, so use an incandescent heat light (a simple light bulb) in addition to the tube. The optimal wattage that is required for which species and under what conditions has not been scientifically determined. The second option is the new screw-in light bulbs (made by Zoo Med® and T-Rex®) that produce UV-B light and heat. These bulbs last about a year. The effective range is dependent on the wattage chosen. These lights give off a great deal of heat and need to be used with care to avoid burning the animals or starting a fire.

HEATING

All reptiles and amphibians are ectotherms (also called heliotherms or poikilotherms), meaning that they are dependent on an external heat source to regulate their body temperature. Cold-blooded is an outdated and misleading term. Each species has its preferred optimal temperature zone (POTZ) required for the animal to be able to digest food, maintain bodily functions, metabolize medications and recover from injuries. To enable the animal to choose the temperature they need, all enclosures should have a heat gradient, with one end being cooler than the other. Always use two thermometers to monitor the temperature in an enclosure; one at the cool end and one at the warmer end. Avoid the flat stick-on thermometers since they can be off by as much as 20 degrees F. Slightly lower nighttime temperatures are normal in nature and cause no harm.

How heat should be provided is something of a debate. Turtles and lizards tend to look for the light as a direction finder for heat, so they do best with the combination UV-B light/heat bulbs described above. Snakes seem to do well with heat pads. To prevent burns, attach the heat pad to the shelf, not the animal's cage. Amphibians are best served by simply keeping their enclosure in a warm room. Heating equipment should be carefully monitored, and lights and heating pads should not be placed directly on glass or plastic.

Never use hot rocks under any circumstances. They are the number one cause of burns in reptiles.

Chapter 5: Reptiles and Amphibians

CLEANING

Animals need to be removed and kept in appropriately warm and humid temporary cages while their enclosures are being cleaned. Daily spot cleaning will reduce the number of more thorough cleanings needed. Major cleaning should be done once a week. If the enclosure contains soil or sand, the surface 0.50 in. (1.27 cm) layer can be scraped off and this will remove the majority of feces, insect chitin, and shed skin. New soil or sand can then be added on top.

Once to twice a month the enclosures must be deconstructed and cleaned in a tub and all the soil and moss should be replaced. The enclosure and any "furniture" should be washed with a mild soap-based cleaner (a detergent such as Dawn®) to remove organic debris, rinsed thoroughly, disinfected, rinsed again and completely dried before returning the animal to the enclosure.

The disinfectant should contain either chlorhexidine (Nolvasan™ or a mild quaternary ammonium also called benzalkonium chloride (Roccal-D™). According to the Environmental Protection Agency (EPA), benzalkonium chloride is effective against common animal bacteria such as *E. coli*, *Staphylococcus*, *Streptococcus*, *Salmonella*, *Pseudomonas* and *Campylobacter* in 30 seconds. Many fungi, molds, and a host of viruses are also destroyed with a contact time of 10 minutes.

Disinfectants labeled as Alkyl (67% C12, 25% C14, 7% C16, 1% C8-C10-C18) Dimethyl benzyl ammonium chlorides 0.08% and Alkyl (50% C14, 40% C12, 10% C16) Dimethyl benzyl ammonium chlorides 0.02 percent with 99.9 percent inert ingredients are completely appropriate and safer than bleach! It sounds complicated, but read a few labels. Many household disinfectants are made from these substances and they have been tested for efficacy and safety. No ventilation is required. Contact with eyes should be avoided, but no goggles are necessary. Gloves should be used for sensitive skinned individuals. These are the compounds that are used by zoos, veterinary clinics, human hospitals, and households.

☠ Bleach is not recommended. Straight bleach is poisonous to animals and humans. The toxic fumes by themselves (without contact) can kill amphibians. OSHA-issued Material Safety Data Sheets (MSDS) state that bleach is "highly toxic to aquatic life." The MSDS requires chemical-resistant gloves, splash-resistant safety goggles and face shield, chemical-resistant clothing, exhaust ventilation, and the possible use of a respirator.

FEEDING OF REPTILES AND AMPHIBIANS

Reptiles and amphibians hunt nearly every group of animal on Earth, from snakes that hunt bats to salamanders that hunt water birds. As a general rule, however, all frogs, toads, salamanders, and snakes are carnivorous, turtles are omnivorous, and lizards can be carnivorous, herbivorous or omnivorous. Even if the animal species' wild diet is only comprised of insects, it will almost always include a great variety of food species. There are notable exceptions such as the eastern hognose snake that eats toads almost exclusively.

This variety is the basis for a balanced diet and it is very challenging to reproduce this diet for a captive animal. Reptile nutrition is a complex field and new discoveries are being made at an astounding rate. In order to maintain healthy reptiles, their diets must constantly be reviewed and updated.

How to present food to amphibians properly depends to some extent on species. In general, amphibians will accept only live food, although large frogs can often be fed dead mice using tongs. Larva and worms can be offered in shallow bowls to frogs. Salamanders will often snap up invertebrates from ambush, so using live invertebrates walking around the substrate is required. Fish, of course, will need to be placed in the amphibians' water, but add them a few at a time.

Proper food presentation for reptiles is food and species dependent as well. Snakes should always be fed dead rodents using tongs. Gloves are helpful at feeding time, since snakes will often strike in the direction of the rodent's smell and sometimes miss and grab an exposed finger. Feed each snake in an individual container. Never feed snakes together or both snakes may try to consume one mouse and this could lead to injury or even death for one of the snakes. If the snake is large enough to take either a single dead rat or several dead mice, always choose the smaller feeder animal in greater number. The snake will absorb more nutrients from the several smaller meals than a single large one. It also costs the snake less energy to digest several small mice so the net energy gain is greater.

It is sometimes useful to put snakes in a "shift cage" (a cage other than its home cage) during feeding time. This also allows for home cage cleaning while the snake enjoys its meal in peace. However, some snakes are too nervous to eat after being handled and they must eat first and then be shifted to another enclosure for cleaning duties. Garter snakes may hunt fish in their water bowl and therefore need a great deal more time for feeding than other species.

For lizards that need to hunt invertebrates, allow the invertebrates to run free within the cage. Vegetable matter can be placed in a shallow dish to use as a "hunting ground" so the lizards do not accidentally consume the substrate with their meal.

Smaller younger animals will need to eat more often than larger older animals. Most frogs, salamanders, turtles, and lizards should eat three to four times a week. Small snakes should be fed at least once a week, especially if they are juveniles. Adult mid-sized snakes are satisfied being fed every other week. Many frogs, salamanders, some turtles, and the smaller lizards can be allowed to have access to food in bowls at all times. All juvenile frogs, salamanders, lizards, and turtles should be fed every day.

Live Food

The most widely available and easily purchased food animals are crickets, mealworms, super mealworms, earthworms, red worms, silkworms, waxworms, house flies, rosies, guppies, goldfish, mice, and rats. Specific feeding choices will be discussed in the individual species section.

Invertebrates

Invertebrate food animals should always be fed themselves before being fed to larger animals. Some evidence suggests that the enzymes in the gut of a hungry invertebrate can be detrimental to the animal that consumes it. Certainly a well-fed food animal will be higher in nutritional value than one that is starving. Dusting inverts with various vitamin and mineral powders just before offering can also increase their food value. Use caution when feeding invertebrates; those that survive will take up residence in the enclosure, may even chew on your animals or escape into your facility.

Crickets are available from most pet stores and on-line from a large number of sources. They can be purchased in various sizes from the extremely small "pinheads" to adult. They are cheap, easy to maintain, readily accepted by many species, low in fat, and high in protein. Crickets should not be the sole source of animal protein in any diet. Their exoskeleton consists of chitin, which can cause intestinal blockages if eaten in too high an amount. Commercially available cricket foods should be fed to the crickets before feeding them to your reptiles. Crickets should not be left in the enclosure if not eaten, as they will readily chew on an amphibian's soft skin, other invertebrate food animals, and the eyes, toes, and lips of an incapacitated or insufficiently warmed reptile. Do not overfeed crickets to your herpetiles!

Mealworms are also commonly available. Large numbers of many sizes can be purchased, and several companies will mail a pre-ordered number to you as often as you wish. This makes trying to raise them an unnecessary exercise. As with crickets, mealworms should be fed whole oats, mixed with a calcium powder, wheat germ, and small bits of apple for moisture. Mealworms are higher in fat than crickets and slightly lower in chitin.

Super mealworms are several times the size of mealworms. They eat the same foods and are lower in chitin than their smaller cousins, therefore a better meal. However, they can pose a problem for small amphibians because super mealworms have fairly strong jaws and can bite the outsides or the insides of your amphibian. A quick pinch to the head usually will incapacitate the mealworm enough to make it harmless. If there is doubt, use the smaller mealworm variety until the amphibian is larger. Reptiles generally partially chew their prey, which kills the mealworm.

Earthworms are a marvelous source of many minerals such as calcium and micro-nutrients. They are comparatively low in fat, high in protein, and full of vitamins. Sufficient moisture and earth to hold and feed them is essential or they will rapidly die. Purchasing earthworms is not always easy, but it will be worth the small effort required. Farmed earthworms have been fed "clean" food for generations and are a better choice than wild earthworms. In the wild, they are exposed to chemicals ranging from fertilizers to motor oil, which their bodies store for great periods of time. This makes wild earthworms a significant source of poisoning when dug and consumed.

Red worms are compost worms and are readily available from compost catalogues or green companies. They are significantly smaller than earthworms, easy to feed to smaller animals, and simple to maintain if the colony is kept in a cool, dark place. These worms usually reproduce fairly rapidly.

Silkworm larva is only sold by a few vendors and usually on-line. They are higher in protein and lower in fat than any of the other larva worms. However, they require an extremely specific diet of mulberry leaves (which are usually sold with the worms) and are much more expensive than the rest.

Waxworms are similar to mealworms, but are softer bodied and higher in fat. Overfeeding of waxworms will cause obesity in many species.

Housefly larva (maggots) are hard to find and are only needed for very small animals. They are certainly easy to feed, but remember, these are maggots that will eat flesh and should not be left in any cage with an injured animal.

Many sources suggest "land plankton" to feed insectivores. These are insects swept with nets from fields. This process is not recommended due to the problems of pesticides, herbicides and parasites as mentioned above.

Fish

Feeder fish are high in protein and low in fat and can often encourage reluctant animals, especially turtles and garter snakes, to eat vigorously. Most pet stores will be delighted to order you a regular weekly supply of any kind of feeder fish. Unfortunately, fish smell, both going in and coming out. If you forget this fact, the children attending your programs will be sure to remind you! Feeding frozen fish is not recommended due to the possibility of it leading to thiamin (vitamin B) deficiency.

Rosies are medium-sized, slender fish that can be found everywhere and are a wonderful source of food. They do not live long without a well-aerated, filtered fish tank, so use them immediately. Guppies are the smallest food fish available and are slightly hardier than the rosies. Goldfish are easily obtained and often recommended. However, if swallowed whole, they have a dorsal spike that can cause slashing damage to the throat and stomach. Do not feed goldfish to animals that do not tear apart their food.

Rodents

Mice in all sizes - pinkies, fuzzies, hoppers, juveniles, and adults - are extremely nutritious, and one of the best foods available. Frozen mice have the same nutritional content as live mice. Feeding live adult mice should only be done under experienced supervision and only if the animal refuses to eat pre-killed.

Rats are not just big mice. Rats, dead or alive, should only be used to feed very large herpetiles. Rats are much higher in fat than mice. Feeding live rats requires supervision at all times. They are very intelligent, and live rats have injured or killed many an animal that was supposed to eat them.

Never use wild-caught mice or rats as food items.

NON-LIVE FOODS

Non-live foods come in two types, processed and "real." The temptation to feed only "real" is not always a good one. The wrong real food is just as damaging as the wrong processed food. Do not forget that the nutritional requirements of the animals and the long-term effects of the foods are still being researched.

Canned cat and dog foods are almost universally condemned as containing too much fat and minerals. These foods may cause obesity, liver and kidney disease, and hardening of organs and tissues. However, good quality dry cat and dog foods may be used as part of a diet.

Processed turtle pellets and trout chow are both useful parts of a balanced diet, but neither one should be used exclusively. They can be used in a limited fashion when a quick feeding is needed and are often useful in getting a difficult turtle to eat.

There are many vegetables and fruits to use when feeding herpetiles, such as dandelion, kale, romaine, shredded carrots and carrot tops, collards, tomatoes, squash, melons, mangos, apple, pears, and all types of berries. Bananas are not recommended, since bananas may lead to addiction in some species and constipation in others.

VITAMINS AND MINERALS

Vitamins need to be considered on a species-by-species basis with a few general rules. Animals that eat whole animals, like snakes, are unlikely to need vitamins. But frogs and toads that feed on invertebrates require vitamins because their diet needs to be more diverse than is possible in captivity. Box turtles require a modest dose of a multivitamin occasionally, while lizards, such as the chuckwalla, may require weekly supplementation. There are many products available such as Herptivite®, Reptivite® or a general animal vitamin called Vionate®. A small amount of vitamin supplementation is probably a good thing in most cases, but it is also a danger if used too often or to excess.

Calcium is one of the most important minerals in a herpetile's diet and supplements are necessary to meet the dietary requirements for many species. Calcium carbonate is one of the better supplements.

WATER

Water must always be available for all species. The water bowl must be easy for the animal to enter and exit and large enough for the animal to completely immerse itself. Stainless steel dog bowls are usually adequate.

Chapter 5: Reptiles and Amphibians

USING THE EDUCATION ANIMAL

When considering any animal for use in education programs, there are a few criteria that should be reviewed. The animal should be healthy and eating regularly and well. Any injury that it may have sustained should be fully healed and not be painful. Healed injuries may be visible to the audience, but they should not be disturbing to view. The animal should be familiar with the handler and not exhibit undue stress when handled casually.

When an animal first becomes a captive, there will be a period of transition. Even stoic reptiles can experience depression. It is necessary to allow the animal to become used to its new surroundings, foods, smells, water taste, and day-to-day routine before it is launched on a career of public appearances. Do not use the animal in presentations before it has fully adjusted to its new environment.

Injured animals brought to a rehabilitator require treatment that is usually painful, always stressful, and most certainly outside the range of the animals' normal experiences. It is therefore worth remembering that there needs to be a period of "normalization." This normalizing time begins when all medical treatments are completed and it has been determined that the animal will not be released.

Move the animal to its new permanent home as soon as possible. Offer it foods you would like it to eat first, resorting to using wild foods only if absolutely necessary. Give it all it needs to do well, but the most important thing is to leave it alone – for weeks. When it has been eating and acting well for weeks, slowly introduce yourself by handling the animal for no more than the 30 seconds it takes to get it to its shift cage. Allow a day for the animal to digest the experience, and make sure its still digesting its food, too. Try again for a bit longer - several minutes in hand and then back to the enclosure. Then move the animal from hand to hand under secure restraint and increase time out of its enclosure. Always watch for stress while handling and after the animal is back in the enclosure. Some animals will come along quickly, a few will take months, and some will never adapt. Always be mindful that this animal was not born to this process, so you must be patient.

Most animals will benefit from "tryouts" where the keeper handles the animal for an increasing period of time, working up to 20 minutes, over a period of two weeks. This amount of time will almost always be more than the animal will actually be needed for in a program, but dealing with the extra stress should be instructive for both handler and animal. Introducing the animal to its travel enclosure in advance will also help it deal with the new challenges.

Start the animal off with a single program and then return it to its enclosure. After several days to a week, use it for two programs. How many times in a row and how many times a week you use the animal will depend on how much stress the animal is experiencing. Refusal to eat is always an indicator of illness or a high stress level. At least one week off is required for any animal exhibiting stress.

When designing your program, check with local and/or state fish and wildlife authorities as to laws governing which species may be touched and under what circumstances. Any audience member touching an animal should disinfect their hands with an alcohol-based cleaner. Soap will not disinfect. It is not in the best interest of the animal to allow it to be touched by members of the audience. Rather, you should supplement your teaching repertoire with skins, skulls, bones, shells, and other items that can be touched and investigated.

AMPHIBIANS

Handling frogs in front of an audience can be a challenging feat. For the comfort of the frog, the educator's hands should be moist and free of chemicals (even soap). Moist hands means the frog will be even more slippery so the frog should be a good size; 3 in. (7.62 cm) or larger (nose to vent length). Carefully open the enclosure and quickly, but gently, cup or pin the frog under one hand. Then slip the thumb and middle finger of the free hand around the frog's waist and pick up. If done correctly, the legs of the frog should hang down in front of the palm of the hand and the body will protrude up over the lower three fingers, facing the audience. The index finger will stick out in front of the frog's chest. If the frog starts to slip, the index finger can be employed to reinforce the middle finger. After a period of time, the frog will become accustomed to this and will not struggle while being shown. Toads can be handled similarly, and they are generally less prone to jump. If either of these species starts to shed excessively, it may be a sign of too much handling.

Frogs and toads are not "pet-able" and the audience should not be allowed to touch. Large frogs can bite. Many frogs and toads have skins toxic enough to cause irritations of mucous membranes, some dangerously so. The handler should use an alcohol gel or wipe to clean hands afterward to avoid spreading frog toxins and to prevent being mistaken for a frog by another animal.

Salamanders should be handled with moist hands as well. Lift them out of their enclosure from the middle of their body and display them on the open palm of your hand. They may try to run off at first, but eventually will settle down as they get used to being handled. Due to their generally delicate nature and occasionally poisonous skins, salamanders should not be touched by the audience. An alcohol cleaner to clean hands is helpful here as well.

SNAKES

Snakes are the easiest herptiles to handle due to the patience many snakes exhibit after becoming accustomed to handling. Before using any snake in a program, its individual fitness for the job should be ascertained. A certain amount of nervousness or even aggression at first is to be expected and does not rule the animal out. Biting, hissing and defecating are normal initial reactions. Handling the snake in several private sessions and then with a small group of friends or family will be needed to fairly assess the snake.

Slowly and gently lift the snake just forward of the center of its body with one hand while supporting the rear with the other hand. Do not approach the face of the snake from the front! Constrictors will be most comfortable with the back half of their body coiled around one arm or wrist. Hold the snake loosely, allowing the body to travel as it is supported with both hands. The head should be allowed to roam about and only gently redirected if it approaches the educator's face. Larger snakes may be allowed to wrap around the waist of the handler. Under no circumstance should a snake ever be put around anyone's neck, whether the educator or audience member. The snake should never be passed around, used to frighten anyone, or have its mouth taped shut!

Handling garter snakes may take a while to become accustomed to, as they cannot hold on to the educator as constrictors can. Wild garters will both bite and defecate regularly on anyone touching them. This behavior may persist for some time after becoming a captive.

Most snakes will well tolerate a person gently stroking its back. It is not in the best interest of the animal to allow it to be touched by members of the audience. For most animals, it will cause unnecessary stress. Remember that humans appear to be predators in the eyes of the animals used in education programs. In the eyes of many audiences, there will be no difference between a wild animal in an educational setting and a wild animal in their yard. If they are encouraged to touch the former, they may be encouraged to touch the latter. Zoonotic exposures are another factor that should be considered for the well-being of the audience.

Chapter 5: Reptiles and Amphibians

TURTLES

Many turtles make fine education animals but should be given several tryout periods to determine if their personality will tolerate being handled as often as needed. Turtles should be approached initially from the rear, lifted from underneath, and supported from below at all times. They can feel support through the lower shell (plastron), and so long as the turtle is held horizontally, it should acclimate well. It is not necessary to allow the feet of the turtle to touch the ground or the hands of the educator, as they will attempt to swim or crawl and can scratch the handler.

Water turtles carry a risk of bacterial contamination, and audience members should not be allowed to touch the turtle. A safer recommendation would be to allow the audience to touch an empty turtle shell that has been thoroughly cleaned.

LIZARDS

Lizards can be nervous animals (especially the US species), making them difficult to handle. Even the smaller species may require both hands to prevent their escape or injury. The initial stages of handling should be dealt with cautiously. Reach quickly for the lizard's middle from above. Grasp the waist firmly but gently, keeping the rear legs and tail together and straight. This will prevent injury to both the lizard and the handler. Support the front legs with the other hand while carefully avoiding the animal's mouth. This very restrictive hold may be gradually relaxed and the lizard may be allowed to rest in the palm of one hand while the other hand is held, gently but firmly, on its back near the hips. This should first be tried in a controlled atmosphere without an audience. Lizards that will not settle down in private should not be used in public. If both lizard and handler are comfortable, it can be attempted with an audience. Keep in mind that many lizards' tails can break off in an attempt to escape. So, never restrain a lizard by its tail.

TRANSPORT OF REPTILES AND AMPHIBIANS

Traveling with reptiles and amphibians to a program requires care, but is fairly simple. Enclosures must be plastic - no other material is as easily cleaned, as durable, waterproof, or as safe for the animals. The enclosure should be opaque, not clear. The less the animal sees, the less stressed it will be, and an opaque enclosure will keep your audience from bothering the animal. Cover the enclosure with a white towel to protect the animal from over-heating in the car when traveling.

A plastic box with a hinged top is superior to other containers, since it will prevent the animal from trying to escape in the direction of the attached top when the box is opened. A small "sweater" or "stuff" box is perfect and should be just larger than the size of the animal. A large enclosure containing a small animal could allow the animal to jump and bang around when jostled. The floor of the enclosure should be covered with several sheets of moist newsprint. The carrier should be clipped or banded so it will close securely, but should not have the ability to create an air-tight seal. Holes are usually NOT needed as long as the container is not made for food storage (food storage containers seal tightly and require air holes). If holes are necessary, a few small holes may be made with a hot nail or wood burning tool. Minimizing the holes keeps the temperature in the carrier stable. Another option would to put the enclosure into a cooler.

Snakes can be transported in cloth bags but these are more restrictive than a plastic box. Bags can tear or wear and they offer no support for the trip, so a sudden stop can send the snake rolling across the vehicle, bag and all. It can also be discomforting to stick an arm down a bag after a snake.
The vehicle will need to be heated or cooled to the desired temperature. A range of 75 to 80 degrees F is usually acceptable to all herpetiles. It is not unusual for the temperatures to vary widely from one area of a car or van to another, so use a thermometer in the animal's area to monitor the temperature. Remember that the smaller the animal, the faster the animals' core temperature will change.

SPECIES CHOICE AND SUITABILITY

Suitability of any reptile or amphibian for education is based on a combination of factors that must be considered before pressing the animal into service. And let us be fair about this; the best that can be hoped for with these animals is toleration.

The animal's constitution and disposition, both as an individual and a species, need to be considered. Many snakes are tough, good-natured, and eat well. Size is another important factor to consider. A spring peeper is not only impossible to see from just a few feet away, but it also will suffer comparatively huge shifts in temperature and humidity just being removed from its enclosure. It will receive high doses of oil and salt from the handler's skin, it will dehydrate rapidly and a slight squeezing can mortally wound it.

Difficulty of care is a major concern. How hard is it to feed and how complicated is its environment to maintain? Some animals will eat only special prey, and others need very specific environmental conditions.

Educators are encouraged to research all individual species and subspecies before making a final decision if the animal is appropriate to use. The animals suggested here are some of the best choices, however, they are not the only ones appropriate to education. These animals are chosen because they are hardy, relatively easy to care for, accept being handled, and are large enough for a group of people to see from a distance.

Turtles

Box Turtles

These robust, helmet-shaped turtles are one of the best choices for educational program use. The box turtle group in the United States includes the Eastern, Gulf Coast, ornate, Florida, and three-toed varieties, all of which are generally good-natured.

A terrestrial enclosure with a moist (not wet) substrate of sphagnum moss (not peat moss), leaf litter, and potting soil (without perlite, vermiculite, or chemicals) is required for these turtles, as they enjoy partially submerging themselves in soil. Box turtles are active, inquisitive creatures, so the enclosure should be enriched with plants, hiding places, and differences in terrain. The temperature gradient for box turtles should be 75 to 78 degrees F at the cool end and 85 to 88 degrees F at the warm end. Humidity should be around 60 to 80 percent and the humidity should be checked with a humidity gauge (easily purchased in a pet store). UV-B lighting is necessary for box turtle enclosures. Water should always be available in an easily entered bowl that is big enough for the turtle to stretch out its entire body. The depth of the water should be around half the height of the box turtle (e.g., the average Eastern box turtle is about 4 in. [10.16 cm] high, so the water depth would be about 2 in. [5.08 cm]).

The *Minimum Standards for Wildlife Rehabilitation* (Miller 2000) suggests that box turtle enclosures for animals in rehabilitative care be five times the turtle's width and length. Based on those calculations, a single box turtle measuring approximately 4 x 6 in. (10.15 x 15.24 cm) would require an enclosure of a minimum of 20 in. (50.80 cm) wide and 30 in. (76.20 cm) long. Since the turtles will spend their entire lives in this enclosure, make it as big as space and money will allow. To prevent escape, the sides should be high or the top should be screened.

Adult box turtles are omnivores, and their diet should consist of 50 percent animal matter, 40 percent vegetables and leafy greens, and 10 percent fruit. Young box turtles are much more carnivorous, and animal matter should be greatly increased in their diet. Animal matter can include dead mice, mealworms, cricket,s and earthworms. There are many vegetables and greens favored by box turtles, including dandelion, kale, romaine, mustard and collard greens, mushrooms, bell peppers, shredded carrots, tomatoes, sweet potatoes, and squash. Avoid spinach and cabbage, as these are too high in oxalic acid. Oxalic acid can prevent proper utilization of calcium in the diet. A selection of fruits can include apples, melons, strawberries, blackberries, raspberries, pears, and many others. Food from all groups can be mixed together on shallow plates and fed to adult turtles three to four times a week. Hatchlings and juveniles should be fed every day.

Chapter 5: Reptiles and Amphibians

Aquatic Turtles

This group of turtles includes some large species such as red-eared sliders, chicken turtles, redbelly and yellowbelly turtles, and Suwannee, river, and hieroglyphic cooters. Smaller aquatics, like painted turtles, are more easily handled than the cooters and sliders.

All aquatics require a large, well-filtered enclosure at least 1.50 to 2 ft. (0.462 to 0.610 m) wide and 3 to 4 ft. (0.92 to 1.22 m) long. Many aquariums are only 1 ft. (0.305m) wide and are not appropriate for adult turtles. If the enclosure is large enough, a few turtles maybe kept together, but they should be closely watched for aggression, and mating is strongly discouraged.

Like box turtles, UV-B lighting is required for aquatic turtles.

Water temperatures should be in the 75 to 82 degree F range with a land basking area temperature around 88 to 90 degrees F. Basking platforms can be created by gluing (using aquarium glue) pieces of rigid tubing to the sides of the tank above the water level and resting a platform on the tubes. A ramp must be added so the turtle can climb up to the platform. External canister filters such as the Eheim® are absolutely necessary to maintain water quality, however, regular water changes are still essential. Fifty percent of the water should be changed every week and a complete water change should be done monthly.

Aquatic turtles must be in water to eat. They are omnivores with a strong leaning toward carnivore. Depending on the species, animal matter can comprise 65 to 90 percent of their diet and vegetable matter 35 percent or less. Animal matter should include trout chow, feeder fish, dead pinky mice, super mealworms, mealworms, and a good commercial pellet such as Reptomin®. The vegetable matter can be romaine, grated carrot, water plants such as water lettuce or water hyacinth, and dandelion. Adult turtles should be fed three to four times a week. Hatchlings and juveniles must be fed every day. Using a feeding bin filled with water is recommended by many keepers, and will reduce the mess in the enclosure.

SNAKES

A plastic sweater box of correct size, with holes melted into the sides and lid for air circulation is nearly the perfect enclosure for most small to medium snakes. The width of the enclosure should be half the length of the snake, and the length of the enclosure should be three quarters to full length of the snake. Newsprint is the best substrate, since it is easy to clean, available, safe and will not be ingested with the food. Inks rarely stick and all newsprint ink is completely safe. A hide box should always be available and can be easily constructed of a cardboard box with the lower side removed. The box should be large enough for the snake to curl up in easily.

Arboreal species should be given climbing branches. Plastic branches are easiest to use, bug free and able to be disinfected. Real tree branches should be collected in the late spring or summer since branches collected in the autumn or winter may have insects hibernating in them. Branches can be bound together using plastic wire ties to construct the correct shape of a tree canopy.

King Snakes

Certainly the best snake species for education, the king snake combines the traits of being easy to feed with being easy to care for and handle.

Temperatures vary among species but most prefer 70 to 82 degrees F with a warmer area of 88 to 93 degrees F. Water must always be available. Kings will almost always accept dead mice and they usually accept them readily and quickly, so watch your fingers! A two to three ft. (0.92 to 1.22 m) king snake will require four or five dead mice every two weeks. When handled, it should be remembered that these snakes eat mice, lizards, snakes, birds, voles, moles, juvenile rabbits, and other prey. If the handler's hand smells enough like a food item, the king snake is very capable of treating the hand as a food item!

Milk Snakes

Milk snakes are smaller relatives of the king snakes. They have similar temperature requirements and the feeding schedule is the same, but with smaller and/or fewer mice. Juvenile milk snakes can be difficult to feed. Very often, small live lizards are required to get the young milk snake to eat. Water should always be available.

Bull, Pine, and Gopher Snakes
These snakes have care and handling requirements similar to king snakes. However, bull snakes may take longer to tame down, and some may never tame. These heavy-bodied snakes can be five to seven ft. (1.52 to 2.13 m) long. They can be fed juvenile dead rats, but only the largest of them should be given adult dead rats. Temperatures are generally 70 to 82 degrees F with a 90 degree F warmer spot.

Rat and Corn Snakes
They are very similar in habits to king snakes, though rat snakes may benefit from having branches for climbing. As long as bull snakes at five to seven ft. (1.52 to 2.13 m), rat snakes are lighter and more slender. Again, very similar in habits to king snakes, although rat snakes may benefit from having branches for climbing. Corn snakes are generally more brightly colored and somewhat more docile than some species of rat snakes. Temperatures are generally 70 to 82 degrees F with a 90 degree F warmer spot.

Rubber and Rosey Boa
These are the only two boas in the US. They are not large snakes. In comparison, most bull or rat snakes are longer and heavier. Boas are shyer than the snakes already mentioned. They need it warmer as well, 80 to 85 degrees F with a 92 to 95 degree F basking area. They are easy feeders and accept mice readily. The enclosure should have multiple hide boxes, climbing branches, and an earth container to allow these snakes to burrow.

Garter and Ribbon Snakes
There are numerous species, subspecies, and geographical variants of garter and ribbon snakes. All are non-constrictor and non-venomous. This means that they do not kill their food prior to eating it, but eat it live. This can be a source of difficulty because it restricts food choices to earthworms and feeder fish. These snakes are recommended only if a steady, dependable, non-wild food source can be maintained. Younger garters may be difficult to train to eat fish out of a water dish, so use a live fish on the end of a tweezers as an enticement. Hand the fish head first to the snake. Garter snakes should never be fed live mice, as they have no defense from the mouse's teeth and claws.

All species may be kept in a typical snake enclosure as described above. Temperatures vary among species but most prefer 68 to 77 degrees F with a warmer area of 88 to 93 degrees F. Water must always be available and it must be cleaned more often if it has food fish in it.

LIZARDS
There are few lizards in the US that can be unreservedly recommended for education. Most are small, swift, nervous, and aggressive all their lives, and no amount of handling will alter them. The best recommendation would be to use an exotic lizard, such as the Australian bearded dragon or Asian leopard gecko, if a lizard is needed in the education program. If a US species must be used, the following can be considered.

Desert Iguanas
These lizards are sensitive creatures and should be handled with great care. Desert iguanas like it hot–enclosure temperatures of 90 degrees F with a basking area of 105 degrees F! Enclosure size needs to be at least 3 x 3 x 2 ft. (0.92 x 0.92 x 0.61 m). They require 4 to 8 in. (10.18 to 20.32 cm) of sand (play sand should be used and can be purchased in most hardware stores) in their enclosures and climbing equipment consisting of rock formations and tree branches. The climbing equipment should be firmly secured to prevent it from falling over onto the lizards. Food is a variety of invertebrates and greens. Water is often lapped from surfaces, so spraying the enclosure once a day is necessary. UV light is a must.

Great Plains Skinks
A large enclosure size is necessary for this skink and should be at l least 3 x 3 x 2 ft. (0.92 x 0.92 x 0.61 m). They require 2 to 4 in. (5.08 to 10.16 cm) of sand as a substrate and rock slabs or branches for climbing equipment. The climbing equipment should be firmly secured to prevent it from falling over onto the lizards. Temperature requirements are 78 to 86 degrees F with a basking area of 95 degrees F. All manner of insects are eaten. The enclosure should be sprayed twice a day and a small water bowl should be provided.

Chuckwallas
Chuckwallas are probably the best US lizard for education, but they are still a handful compared to exotic pet species. A large terrestrial enclosure, 4 x 3 x 3 ft. (1.22 x 0.92 x 0.92 m), is required and should have a sand

substrate, rocky structures and branches for climbing, and several above-ground hiding places. Temperatures of 85 to 92 degrees F with a basking spot of 100 degrees F are needed and UV light is mandatory. Greens and fruits should be offered and the lizard observed closely to see what it eats. Some chuckwallas eat well, while others only eat yellow flowers! Chuckwallas get most of their moisture from foods, but a water bowl should be provided.

Amphibians

Enclosures for amphibians start with an appropriately sized plastic or glass container. Most amphibians live at the edges of the pond and prefer shallow water, so the enclosure should be half water and half land. To create a large half-and-half tank, glue a plastic container to the sides of the tank just above the water level. Fill this with a substrate of sphagnum moss, potting soil, (minus the perlite and vermiculite), leaf litter, and tree bark, and add a ramp from the water to the container. This set up will give the animals a great deal of swimming space, but will require a great deal of water filtration and constant "touch ups"-picking the sphagnum out of the filter, netting it and shed skin out of the water, cleaning up dead, uneaten food insects and fish, and collecting soil that has fallen into the water. With deep levels of water, make sure that all animals in this enclosure swim very well or they could drown.

Another idea is the "island/pond", which involves filling a tank with water to 30 to 50 percent capacity and creating an island for hauling out on. The island can be a "milk crate" of appropriate size or some other construction that turtles can climb out on, but the "island" should be made of plastic. Plastic is light to remove or replace, is less accumulative of debris, and can be rinsed and disinfected. Stone or brick should not be used, as they will collect feces and breed bacteria that will foul the water in spite of a good filter.

An easier alternative would be to fill the container with substrate and sink a large bowl or deep pan to serve as a water area. Rounded rocks and sphagnum are piled beside the bowl to form an access slope. If the bowl is deep, a slope inside the bowl should also be constructed. This enclosure has a great deal less water but is also much easier to keep clean. Most of the work will simply be changing the water bowl every day.

Filtration is necessary with any semi-aquatic tank. There are many types of filters; under-gravel, submersible, overflow, biological, and more, but all were invented for fish. Filtration for amphibians should be used at many times the recommended level and rate for fish in the same size environment.

The water itself should be dechlorinated if it does not come from a well. This can be accomplished with a chemical dechlorinater or by leaving the water in open containers for 24 hours. Amphibians are not as sensitive to nitrates, nitrites, and ammonia as most fish, but a significant build-up could be a problem, so partial water changes will be necessary weekly. A total water change will be needed monthly, or sooner if the filter gets clogged or is not up to the load placed upon it. A substrate of sand or gravel can be used at the bottom of the water but it may clog the filter, cause obstructions in the animals if ingested, and can act as a breeding ground for some parasites.

The combination of materials used and the substrate depth depends on the burrowing needs of the animals to be housed. Salamanders dig burrows, many toads prefer to be partially submerged in earth, and most frogs will sit atop or just under the moss. Plastic plants can be added for cover or minor climbing. Plastic plants are superior to live plants since they can be cleaned and will not harbor pests. Additional cover materials should be included using halved clay flower pots, halved plastic bowls, or small pieces of slate. Use smooth, cheap materials for easy cleaning and inexpensive replacement.

A food bowl is also helpful, as many species will eat live insects or worms trapped in the bowl.

Keep in mind that many of the creatures are crepuscular (active only at dawn or dusk) or nocturnal, so high amounts of light are not only unnecessary but stress inducing. Also remember that nearly all amphibians like considerably cooler temperatures than the reptiles that inhabit similar environments. Even moderate heat may be enough to fry or dry your amphibian!

The level of humidity will depend on how much water the soil and moss is soaked with and how quickly the air absorbs it. Humidity is essential to these animals and should be checked daily with a small hydrometer.

Salamanders

Members of the *Ambystoma* group are the largest terrestrial salamanders in the US and include the Jefferson's, tiger, marbled, and spotted salamanders. Still, salamanders are relatively tiny and will work for small group education only. A terrestrial enclosure about 1 x 1 ft. (0.305 x 0.305 m) is adequate for a single animal. Large tigers or multiple animals should have larger quarters to insure they do not harm one another. Temperatures need to stay mild, 68 to 75 degrees F, with low light intensities. Humidity should be high, since most of these are forest floor dwellers and burrowers. Food items include small invertebrates, which need to be sized according to the individual consuming them.

Toads

The *Bufo* group is the largest toad grouping in the US and contains the American, Fowlers, marine, Colorado River, and green toads, among others. The larger individuals are excellent animals for education. All are hardy and feed easily on all varieties of invertebrates, which they will pick out of a shallow bowl. A 1 x 2 ft. (0.305 x 0.62 m) terrestrial enclosure kept at 65 to 75 degrees F could house several medium-sized specimens. The substrate should be a slightly damp mixture of moss, soil, and leaves with a water section. Be sure the toads are the same size, since larger toads will eat the smaller ones. No more than reflected light from the larger room is needed. Long-term captive specimens become so calm when handled they must be encouraged to jump!

Frogs

The largest frog grouping in the US is the *Rana* group. Most common frogs are bullfrogs, greens, leopards, and pickerels. The larger frogs from this group will become tractable enough to use in education, though not nearly as well-behaved as the toads. A large semi-aquatic enclosure, 3 x 3 ft. (0.92 x 0.92 m) or larger for exceptional specimens, will be needed for the bulls, greens, woods, and pig frogs. Temperatures should be in the 70 to 80 degrees F range with high humidity and moderate lighting. These frogs will eat all types of invertebrates and will usually take dead mice from tongs.

NOT RECOMMENDED FOR EDUCATION PROGRAMS

The crocodilians, venomous snakes, and venomous lizards should not be used for education programs. Tree frogs, ground snakes, green snakes, woodland salamanders, and most native skinks are all too small to be practical. Spadefoot toads, horned lizards, chorus frogs, narrowmouth frogs, and the American tortoises are sensitive creatures that can die from the stress of educational use. Snapping turtles, musk turtles, amphiuma, hellbenders, alligator lizards, soft-shelled turtles, water snakes, and collared lizards are all very willing to bite. Sea turtles should never be used due to their size, sensitivity, and protected status.

Literature Cited

Abate, Ardi. 2000. *Thoughts for Food: A step by step manual for providing healthy, nutritious and varied live food to insectivorous reptiles, amphibians, birds, mammals and other creatures.* Chameleon Information Network, San Diego, CA.

Coborn, John. 1992. *The Proper Care of Amphibians.* T.F.H. Publication, Inc, Neptune City, NJ.

Conant, Roger and Joseph T. Collins. 1991. *Peterson Field Guides: Reptiles and Amphibians: Eastern/Central North America.* Third Edition. Houghton Mifflin Company, Boston. ISBN 0-395-58389-6 (pbk)

Miller, E. A., ed. 2000. *Minimum Standards for Wildlife Rehabilitation, 3rd Edition.* National Wildlife Rehabilitators Association, St. Cloud, MN.

Oldfield, Barney and John J. Moriarty. 1994. *Amphibians and Reptiles Native to Minnesota.* University of Minnesota Press, Minneapolis, MN. ISBN 0-8166-2384-8

Tyning, Thomas F. 1990. *Stokes Nature Guides: A Guide to Amphibians and Reptiles.* Little, Brown and Company, Boston. ISBN: 0-316-81713-9 (pbk)

Chapter 6

BIRDS

There are about 800 species of native birds found in North America, adjacent islands, and offshore waters (Sibley 2000). Many of these species come under the care of wildlife rehabilitators, and fairly large proportions of these birds are permanently disabled and become non-releasable. A small percentage of these birds can be placed in educational facilities or used in education programs. Rehabilitated birds are not the only birds eligible for use as education animals. Different laws apply to non-native and captive-bred native birds, and thus are regulated differently than native birds protected by the Migratory Bird Treaty Act (MBTA). Check with your regional USFWS office for applicable permit regulations.

If you are reading this book, you presumably have an interest in learning what species are suitable for education programs and how to determine how to ensure an individual bird's success. A few suggestions for getting started are included in this chapter, but all are built on the same theme: to become an excellent educator using birds, you must study birds and understand what it takes to have a successful education program.

SUITABILITY OF SPECIES

Some bird species or families are known to be unsuitable for education programs for numerous reasons. Intolerance to humans, stress, or confinement are only a few of the reasons some bird groups are not recommended as education animals. Many bird species are not discussed here because of their unsuitability. The following families or species groups are to be avoided for educational programs based on natural history information and prior experience. Of course, there are always exceptions, and not all of the species included in these families or groups are inappropriate, however, the majority of birds will not work as education animals.

Birds that are generally unsuitable for education birds:

Cuculidae	cuckoos and their allies (some species may work)
Apodidae	swifts
Trochilidae	hummingbirds
Picidae	woodpeckers
Passerines	(many families) including perching songbirds, swallows, crows, magpies, ravens
Gaviidae	loons
Podicipedidae	small and large grebes
Seabirds	(many families) pelicans, gannets, boobies, cormorants, anhinga, frigatebirds, tropicbirds
Wading birds	(many families) herons, bitterns, egrets, storks, ibis, spoonbills

Severely debilitating injuries or profound blindness are not acceptable in education birds. Birds with otherwise adequate physical condition that cannot tolerate the stress of captivity and close human contact are also unacceptable. The adaptive behavior of some species makes it difficult to maintain them in captivity with a permanent injury. For example, a bird that is adapted to hunting insects on the wing may never eat from a bowl or fingers.

Education birds must be trained or conditioned to be handled in front of an audience. A great blue heron and a red-tailed hawk both present a degree of danger to a handler, but the red-tailed hawk can be conditioned to tolerate being used in a program, where the blue heron is less likely to "behave" in front of a group. The impression your bird makes on the audience is worth considering in detail. For example, a crow may be easy to handle, perhaps even a bit too easy. These birds must appear "wild" and not give the impression of being cute pets.

The remaining sections of this chapter contain more specific information on the housing of raptors, waterbirds, and passerines (songbirds and perching birds) and other miscellaneous avian groups. It is worth repeating that you must check with the local or regional office of your state's wildlife or natural resources agency, and the regional US Fish and Wildlife Service before you try to acquire any bird protected by MBTA for educational purposes. Birds are more regulated than any other taxa, and there are many rules and regulations that you must comply with.

Theoretically, you should design your education program and define your message before accepting an animal or bird. Trying to "fit in" or design a program around an otherwise excellent education animal is not the best practice and will not provide you with the professional program you are seeking.

Another thing to consider before accepting any bird for educational use is the permanent injury that makes it non-releasable. Some injuries make it difficult for the bird to be handled or to live comfortably in captivity.

- Your federal permit authorizes possession of specific birds, so you need prior permission to accept any bird. Current regulations clearly define what types of injuries warrant euthanasia, and what types are acceptable for attempted rehabilitation activities.

- Wing amputees above the elbow are no longer permitted by USFWS.

- Full or partial leg amputees have difficulty balancing on one leg. Larger birds cannot support themselves on one leg all the time without detrimental side-effects. Unfortunately, these creatures are not suitable for release and not suitable for educational birds. They will eventually develop many foot problems such as sores, open wounds, or pressure spots (bumblefoot), which cause the tissue to break down and develop topical and systemic infections.

- Birds that are blind in one eye can learn to live comfortably in captivity. The handlers need to recognize and adapt to the animal's blindness, as this disability may make the bird more nervous. Specifically, you must be aware that often they cannot see something and are startled when it suddenly "appears" before them.

- Birds that are blind in both eyes need to be assessed on an individual basis. Check with your regional USFWS office for regulations regarding this injury and the limited exceptions for obtaining a permit for such birds. If the individual is calm, it may work as an educational animal. Unfortunately if it is nervous, life may be extraordinarily scary and unfair for the bird. If the bird does work, an enormous amount of management will have to be done for this bird to keep it comfortable and healthy.

- Amputated or missing toes may not impair a bird in captivity. Raptors, since they depend on their talons for survival, are vulnerable if certain toes have to be amputated.

- Partial amputation or mutilation of the beak is an injury that a bird may survive with in captivity. An education bird candidate with this condition is successful only if its management needs and medical needs can be met. Specific problems are mouth and tongue drying out, feeding process, preening activity, and other behaviors.

- If the bird was raised by humans in the wrong part of its development, then imprinting can be a consideration. The bird may be more accepting of a captive situation, but again, it may not be. The adult imprinted bird may become aggressive and territorial.

When considering a bird for use in an education program, look for other birds of the same species being kept in a captive educational situation successfully. If you cannot find other examples, that particular species may not be suited to captivity or an education program life. Talk to bird trainers, falconers, zoo education personnel, and nature center personnel when researching species suitability for education programs.

RAPTORS

Raptors are commonly called birds of prey, and include the hawks, eagles, falcons, vultures, osprey, and owls of the world. Many species of raptors have been used for the sport of falconry. Falconry is the use of raptors, typically hawks and falcons, for hunting purposes. Falconry has been around for over 4000 years, probably beginning in the Arab world (Beebe and Webster 1994).

Many of the techniques to house, feed, and hunt with raptors have been time-tested and improved upon with modern technology, science, and medicine. Different types of raptors are commonly used in education programs. Some birds adapt very well to a life in captivity and can be incredibly useful tools for environmental education, however, most will need a lot of training to become comfortable perched on the glove in front of a crowd.

For the purposes of housing, food, and training considerations, raptors are put in three size and behavior categories (Table 9).

TABLE 9 – GENERAL RAPTOR CATEGORIES

Size	A sample of species included in that size
Small (less than 200 grams)	American kestrel, burrowing owl, saw-whet owl, screech owl, merlin
Medium (201 to 1500 grams)	red-tailed hawk, great horned owl, barn owl, barred owl, goshawk
Large (more than 1501 grams)	eagle, vulture, osprey

Editor's note: This publication addresses those animals used in on-site and off-site education programming. Any cage sizes noted are a minimum size to be used when animals are not in transport carriers. This publication does not address animals used in static displays, who have much different requirements for permanent caging.

HOUSING

All permanently injured animals used in educational circumstances, including raptors, must have facilities that they call their home reflecting their natural history as well as their disability needs. Each bird should have enough room in its mew, or housing area that provides protection from the weather, to move around and to feel secure. Birds of prey should be kept in enclosures that meet or exceed falconry standards described in the Federal Regulations 50 CFR 21.29. Guidelines for housing and care are also described in *Care and Management of Captive Raptors* (Arent and Martell 1996). The enclosure must be large enough for the bird to open its wings without touching any wall of the enclosure. Some wild birds are more safely housed in enclosures that are smaller rather than larger as they adjust to being in a mew (Arent, Lori, personal communication).

Outside Mews

The mew can be rectangular, square, or any other shape as long as it fits the requirements of the bird. At least one back wall should be solid, for example, made of painted plywood. One solid wall adjoining the first solid wall is even better for security and weather protection. The bird is protected from the harshest elements if these two adjoining walls are placed so the prevailing winds hit this barrier from the outside. Alternately, you should have the back wall solid, and the back third to half of the two adjoining walls solid. If all walls are solid, windows must be provided at regular intervals for ventilation and weather exposure. All of these configurations provide security and protection.

Partial exposure to the elements is important for ventilation, and for the raptor's well-being and health. Mew designs should allow raptors to move into and out of the weather according to their comfort level. For example, if they choose to sun themselves, they have an area to do so, however, if it is too hot for them, they can retreat to another part of the mew or into a hutch.

The remaining walls of the mew can be constructed of non-solid materials. Wood lath or slats can be placed vertically from floor to ceiling for a wall. The same materials can be used for windows in a solid wall. Doweling, sturdy PVC pipe, or smooth conduit pipe can be used for window construction as well. If using this type of vertical bars for windows or walls, measure the spacing carefully to prevent escapes and predation attempts (Table 10). Chicken wire, hardware cloth or other type of metal mesh are not acceptable as window coverings. These metal meshes can harm the bird if it comes in contact with these materials.

TABLE 10
OPENING SIZES FOR MESH OR BARS ON A RAPTOR CAGE

Type of bird	Gap for mesh or between vertical bars
Small raptors	0.50 in. (1.27 cm)
Medium raptors	1.50 in. (3.81 cm)
Large raptors	2 in. (5.08)

Editor's note: This publication addresses those animals used in on-site and off-site education programming. Any cage sizes noted are a minimum size to be used when animals are not in transport carriers. This publication does not address animals used in static displays, who have much different requirements for permanent caging.

The roof, whether open or semi-solid, should be made of materials that will protect the bird from predators, let snow through, and will not harm the bird. The ceiling or roof of the mew can be solid slanting construction, as long as the bird is provided with adequate ventilation and exposure to natural elements. It is beneficial to have a partial roof, but the entire roof does not need to be solid.

Wood slats can be used to make a semi-solid roof. Use the same spacing between slats as for the walls. Chain link or 1 x 2 in. (2.54 x 5.08 cm) mesh can cover the slats to provide better protection from predators. Do not allow nails, screws, or anything sharp to protrude into the cage. It may injure the bird. Walls should extend approximately 6 in. (15.24 cm) below the surface of the soil. The section of the wall buried can be made of cement, 1 x 2 in. (2.54 x 5.08 cm) galvanized wire, or chain link fencing. These materials are then covered with soil, sand, or rocks. The wire or fencing material can go straight down into the ground or placed at a 45 degree angle from the wall to prevent entry of digging predators.

Mosquito-proof the mews during the summer months or move the raptor indoors when incidence of mosquito activity is high. These precautions will help prevent the transmission of West Nile virus and avian malaria to your raptor.

The enclosure should provide easy access for maintenance of bird and cage. Consider having the lower sill of the door off the ground for snow clearance and moving the top of the opening a little lower to discourage a scared bird from flying out over your head. An outdoor enclosure should have some type of double door system installed. This construction can resemble a cage within a cage around several mews or a vestibule in front of the door at each mew. A double door construction will contain any escapee from the mew, and provides a "first line of defense" against predators.

The mew flooring needs to be easily cleaned and to drain well. Cement as the base flooring can work if there is at least 3 to 4 in. (7.62 x 10.16 cm) of another substrate on top of it to provide cushion for the bird's feet. The additional substrate allows the feces (mutes) to move away from the bird's feet.
Pea gravel is the most common substrate used on top of concrete, soil, or dirt. This rock can vary from 0.50 to 1 in. (1.27 to 2.54 cm) in diameter and is rounded, but irregular, in shape. Slightly bigger rock can be used, (1.25 to 2 in. [3.175 to 5.08 cm] in diameter). Larger sized rocks cause foot problems and should not be used. Sand, grass, or artificial turf can work for floor substrate. Sand requires care, as impaction can result from ingesting sand-coated food.

Guidelines to the general minimum sizes for raptor enclosures are found on the next page (Table 11). The measurements in Table 11 are offered as minimums, but all birds should be able to completely turn around with wings and tail extended without touching the walls, floor, or roof of the cage.

TABLE 11
MINIMUM ENCLOSURE SIZES FOR RAPTORS IN CAPTIVITY (Arent and Martell 1996)

		Length ft. (m)	Width ft. (m)	Height ft. (m)
Small birds	Flighted	6 (1.83)	6 (1.83)	7 (2.134)
	Nonflighted	3 (0.93)	3 (0.93)	3 (0.93)
Medium size birds	Flighted	12 (3.66)	6 (1.83)	7 (2.134)
	Nonflighted	6 (1.83)	6 (1.83)	7 (2.134)
Large size birds	Flighted	40 (12.20)	10 (3.05)	9 (2.74)
	Nonflighted	12 (3.66)	10 (3.05)	9 (2.74)

Editor's note: This publication addresses those animals used in on-site and off-site education programming. Any cage sizes noted are a minimum size to be used when animals are not in transport carriers. This publication does not address animals used in static displays, who have much different requirements for permanent caging.

The external dimension for mews provides only the very basic parameters for enclosure construction. Included in each enclosure should be many other elements, such as perches, hutches and tethering areas for each individual's comfort. Use your imagination and careful observations of the bird to construct as secure and comforting "home" as possible.

Enclosure Elements

Perches

Perches come in all shapes, sizes and materials (Table 12). Generally they are very flat, rounded, or beveled. It is a good idea to have several perching options for the bird. Provide a variety of perches and place them strategically to encourage the bird to use them. Because birds usually sit where they want to, and not on the perch best suited to them, observe where the bird sits most often and make that perch the healthiest for that bird's feet.

Rounded or beveled perches should fit the foot of the bird sitting on them. A good rule of thumb is the bird's foot should not encircle the perch more than 0.50 to 0.75 in. (1.27 to 1.905 cm) around a rounded perch. Proper sizes and some materials for perches are found below. Natural branches with rough bark can make very suitable perches. Follow the size guidelines and do not use branches with runny sap. All perches must be re-roped, re-covered, or replaced on a regular basis.

Block perches usually stand on the ground and are flat on top. They can be as simple as a flattened stump with turf on the top or as complicated as a beautifully turned piece of wood (also flat on the top) on a nice stand. Block perches can be used in mews where a bird is free-lofted (flying loose in the mew) or a bird can be tethered to it for training or weathering purposes. Shelf perches are also flat but are usually mounted onto the wall of the mew. Shelf perches are rounded in front and are generally attached flush with the wall of the mew.

TABLE 12
RECOMMENDED PERCH SIZES FOR CAPTIVE RAPTORS

Species	Surface size (inches)	Cover size (inches)
American kestrel	0.375 in. (0.953cm) dowel 6 in. (15.24 cm) diameter block perch	0.25 in. (0.635 cm) rope or artificial turf
Bald eagle	Modified 2 x 4 in. (5.08 x 20.26 cm) beveled so the top is 1 in. (2.54 cm) thick	0.50 in. (1.27 cm) rope
Barn owl	Modified 2 x 4 in. (5.08 x 20.26 cm) beveled so that the top is rounded to 0.75 in. (1.905 cm) top	0.375 in. (0.953cm) rope or artificial turf
Barred owl	Modified 2 x 4 in. (5.08 x 20.26 cm) beveled so top is 0.50 in. (1.27 cm) thick	0.375 in. (0.953cm) rope or artificial turf
Burrowing owl	6 in. (15.24 cm) diameter block perch	artificial turf
Golden eagle	Modified 2 x 4 in. (5.08 x 20.26 cm) beveled so top is 1 in. (2.54 cm) thick	0.50 in. (1.27 cm) rope or artificial turf
Great horned owl	Modified 2 x 4 in. (5.08 x 20.26 cm) beveled so top is 0.75 in. (1.905 cm) thick	0.375 in. (0.953 cm) rope
Northern goshawk	0.75 in. (1.905 cm) dowel	0.25 in. (0.635 cm) rope
Peregrine falcon	1 ft. (2.54 cm) diameter shelf or block perch	Artificial turf
Prairie falcon	1 ft. (2.54 cm) diameter shelf or block perch	Artificial turf
Red-tailed hawk	Modified 2 x 4 in. (5.08 x 20.26 cm) beveled so top is 0.75 in. (1.905 cm) thick	0.375 in. (0.953 cm) rope
Rough-legged hawk	Modified 2 x 4 in. (5.08 x 20.26 cm) beveled so top is 0.75 in. (1.905 cm) thick	0.375 in. (0.953 cm) rope
Saw-whet owl	0.375 in. (0.953 cm) dowel	0.25 in. (0.635 cm) rope
Screech owl	0.375 in. (0.953 cm) dowel	0.25 in. (0.635 cm) rope
Turkey vulture	24 in. (5.08 m) diameter block	Artificial turf

Editor's note: This publication addresses those animals used in on-site and off-site education programming. Any cage sizes noted are a minimum size to be used when animals are not in transport carriers. This publication does not address animals used in static displays, who have much different requirements for permanent caging.

Hutches and Shelter Boxes

Hutches and shelter boxes are very important to the raptor in a captive situation because they offer shelter and security (Table 13). In cold weather climates, such furniture can help the bird conserve body heat. Shelter boxes are generally mounted on the wall of the mew and have three sides, a roof, and are open on the bottom. The perch either attaches to the wall perpendicular to the wall, or it is attached to the walls of the box itself and is parallel to the wall of the mew the box is attached to. Hutches are generally on the ground and have three sides, a top, and no bottom, and are furnished with a perch.

Perches can be attached to the top of both of these types of shelters for additional perching options. These boxes are generally made out of painted plywood. Hutches may also be heated if needed during the cold weather months. Make sure the bird cannot touch the heating element and that the bird can change its position relative to the heat source.

TABLE 13
RECOMMENDED MINIMUM SHELTER BOX/HUTCH SIZES FOR CAPTIVE RAPTORS

Species	Depth in. (m)	Width in. (m)	Height in. (m)
Small birds	12 (0.305 m)	12 (0.305 m)	12 (0.305 m)
Medium birds	15 (0.38 m)	24 (0.61 m)	24 (0.61 m)
Large birds	35 (0.89 m)	35 (0.89 m)	35 (0.89 m)

Editor's note: This publication addresses those animals used in on-site and off-site education programming. Any cage sizes noted are a minimum size to be used when animals are not in transport carriers. This publication does not address animals used in static displays, who have much different requirements for permanent caging.

Water

Most raptors do drink and enjoying bathing, so you need to supply a suitable container for these activities. Rubber pans and plastic cement mixing trays work well. This container should be as wide as the bird is long and the water level no greater than the bird's leg length.

Weathering Areas (Outdoor Tethering Area)

Weathering areas are usually grassy areas where a raptor is tethered to a perch, with a water pan nearby and a hutch to retreat into. The area is roped or fenced to keep people and other animals a certain distance away. Weathering areas are used to give the raptor more sunshine (usually) than they are able to get in the mews. These areas also provide a way for the public to view the raptor. Many raptors can be tethered together in the same weathering area, but spaced appropriately so as not to get tangled together, or hurt one another. The weathering area can be covered with netting above and to the sides to help with predator protection. Aerial predators may think a kestrel would be a nice meal, tethered or not!

A weathering area should be supervised while the birds are in it. A handler needs to be nearby to occasionally check on the birds. Many times birds become tangled, or worse, and need to be returned to the mew. Raptors can be tethered to a block perch or a bow perch (half circle usually roped or covered with turf) in the weathering area (Table 14). The water pan should be situated so that the bird can reach and stand in the middle of the pan, but no further. If the tether is too long, the bird can become tangled over the far end of the pan.

Do not tether small raptors near large ones, as the smaller birds will feel threatened. Visual barriers can be used to help reduce stress between two birds that are aggressive toward one another. Small birds in a weathering area should be directly supervised at all times.

A raptor can be tethered safely if the equipment is correctly attached to the bird's legs. Because raptors have very strong legs and toes, bracelets and jesses are safe to use and well tolerated. The use of jesses and other equipment on the legs of non-raptor bird species is not generally recommended.

TABLE 14
RECOMMENDED OUTDOOR PERCH DESIGN AND SIZE FOR TETHERING A BIRD

Animal	Design	Size
Medium to large falcon	Block	5 to 8 in. (12.7 to 20.32 cm) top diameter 4 in. (5.08 cm) bottom diameter 11 in. (27.94 cm) high
Small falcon	Block	3.5 to 4.5 in. (8.89 to 11.43 cm) top diameter 2.5 in. (6.35 cm) bottom diameter 7 in. (17.78 cm) high
Small hawks	Bow	1 to 1.5 in. (2.54 to 3.81 cm) diameter At least 2.5 ft. (0.762 m) long 8 to 10 in. (20.32 to 30.48 cm) high
Large hawks	Bow	At least 3.5 ft. (8.89 cm) long 12 to 14 in. (30.48 to 35.56 cm) high

Tethering a raptor

Many raptors used for educational purposes are constantly tethered in the mew and in the weathering area. This practice is a very safe way of managing birds of prey. The birds can become very comfortable tethered when handled regularly. Offer many different perching surfaces or rotate perch type daily. Block perches should be a little smaller than normal in diameter if the bird is tethered all the time to help prevent tail feather breakage. For example, a falcon block perch should be around 8 in. (20.32 cm) in diameter.

One method of managing raptors combines tethering the bird the entire period of time that the individual is being used in programs and free-lofting the same bird in a mew during any time "off" (1 to 2 months). As always, it is recommended you consult with falconers, educators, and others who handle raptors in public displays to gain the benefit of their experience. Raptors handled this way must meet federal and state guidelines for falconry.

FEEDING

Raptors are carnivorous predators. In the wild, raptors generally consume the whole of their catch; bones, fur, feathers, internal organs, and everything else. Every 18 to 24 hours they will cast a pellet that contains some of the items they cannot fully digest. Pellet content, consistency, and frequency can be clues into the health of the raptor. A variety of food items are available to feed raptors, including mice, rats, hamsters, gerbils, rabbits, quail, other poultry, and in some cases, fish. Most birds can be fed a variety of food, and doing so provides enrichment and proper nutrition. Of course, some raptors have specific dietary needs (osprey only eat fish, for example), and you must meet those specific needs.

Freshly killed prey is preferable because it may have optimal nutrients. If feeding mainly frozen food items, it is recommended to include in the bird's diet a vitamin supplement daily like Vitahawk™.

Frozen food should be thawed in the refrigerator overnight or be rehydrated and thawed slowly in cold (not hot) water. All food should be fed within a 24 to 36 hour period after thawing. Food should be presented at room temperature and not too cold. Offer whole animals (bones, fur, feathers, organs, etc.) to ensure the bird receives a proper balance of vitamins and minerals, as well as casting material. Do not feed live prey items. If you are not sure if the food is in good condition, do not use it! Food items with tissue discolorations, freezer burns, fecal contamination, or a bad smell should be rejected. It is not recommended to feed road kill or animals from unknown sources.

Raptors are birds of habit. Try to feed the birds in the same place and at the same time every day. Food requirements of raptors vary greatly not only according to the size of the bird, but also the time of the year, the activity level of the bird, the weather, molting, and even its gender. Weigh your birds periodically (at least twice per week if they are not flying, daily if they are) to determine their optimal food consumption. Keep daily records including type and amount of food offered each at feeding. Raptors usually are fed once per day. In very cold weather, small birds may need to be fed more than once a day.

Generally, you should plan on feeding raptors a percentage of their body weight that varies with overall size (Arent and Martell 1996). Here is a general guide to what percentage of body weight to feed daily (Table 15):

TABLE 15 – GENERAL NUTRITION FOR RAPTORS

Size of Raptor	Percentage of body weight fed daily
100 to 200 gm (4 to 8 oz)	20 percent
200 to 800 gm (8 oz to 1.8 lbs)	15 percent
800 to 1,200 gm (1.8 to 2.8 lbs)	10 percent
1,200 gm (2.8 lbs) and above	6 to 8 percent

CLEANING

Raptor mews should be cleaned daily and mutes (fecal material), castings, feathers and old food removed. Uneaten food should be removed before the end of each day. This prevents the bird from eating it early the next morning. Uneaten food attracts unwanted flies and other insects, and scavengers smelling the "free" food.

All cages should be on a disinfection schedule for walls, perches, and water pans. This schedule may have to be modified during cold winter months when you are unable to use water to spray down the mew. During the summer, water and sunshine will help to prevent bacteria from growing between disinfections.

HANDLING AND TRANSPORT OF BIRDS FOR PROGRAMS

Handling

Gaining experience handling and training raptors is strongly recommended before you acquire a raptor as an education animal—even if the bird is already trained. Handling techniques are complex and are not covered in this text. Making or applying falconry equipment is also a complicated subject, and there are many sources that you can use to find more information. Please refer to the books listed in the suggested readings, and talk to people who have experience working with raptors as falconry birds and as education birds.

Raptors are handled on the top of the closed fingers of a gloved hand. The hand is held at about an 85 to 90 degree angle from the body with the elbow bent. Hold the jesses between the index finger and thumb of the hand holding the bird, passed between the third and fourth fingers, where they are attached to the swivel and the leash. Before doing full programs, birds should be fully comfortable on the glove and in front of people, as well as trained to go into and out of a travel crate. The birds should be trained to sit on a scale and be weighed. At a minimum, weigh your raptors once a week. Birds that are being trained using weight management should be weighed once per day. Table 16 gives the definitions of some common terms.

TABLE 16 – GENERAL DESCRIPTIONS OF COMMON EQUIPMENT

Term	Description
Jesses	Jesses are straps made of leather or nylon cord (like parachute cord) that assist in keeping the bird on the glove when it is being held or tethered. Two types of jesses can be used. Traditional jesses are of one piece and are attached to the leg above the foot with a length of strap left for the handler to hold or to attach to a swivel and leash to tether to a perch. These types of jesses should not be used on birds that are free flown or on education birds that can fly, as they can become tangled in branches or other objects. Aylmeri jesses consist of a separate bracelet that is attached around the bird's leg above the toes. This piece is made from soft leather and is attached to itself with a grommet. The jess is then passed through the grommet. Each bird has one jess per leg.
Swivel	The swivel connects the bird's jesses to the leash when it is tethered. A swivel is two stainless steel rings separated by a piece of steel and it rotates to help prevent the jess from tangling or becoming knotted on itself.
Leash	The leash can be made from climbing rope, parachute cord, or leather. This piece is used to tether the bird to a perch.
Glove	Wear a glove every time the raptor is on your fist. Gloves are available in different sizes and thicknesses. Leather gloves provide the best protection for the handler and give the raptor a good perch to sit and grip onto. Wearing a glove during programs demonstrates clearly that the raptor is not a pet. It makes you appear more professional by showing that safety for the handler and the bird is important. It shows that the bird, although in captivity, is still a wild animal.
Hood	A hood is a formed (by sewing or gluing) leather helmet designed to comfortably fit over the head and the eyes of falcons and hawks. It is designed to keep this type of bird calm when being handled or moved.
Spray Bottle	Use a bottle to spray a light mist of water on the raptor's legs and near its mouth when it is stressed or too warm to help it cool down.
Scale	Weighing raptors is a good way to keep track of their overall health (see General Health).
Falconer's Knot	This knot is extremely important to learn, as it is used to tether a bird. You have to apply it with one hand and you take it out with one hand.

Transport

In most cases, you will have a separate travel enclosures for transporting birds to and from program locations. These travel enclosures can be plastic dog crates, handmade wood "giant hoods," or similar containers. For small birds, modified cardboard boxes may work just fine. Some birds do quite well traveling on a perch solidly mounted in the travel carrier, while others do better if there is no perch. Generally, there should be plenty of ventilation into the enclosure. The interior of the crate should be dark or very dim when the door is closed to help keep the bird calm, and the door should be located on the side of the enclosure.

The size of the transport enclosure is important (Table 17). It must allow the bird to perch and mute (defecate) properly without damaging any feathers, but not be so large as to allow the bird to do a lot of jumping around. Length of tail and calmness of the bird are two factors in determining the correct size for the enclosure. The best crate size can be determined by talking to experienced trainers and by knowing the individual bird.

TABLE 17
MINIMUM SIZE RECOMMENDATIONS FOR SEVERAL TYPES OF RAPTOR TRANSPORT CARRIERS GIVEN AS W x L x H

Size of bird	Dog kennel in. (m)	Giant hood in. (m)	Plywood carrier in. (m)
Under 200 gm	20 x 11 x 12.5 in. (0.51 x 0.28 x 0.32 m)	12.5 x 12.5 x 14 in. (0.32 x 0.32 x 0.36 m)	------ ------
200 to 2000 gm	26 x 20 x 20 in. (0.66 x 0.51 x 0.51 m)	19 x 17 x 25 in. (0.48 x 0.43 x 0.635 m)	27 x 14 x 20 in. (0.69 x 0.36 x 0.51 m)
Over 2000 gm	40 x 31 x 30 in. (1.02 x 0.79 x 0.76 m)	23 x 22 x 30 in. (0.58 x 0.56 x 0.76 m)	27 x 14 x 20 in. (0.69 x 0.36 x 0.51 m)

WATERBIRDS

Waterbirds are defined as birds that spend a lot of their lives in, on, or near the water. Most waterbirds do not work well for education birds. For example, some are very colonial in nature and will suffer from stress if housed alone, while some rely on water which makes it impractical to take them out on programs. However, some species may work very well for on or offsite education programs. In the introduction of this chapter several bird families or groups were given as "unsuitable" for use as education animals. Below you will find more detail on the unsuitable families within the waterbird group.

Waterbird families that are not recommended for education birds

Gaviidae (loons)
These birds spend the majority of their time in the water. Their feet are located far back on their bodies which makes standing and walking on land for any period of time very difficult. These birds, especially adults, can suffer from high stress. These birds have an incidence of contracting aspergillosis, a disease caused by airborne fungus, that can terminally compromise their lungs and air sacs.

Podicipedidae (grebes)
Grebes are similar to loons, as they spend much of their time on the water, and their legs are situated toward the back of their bodies. Grebes are perfect for diving and catching fish but not easy to maintain in captivity. These birds do not tolerate stress well.

Diomedeidae (albatrosses)
These birds are colonial and spend most of their life at sea. They have enormous wingspans from 5 feet 10 in. (1.75m) to 12 ft. (3.7m) (Sibley 2001).

Procellariidae (petrels and shearwaters) and **Phaethontidae** (tropicbirds)
These birds are very similar to the albatrosses, colonial and spend the majority of their life over and on the water.

Fregatidae (frigatebirds)
Frigatebirds spend most of their time at sea. These birds do perch on branches, but have very delicate fragile long wing and tail feathers that would be difficult to keep intact.

Aramidae (limpkins)
These secretive birds are prone to stress.

Rallidae (rails, gallinules, and coots)
These birds are very secretive and prone to stress.

Haematopodidae (oystercatchers) and *Recurvirostridae* (stilts and avocet)
Oystercatchers are flock birds and suffer from high stress in captivity.

Anatidae (swans, geese, and ducks)
Some of the individuals in this family will work for education birds, for example, mallards and Canada geese, but many others suffer unreasonable stress. Most swans will be difficult because of their size and defenses.

Ardeidae (egrets, bitterns, and herons).
These birds can be susceptible to high stress. Their beaks can be a danger as well.

Charadriidae (plovers, killdeer) and
Scolopacidae (sandpipers, phalaropes, dowitchers, snipe, turnstones, stints and woodcock).
All of these birds suffer high stress in captivity, and some species are very gregarious.

Laridae (skuas, jaegers, gulls, and terns).
Some of these individuals may do well as education birds (gulls in particular), but all in this family are gregarious and the terns are more shy and easily stressed.

Waterbird families suitable for selected educational programming

Pelecanidae (pelicans).
Certain pelicans can socialize with people to the point that they may be comfortable doing programs. Drawbacks to using pelicans as education birds include a quick snap of their beak that could injure an unwary handler or bystander and fecal material that is very odorous (as in all fish-eating birds).

Sulidae (gannets and boobies) and **Phalacrocoracidae** (cormorants).
These birds are smaller than pelicans and would be easier to transport, but still will have odorous fecal material.

Ciconiidae (storks) and **Gruidae** (cranes).
These are very large animals and are hard to transport. Handlers and observers must be wary of their beaks. These birds would do better in a group, and they are not suitable for the beginning handler.

Threskiornithidae (ibises and spoonbills).
These birds must be kept in a flock situation. Injured adults may be too wary of humans for program use, but juveniles and imprinted birds may be suitable. These birds will be hard to transport because they prefer being in a flock, and they are not suitable for a beginning handler.

Alcidae (auks and puffins).
These waterbirds are smaller in size and are more easily transported. Auks, however, spend almost all their time in the water, and there may be some high stress experienced by these birds.

HOUSING FOR WATERBIRDS

General guidelines on sizes of cages and some cage furniture are important for keeping suitable waterbirds comfortable and healthy (Table 18). Please read carefully the codes and notes associated with them. The information provided is modified from the *Minimum Standards for Wildlife Rehabilitation*, 3rd Edition (Miller 2000) and from the Florida Game and Freshwater Fish Commission to accommodate the special needs of education birds (Regulations 68A-6.004 on Standard Caging Requirements for Captive Wildlife: Specific Authority Art. IV, Sec. 9, Fla. Const. Law Implemented Art. IV, Sec. 9, Fla. Const. 372.921, 372.922).

TABLE 18
MINIMUM HOUSING GUIDELINES FOR WATERBIRDS USED IN EDUCATION

Family	Species	Minimum cage size (W x L x H)	Codes
Pelecanidae	white pelican	Aviary with pool: 144 sq. ft. (44 sq. m) with half of the area a pool 18 to 24 in. (0.46 x 0.61 m) deep. 2 birds maximum**	M, W, PT, AP, SO
	brown pelican	Aviary with pool: 144 sq. ft. (44 sq. m) with half of the area a pool 18 to 24 in. (0.46 x 0.61 m) deep. 2 birds maximum**	M, W, PT, AP, SO
Sulidae	gannet	Aviary with pool: Aviary: 8 x 16 x 8 ft. (2.44 x 4.88 x 2.44 m), (128 sq. ft. [39 sq. m]) Pool: 8 ft. (2.44 m) diameter, 2 ft. (1.83 m) deep, 6 birds maximum*	M, W, PT, AP, SO, ST
	booby	Aviary with pool: Aviary: 8 x 16 x 8 ft. (2.44 x 4.88 x 2.44 m) (128 sq. ft. [39 sq. m]) Pool: 8 ft. (2.44 m) diameter, 2 ft. (1.83 m) deep, 6 birds maximum*	M, W, AP, SO, ST
Phalacrocoracidae	cormorant	Aviary with pool: Aviary: 8 x 16 x 8 ft. (2.44 x 4.88 x 2.44 m) (128 sq. ft. [39 sq. m]) Pool: 8 ft. (2.44 m) diameter, 2 ft. (1.83 m) deep, 6 birds maximum*	M, W, AP, SO, ST
Ciconiidae	wood stork	Aviary with wading pool: 144 sq. ft. (44 sq. m) floor space with 14 sq. ft. (4.27 sq. m) pool 6 to 10 in. (15.2 x 25.4 cm) deep** 4 birds maximum	M, W, AW,
Threskiornithidae	ibis	Aviary with wading pool: 144 sq. ft. (44 sq. m) floor space with 14 sq. ft. (4.27 sq. m) pool 6 to 10 in. (15.2 x 25.4 cm) deep** 4 birds maximum	M, W, AW, FL
	spoonbill	Aviary with wading pool: 144 sq. ft. (44 sq. m) floor space with 14 sq. ft. (4.27 sq. m) pool 6 to 10 in. (15.2 x 25.4 cm) deep** 4 birds maximum	M, W, AW, FL
Gruidae	sandhill crane	Aviary with wading pool: 144 sq. ft. (44 sq. m) floor space with 14 sq. ft. (4.27 sq. m) pool 6 to 10 in. (15.2 x 25.4 cm) deep** 4 birds maximum	M, W, AW

TABLE 18, Continued

Family	Species	Minimum cage size (W x L x H)	Codes
Anatidae	Canada goose	Aviary with wading/swimming pool: 150 sq. ft. (46 sq. m) floor space and 15 sq. ft. (4.6 m) of pool area** 2 ft. (0.61 m) deep*. 4 birds maximum**	M, W, AP
	mallard	Aviary with wading/swimming pool: 75 sq. ft. (23 sq. m) of floor space and 7.5 sq. ft. (2.3 sq. m) of pool area** 8 to 10 in. (20.32 to 25.4 cm) deep* 4 birds maximum**	M, W, AP
Laridae	gull, less than 14 in. (35.6 cm) from tip of beak to tip of tail with neck extended.	Aviary with pool Aviary: 6 x 12 x 8 ft. (1.83 x 4.6 x 2.44 m) (72 sq. ft.[22 sq. m]) Pool: 45 in. (114.3 cm) diameter, 10 in. (25.4 cm) deep. 6 birds maximum.*	M, W, SO
	gull, more than 14 in. (35.6 cm) from tip of beak to tip of tail with neck extended.	Aviary with pool Aviary: 8 x 16 x 8 ft. (2.44 x 4.88 x 2.44 m) (128 sq. ft. [39 sq. m]) Pool: 45 in. (114.3 cm) diameter, 12 in. (30.5 cm) deep. 4 birds maximum.*	M, W, SO
Alcidae	puffin	Aviary and pool: 100 sq. ft. (254 sq. m) floor space with 50 sq. ft. (127 sq. m) Pool: 3 ft. (0.93 m) deep 2 birds maximum.**	M, W, SO

KEY:

* * ~ (Miller 2000)

* ** ~ Florida Game and Freshwater Fish Commission regulations

* **M** ~ More birds. For any additional birds, increase the cage size by 25 percent**

* **W** ~ Wingspread. The bird needs to be able to spread its wings and turn around without touching the sides of its enclosure.

* **SO** ~ Surface overflow of pool required to maintain water quality

* **AP** ~ Need enclosures that contain pools to swim in as well as standing and perching surfaces

* **AW** ~ Need enclosures with shallow wading pools and a variety of perches, especially up high.

* **ST** ~ Stiff-tailed birds need stumps or stump-like perches to avoid breaking/soiling tail feathers.

* **FL** ~ Bird needs to be in a flock situation.

* **PT** ~ Bird should be allowed pool time as long and as often as medical condition allows (kiddie pool). This may include cold or warm water pools as appropriate for individual.

Editor's note: This publication addresses those animals used in on-site and off-site education programming. Any cage sizes noted are a minimum size to be used when animals are not in transport carriers. This publication does not address animals used in static displays, who have much different requirements for permanent caging.

FLOORING

The enclosure floor is very important for healthy feet as well as the overall health of the bird. Sand, sod, rubber mats, and mats designed for dogs or cats may be used for flooring. The ideal flooring material has "give" to it so it is more forgiving to the bird's feet and drains water and fecal material away from feet and feathers. The flooring should not collect water, feces, and leftover food. Improper flooring can harbor harmful bacteria, insects, and rodents and thus be detrimental to the health of the bird. Unless the bird's injuries make it dangerous to have a pool, all waterbirds should have pools of sufficient width and depth for their comfort.

PERCHES

Rocks, natural branches, and wrapped doweling are suitable perches. The species determines the proper size and shape of the perches. An appreciation of the bird's natural history is important, but the individual's feet may determine what works best. Usually, different size perches made of different materials can help maintain the bird's feet. Any redness, thinning, cracking, or wear spots noticed on the bottom of the bird's feet usually indicates incorrect perching options. Observe where the bird is perching, as that particular perch may be the culprit. Perches should be changed on a regular basis as they get worn.

FEEDING

Most waterbirds are carnivores and/or omnivores.. Examples of food items include fish of varying sizes and species, rodents, appropriate insects and worms, leafy greens, grains, and commercial duck and geese food. You will need to research the natural foods of your bird and talk to experienced people that have successfully cared for that type of waterbird. If the majority of the diet is dead fish, the bird's diet will need additional Vitamin B1. Fish meat contains an enzyme that destroys Vitamin B1. Consult with a veterinarian for the correct dosage of vitamin B1. Many waterbirds prefer to feed in the water, but these birds can possibly be conditioned to accept at least some food from a shallow pan.

CLEANING

Most enclosures used for waterbirds need to be cleaned frequently. Many of these birds defecate in the same water used for bathing, swimming, and drinking. Fresh water circulating into the enclosure, and out through an overflow, is one way to keep better water quality. You need to clean water containers and pools at least once a day, removing the leftover food and fecal material. Thoroughly clean and disinfect the bird's enclosure on a regular schedule in addition to the daily cleaning routine.

Handling and transportation of waterbirds for programs

Unlike raptors, few if any waterbirds will be handled on the glove or in hand. These birds will feel more comfortable on a perch or flat surface, like the ground or a tabletop. A rock, stump, or other perch that is brought from their enclosure may be the most reassuring for your bird, especially in a program setting.

Transporting most waterbirds in plastic dog kennels works very well. Choose a size large enough for the bird to turn around while standing comfortably. A perch or part of a stump may be attached to the sides of the kennel for the bird to perch on (if needed). Attach the perch to the kennel securely to prevent injuring the bird during transport. The floor of the kennel should have a removable non-skid mat that can be removed for cleaning.

Tall birds with long legs and necks (like cranes) may need a custom transportation kennel. Provide plenty of ventilation holes in any custom constructed kennel and leave enough room for padding on the sides or top if necessary. Large birds (like pelicans) make transport away from the facility on a regular basis difficult, perhaps even impossible. A proper crate may be too tall or too heavy to transport conveniently Carefully consider the feasibility of transporting very large waterbirds. Unless these large birds are to be used "on site"

PASSERINES AND MISCELLANEOUS AVIAN FAMILIES

exclusively, a smaller bird would be a better choice to use as an education animal.

Most of the passerines and other avian families not already covered in this guide are not suitable for educational programs, either because of physical size or intolerable stress. Only experienced handlers should attempt to use non-raptor species in educational programs.

Three categories are discussed in this section; families not suitable for educational programming, families that could be suitable for education, and families with no recommendation (lack of information or previous examples). In almost all cases, juvenile birds generally do better adjusting to life around humans than adult birds.

Passerine families that most species are not recommended for program birds

Cuculidae	cuckoos and anis
Caprimulgidae	nightjars
Apodidae	swifts
Trochilidae	hummingbirds
Alcedinidae	kingfishers
Tyrannidae	tyrant flycatchers
Alaudidae	larks
Hirundinidae	swallows
Muscicapidae	wrentit
Paridae	titmice and chickadees
Aegithalidae	bushtits
Certhiidae	creepers
Sittidae	nuthatches
Troglodytidae	wrens
Muscicapidae	thrushes
Motacillidae	pipits and wagtails
Cinclidae	dippers
Ptilogonatidae	silky flycatchers
Pycnonotidae	bulbuls
Vireonidae	vireos
Emberizidae	warblers and sparrows
Estrildidae	weaver finches
Passeridae	weavers
Fringillidae	finches
Mimidae	mimic thrushes

Passerine families that have some species suitable for educational programming

Phasianidae	grouse, ptarmigans
Columbidae	pigeons and doves – some
Picidae	woodpeckers
Corvidae	jays, crows, magpies
Laniidae	shrikes
Bombycillidae	waxwings
Sturnidae	starlings

Passerine families with no recommendations for educational programming

Remizidae	verdins
Prunellidae	accentors

HOUSING

Because of the numerous different families of passerines, the amount of information about housing is very complex (Table 19). Some passerine families not recommended for educational programming are included here, and does not mean they are suitable.

TABLE 19
GENERAL HOUSING REQUIREMENTS FOR PASSERINES USED IN EDUCATION

Family	Species	Minimum Cage Size (W x L x H)	Codes
Phasianidae	ring-necked pheasant	8 x 12 x 8 ft. (2.44 x 3.66 x 2.44 m) for up to 4 birds, only 1 male	H, P, S, F, B
	wild turkey	10 x 12 x 8 ft. (4.88 x 3.66 x 2.44 m) for 1 to 2 birds, only 1 male	H, P, S, F, B
Columbidae	pigeons/doves	If flighted: 16 x 8 x 8 ft. (4.88 x 2.44 x 2.44 m) (max number in this cage about 8 for pigeons, 12 if doves) If non-flighted: 16 x 16 x 16 in. (41 x 41 x 41 cm) for 1 bird. Add 25 to 50 percent more space per additional bird	H, P, B
Cuculidae	greater roadrunner	4 x 4 x 4 ft. (1.23 x 1.23 x 1.23 m) for 1 bird.	F, P, S
Picidae*	woodpeckers 9 in. (23 cm) or less	4 x 4 x 8 ft. (1.23 x 1.23 x 2.46 m) for 2 to 4 flighted birds	C, B
	woodpeckers 9 in. (23 cm) or larger	8 x 16 x 8 ft. (2.44 x 4.88 x 2.44 m) for 2 to 4 flighted birds	C, B
Corvidae*	corvids smaller than 17 in. (43.2 cm)	8 x 16 x 8 ft. (2.44 x 4.88 x 2.44 m) for up to 6 flighted birds	P, E, B
	corvids larger than 17 in. (43.2 cm)	10 x 30 x 15 ft. (3.05 x 9.14 x 4.6 m) for up to 6 flighted birds	P, E, B
Muscicapidae	American robin	4 x 4 x 8 ft. (1.23 x 1.23 x 2.46 m) for up to 4 flighted birds 4 x 4 x 4 ft. (1.23 x 1.23 x 1.23 m) for 1 to 2 birds if nonflighted	P, B
Laniidae*	shrike	4 x 4 x 8 ft. (1.23 x 1.23 x 2.46 m) if flighted for 1 bird 3 x 3 x 3 ft. (0.92 x 0.92 x 0.92 m) if nonflighted for 1 bird	P, B
Bombycillidae	waxwing	4 x 8 x 8 ft. (1.23 x 2.46 x 2.46 m) for up to 4 to 6 flighted birds 3 x 3 x 3 ft. (0.92 x 0.92 x 0.92 m) for up to 4 non-flighted birds	P, B, FL
Sturnidae	starling	4 x 4 x 8 ft. (1.23 x 1.23 x 2.46 m) if flighted for up to 4 to 6 birds 3 x 3 x 3 ft. (0.92 x 0.92 x 0.92 m)	P, B, E

Chapter 6: Birds

if non-flighted for 4 to 6 birds

TABLE 19, Continued

Emberizidae*	Northern cardinal	4 x 8 x 8 ft. (1.23 x 2.46 x 2.46 m) for up to 4 to 6 flighted birds 3 x 3 x 3 ft. (0.92 x 0.92 x 0.92 m) for up to 4 non-flighted birds	P, H
	grackle, blackbird, cowbird	4 x 8 x 8 ft. (1.23 x 2.46 x 2.46 m) for up to 4 to 6 flighted birds 3 x 3 x 3 ft. (0.92 x 0.92 x 0.92 m) for up to 4 non-flighted birds	P, H

Editor's note: This publication addresses those animals used in on-site and off-site education programming. Any cage sizes noted are a minimum size to be used when animals are not in transport carriers. This publication does not address animals used in static displays, who have much different requirements for permanent caging.

KEY:

* ~ Not all species or individuals will make good education animals.

H ~ Provide places for the animal to hide. These hides can be made from natural material or human made material.

P ~ Provide 2 or more perches of varying sizes. Material may be natural branches, hemp or sisal rope (0.25 to 0.75 in. diameter) (0.635 to 1.9 cm), dowel rods covered in Vetwrap ™ or similar material.

C ~ Birds such as woodpeckers require angled and vertical logs for climbing and hollow logs for resting. These logs help maintain beak and foot health.

F ~ Flooring requirements. Use sand, Astroturf ™, natural dirt/sod.

E ~ Provide lots of enrichment and toys. Examples would include non-toxic parrot toys or shiny objects like spoons.

S ~ Provide shallow pan for dust/sand bath

B ~ Water bathing pan needed appropriate for species and disability and shallow enough for the bird to stand but long and wide enough so the bird can easily crouch and splash wings, back and head with water. **Caution:** birds with balance problems should only be provided bath pans under DIRECT supervision, otherwise they may drown.

FL ~ Flock bird and needs to be housed with others to be comfortable

Feeding

Passerines and the other families of birds discussed in this section require a large variety of food items. What type and what quantity of food to offer is best determined through research and consultation with experienced caregivers. The healthiest choice for your bird is to replicate the natural diet as close as is practicable. The birds should be fed at similar times that they would feed in the wild. For example, if the bird feeds throughout the day normally, food should be offered throughout the day, or if the bird feeds mostly in the morning or evening, then offer the food accordingly. Placing the food in locations where the bird would forage in the wild will encourage feeding. Research the natural history to determine if the bird forages on the ground, low in the bushes, or higher in the trees, for example, and then place food dishes within the enclosure to meet those preferences.

It is useful to record the amount and types of food fed and consumed. Weigh the bird on a regular schedule and compare changes with your feeding records to determine if the bird is eating enough, too little—or too much! Uneaten moist items or food that may spoil quickly should not be left in the cage for more than 3 to 4 hours. If the weather is warm, then the uneaten food should be removed even more quickly to prevent spoilage and unwanted insects.

CLEANING

Cages should be cleaned at least once a day. Set a schedule for completely cleaning and disinfecting the cage on a regular basis as well. All food and water dishes should be cleaned daily, and bath water should be cleaned at least several times per week and more often if needed. Perches should be regularly cleaned and replaced as necessary.

HANDLING AND TRANSPORTATION FOR PROGRAMS

The bird should have some type of transport container. This container should have ventilation, perches appropriate for the species, and should prevent visual over stimulation. The bird should feel safe and secure in the transport enclosure. The container should have a removable covering that reduces stress and increases security for the bird when needed. Covering the container with a dark towel is one easy method.

Transport enclosures can be constructed of many types of materials. Metal mesh, barred, or wire transport enclosures are not recommended, as feathers, ceres, and feet are easily damaged by this material. Commercially available plastic kennels used for domestic pets work well when the metal door is covered with cloth or otherwise modified. Custom enclosures made of sealed wood are acceptable, with adequate ventilation and padding. Any enclosure must be adequate in size to allow the bird to perch and turn around without touching tail or folded wing on any side, top, or floor.

The transport container may double as a display enclosure for the bird in a classroom setting. If the container is plexiglass, for example, it may give good viewing, keep the bird secure and safe, and can be covered if the bird is over stimulated. If you are constructing a transportation enclosure to use for display, it will need to be larger than a normal transport enclosure to allow the bird to move around more naturally.

Some birds may be large enough to be trained to sit on a branch or on a hand. If you plan to present a passerine or other non-raptor bird in this manner, a method is needed to keep the bird safe. The bird becoming "spooked" and trying to fly to safety (whether the bird flies or not) can result in disaster, and you need to be prepared. Unlike raptors, smaller passerines cannot be jessed, so there is a danger of the bird, even a well trained bird, being injured or lost if it becomes scared.

Literature Cited

Arent, L., and M. Martell. 1996. *Care and Management of Captive Raptors*. St. Paul, MN: The Raptor Center.

Beebe, F. L., and H. M. Webster. 1994. *North American Falconry and Hunting Hawks*. Topeka, KS: Jostens Printing and Publishing.

Florida Game and Freshwater Fish Commission. 68A-6.004 *Standard Caging Requirements for Captive Wildlife. Florida Game and Freshwater Fish Regulations*. Specific Authority Art. IV, Sec. 9, Fla. Const. Law Implemented Art. IV, Sec. 9, Fla. Const. 372.921, 372.922.

Miller, E. A., Ed. 2000. *Minimum Standards for Wildlife Rehabilitation, 3rd Edition*. St. Cloud, MN: National Wildlife Rehabilitators Association.

Sibley, D. A. 2000. *National Audubon Society's The Sibley Guide to Birds*. New York, NY: Alfred A. Knopf.

Additional Reading

Abate, A. 2000. *Thoughts for Food: A step by step manual for providing healthy, nutritious, and varied live food to insectivorous reptiles, amphibians, birds, mammals, and other creatures. San Diego, CA:* Chameleon Information Network.

A Manual for the Apprentice Falconer. 1990. Arizona Falconer's Association. Phoenix AZ.

Appelhof, M. 1984. *How to Raise Worms to Feed Amphibians, Reptiles, Birds, and Small Mammals. Wildlife Rehabilitation, Vol 3*. National Wildlife Rehabilitators Association, St Cloud, MN. pp 23-28.

Bent, A. C. 1964. *Life Histories of North American Petrels and Pelicans and their Allies*. New York, NY. Dover Publications.

Brue, R. N. 2001. A Primer on Avian Nutrition. *IAATE Flyer*. Newsletter of the International Association of Avian Trainers and Educators. 8(4).

Clancy, G. 1996. *The Complete Hunter: Wild Turkey. The Hunting and Fishing Library*. Minnetonka, MN: Cowles Creative Publishing.

Clark, W. S., and B. K. Wheeler. 1987. *Peterson Field Guides: Hawks of North America*. New York, NY: Houghton Mifflin.

Corazalla, M. K. 1995. Creative Approaches in Supplying Food for Rehabilitating Wildlife. *Wildlife Rehabilitation*. 13: 27-38.

Crawford, W. C. 1984. The Theory of Imprinting—Its Implications and Ramifications in Raptors. *Wildlife Rehabilitation*. 3:89-92.

Duke, G. E. 1990. A Brief Review of Digestive Physiology of Fowl and Raptors. *Wildlife Rehabilitation*. 8: 223-225.

Dunn, P., D. Sibley, and C. Sutton. 1988. *Hawks in Flight*. Boston, MA: Houghton Mifflin.

Eckert, A. 1973. *The Owls of North America*. Garden City, NY:Doubleday.

Ehrlich, P. R., D. S. Dobkin, and D. Wheye. 1988. *The Birder's Handbook: A Field Guide to the Natural History of North American Birds*. New York, NY: Simon and Shuster.

Evans, L. 1993. Waterbird Diet Guide. *Wildlife Rehabilitation Today*. 4(4): 41-42.

Facts Every Bird Owner Should Know About Avian Nutrition. 2001. IAATE Flyer. Newsletter of the International Association of Avian Trainers and Educators. 8(4).

Farrand, J. Jr., ed. 1983. *The Audubon Society Master Guide to Birding; An advanced field guide to the birds of North America in three volumes. Volume 1 Loons to Sandpipers.* New York: Knopf.

_____. 1983. *The Audubon Society Master Guide to Birding; An advanced field guide to the birds of North America in three volumes. Volume 2 Gulls to Dippers.* New York: Knopf.

_____. 1983. *The Audubon Society Master Guide to Birding; An advanced field guide to the birds of North America in three volumes. Volume 3 Old World Warblers to Sparrows.* New York: Knopf.

Fitzpatrick, J., G. Buhl, and L. Polglase. 1991. Considerations in Raising Feeder Rats (*Rattus norvegicus*). *Wildlife Rehabilitation.* 9:87-90.

Gaunt, A.S. and L.W. Oring, eds.1999. *Guidelines to the Use of Wild Birds in Research.* Washington, DC: The Ornithological Council.

Grant, P. J. 1986. *Gulls: A Guide to Identification.* 2nd edition. Boston, MA: Academic Press, Harcourt Brace.

Hayman, P., J. Marchant, and T. Prater. 1986. *Shorebirds: An Identification Guide.* Boston, MA: Houghton Mifflin.

Heinrich, B. 1989. *Ravens in Winter.* New York, NY: Vintage Books.

Henderson, C. L. 1995. *Wild About Birds: The DNR Bird Feeding Guide.* St. Paul, MN: Minnesota Department of Natural Resources.

Jenkins Hardy, L. 1991. Management and Maintenance Suggestions for Herons and Egrets. *Wildlife Rehabilitation.* 9:41-46.

Johnsgard, P. A. 1990. *Hawks, Eagles, and Falcons of North America.* Washington, DC: Smithsonian Institutional Press.

Kimsey, B., and J. Hodge. 1992. *Falconry Equipment.* Kimsey/Hodge Publications.

Miller, E. A. 1996. Captive Care of Mourning Doves. *The NWRA Quarterly.* 14(2):1-6.

Moore, A. T., and S. Joosten. 2002. Raptor Caging Considerations. In *NWRA Principles of Wildlife Rehabilitation,* 2nd ed. St. Cloud, MN: National Wildlife Rehabilitators Association. Pp 6.53-6.56.

_____. 2002. Food for Raptors. In *NWRA Principles of Wildlife Rehabilitation,* 2nd ed. St. Cloud, MN: National Wildlife Rehabilitators Association. Pp 9.107-9.109.

Morzenti, A.1998. *Captive Raptor Management: Common Raptors of the United States.* 2nd ed. Wildlife Publications. Madison, WI: Omnipress

Murnane, R. D. 1991. Common Nutritional Disorders of Wildlife. *Wildlife Rehabilitation.* 9:105-116.

National Geographic Society Field Guide to the Birds of North America 2nd *Edition.* 1987. Washington, DC: National Geographic Society.

Nero, R. W. 1980. *The Great Gray Owl: Phantom of the Northern Forest.* Washington, DC: Smithsonian Institutional Press.

Neumann, K. *Educating with Raptors: A Resource Booklet.* Carroll, IA: Stone Printing.

Orendorff, B. 2002. Portable/Expandable Pre-Release Enclosure. In *NWRA Principles of Wildlife Rehabilitation* 2nd ed. St. Cloud, MN: National Wildlife Rehabilitators Association. Pp 6.11-6.22.

Parker, K. 1992. Ethics of Killing and Food Acquisition, Preparation, and Storage for Owls. *Wildlife Rehabilitation.* 10:121-127.

_____. 2002. Some Considerations In Enclosure Design and Construction. In *NWRA Principles of Wildlife Rehabilitation.* 2nd ed. St. Cloud, MN: National Wildlife Rehabilitators Association. Pp 6.11-6.16.

Reiter, J. L., and S. D. Crissey. 1991. Nutrient Considerations of Diets for Fish-eating Animals. *Wildlife Rehabilitation*. 9:117-125.

Rule, M. 2002. Nutritional Considerations for Captive Songbirds. In NWRA *Principles of Wildlife Rehabilitation*. 2nd *Edition*. St. Cloud, MN: National Wildlife Rehabilitators Association. Pp 7.19-7.30.

Sibley, D. A. 2001. *The Sibley Guide to Bird Life and Behavior*. New York, NY: Knopf.

Snyder, N. 1991. *Birds of Prey: Natural History and Conservation of North American Raptors*. Stillwater, MN: Voyageur Press.

Sternberg, D. 1995. *The Complete Hunter: Upland Game Birds*. The Hunting and Fishing Library. Minnetonka, MN: Cowles Creative Publishing.

Tinbergen, N. 1960. *The Herring Gull's World: A study of the Social Behavior of Birds*. New York, NY: Harper and Row.

Thorne Bolduc, K. 2002. The Differences between Imprinting, Habituation, and Tameness. In NWRA *Principles of Wildlife Rehabilitation*, 2nd *ed*. St. Cloud, MN: National Wildlife Rehabilitators Association. Pp 9.77-9.79.

Toops, C. 1990. *Voyager Wilderness Books; The Enchanting Owl*. Stillwater, MN: Voyager Press.

Tseng, F. S. Waterfowl Nutrition. In NWRA *Principles of Wildlife Rehabilitation*, 2nd *ed*. St. Cloud, MN: National Wildlife Rehabilitators Association. Pp 7.31-7.38.

Upton, R. 1991. Falconry: Principles and Practice. London, UK: Adam and Charles Black.

Weidensaul, S. 1996. Raptors: The Birds of Prey. New York, NY: Lyons and Burford.

Wheeler, B. K., and W. S. Clark. 1995. A Photographic Guide to North American Raptors. New York, NY: Academic Press, Harcourt Brace.

White, J. 1991. Basics of Captive Care of Common Murres (Uria aalge). Wildlife Rehabilitation. 9:41-46.

Woodford, M.H. 1967. A Manual of Falconry. London, UK: Adam and Charles Black.

Chapter 7

MAMMALS

OVERVIEW

There are over 440 different mammal species in North America (Wilson and Ruff 1999). However, there are few mammals suitable for educational programs, even from the wide range of species available. As with all wildlife, only non-releasable mammals are to be considered for use as education animals. Often this factor becomes a conundrum, since in many cases the reason a mammal is suited for education programs also makes that individual releasable. Many difficulties may lie ahead for anyone considering the use of wild mammals in an education program.

As with any education animal, you must know, understand, and comply with all state and federal regulations regarding that particular species. Most mammals are covered by state regulations. Endangered and threatened species are covered by federal regulations, and all housing must be in accordance with the United States Department of Agriculture Animal and Plant Health Inspection Service (APHIS) standards. (www.aphis.usda.gov). It is always best to confirm compliance with the law before acquiring any new animal. Some other barriers to using wild mammals are the extreme stress suffered by mammals when being handled, the aggressive behavior exhibited by many species, and the need for expert handling skills when using mammals.

The use of mammals in education programs poses some risks to the handler and audience members through zoonoses. Zoonoses are diseases that can be transmitted to any handler and possibly any bystander or audience member. Rabies, for example, is a viral disease that cannot always be detected in a "healthy" mammal but may be transmitted through a bite or saliva. Rabies is one example of the most serious zoonoses that can be transmitted from wildlife to humans or domestic animals.

A concern about transmission of rabies to humans has arisen due to epizootics of rabies in certain regions of the United States. The following policy statement was adopted by the NWRA Board of Directors on March 18, 1992 and amended on November 17, 2002. "The Board of Directors of the National Wildlife Rehabilitators Association is concerned about health risks to wildlife rehabilitators and rescuers who handle high-risk rabies vectors in the midst of an epizootic. Since these species often do not exhibit obvious clinical signs and since non-bite rabies transmission is possible, every wildlife rehabilitator in these areas must decide on a safe and humane policy towards these species. State wildlife agencies and public health departments should be consulted and their regulations should be respected." This policy was made with wildlife rehabilitators in mind, but it applies equally to the use of mammals for educational programming.

Anyone that handles wild mammals should seriously consider pre-exposure rabies immunization. A physician should be contacted regarding pre- and post-exposure prophylaxis (vaccination). More information can be found through each state's health department.

Many mammal species fall into the "not suitable for education program" category for various reasons. For example, an educational program setting may not be safe or comfortable for either these animals or the audience. Static display settings are best suited for many of these mammal groups. Some of the mammals in the "suitable" category have a greater chance of successfully adapting to life as an education animal if the individual is young when permanently injured. Young animals tend to be more "flexible" in adapting to new situations.

Mammalian Orders that are clearly not suitable for education programs, with a few exceptions, include the following:

Insectivora moles and shrews
Carnivora seals and sea lions, bears, weasels, skunks, cats, wolves, and foxes, although some in this Order are acceptable, see below
Cetacea whales, dolphins, and porpoises
Sirena manatee and dugong
Artiodactyla even-toed hoofed mammals
Rodentia squirrels, mice, rats, beavers, porcupines, and voles, although some in this Order are acceptable, see below
Lagomorpha pikas, hares, and rabbits

Wild rodents like mice, rats, and squirrels are prey animals and can experience extreme stress when handled, especially in the presence of large groups. Since mice and rats can be very useful in programs because of their size, the use of laboratory or pet mice and rats raised to be handled by humans is a better alternative than wild species. The laboratory type of rodent is easy to house and feed, and can tolerate the stress of handling during presentations with more comfort than their wild counterparts. The care of domestic rodents is readily available in many publications, but read all references carefully and be sure to provide excellent care for these creatures.

Prairie dogs *(Cynomysludovicianus* spp. and *Cynomys gunnisoni* spp.) are not recommended or discussed in further detail because of the outbreak of Monkeypox (*Orthopox virus*) in pet prairie dogs within the United States. Because of the outbreak in 2003, there is a moratorium on transporting prairie dogs. For more information contact the Centers for Disease Control (CDC) and your local health department.

Mammalian Orders more suited for use as education animals include the following:

Dipelphimorpha opossums
Xenarthra sloths and armadillos
Chiroptera bats
  Specifically, the following species of bats are recommended:
  Big brown bat *Eptesicus fuscus*
  Evening bat *Nycticeius humeralis*
  Eastern pipistrelle *Pipistrellus subflavus*
  Silver-haired bat *Lasionycteris noctivagans*
  Little brown bat *Myotis lucifugus*
  Other *Myotis* sp.
  Brazilian free-tail *Tadarida brasiliensis*
  Big-eared bat *Plecotus* sp.
  Pallid bats *Antrozous pallidus* spp.
Carnivora raccoons, ringtails, coatis, and fox may be acceptable
  (Some members of the families Otariidae and Phocidae [sea lions and seals] may be acceptable, especially for educators on the West Coast)
Rodentia squirrels, beavers, porcupines, nutria, and muskrat may be acceptable

Nutria *(Myocastor coypus),* an introduced species, is included here because it is now very common in the southern United States. This species originally is found in South America and was introduced in the 1940s (Burt and Grossenheider 1980).

Sea lions and seals (marine carnivores) are not suited for the novice handler, and only experienced educators with adequate facilities should handle these mammals. Many individuals from these families are used in education programs, but they require considerable training. Housing must be in accordance with the APHIS standards (www.aphis.usda.gov.). Raccoons and coatis are also considered to be more suited to experienced handlers.

Disabilities and Considerations

The type of permanent injury the individual suffered is a factor when determining the animal's suitability for an educational program. Some types of injuries make it difficult for the handler to properly manage the animal. In the most extreme cases, the injury may be severe enough that the mammal suffers continually while living. Adult animals that are permanently disabled are most often not suitable for use as education animals, depending on the severity of the disfigurement. Severely disfigured animals are generally not suitable for use in front of an audience.

TABLE 20 – INJURIES AND CONSIDERATIONS

Injury	Consideration
Full leg amputation	These mammals have some difficulty balancing and regaining upright posture if they do lose their balance; however, some individuals may learn to compensate for their impairment.
Wing amputation (bats)	Tolerance and adaptation to this injury varies by bat species. Consult with experienced bat rehabilitators or people who use bats as education animals to ascertain if your species will make the transition successfully.
Partial blindness	Partially blind mammals can usually learn to live comfortably in captivity, but handlers must plan movements to accommodate this impairment. For example, an animal may be nervous when a person or object suddenly "appears," so the handler should make a noise or otherwise let the mammal know of their presence.
Total blindness	Successful adjustment to this injury varies by individual. If the individual is calm, then a career as an education animal is possible. If the animal remains nervous, life as an education animal may be inhumane. Even if the animal is calm, an enormous amount of care is needed to keep the individual comfortable and healthy.
Missing toes	If there are only a few toes missing, it may not impair a mammal at all. The animal may be releasable and not eligible for permanent captivity or education.
Missing or broken teeth	A mammal with these injuries may be an education candidate only if its management and medical needs are resolved (mouth and tongue drying out, adequate feeding, grooming, and other considerations).
Human Imprinted or Improper Socialization	These mammals may be more accepting of a captive situation or not, depending on when the improper socialization occurred during development. As the mammal reaches maturity, it may become aggressive and protective of its human handler. These animals may be even more aggressive than a properly socialized individual of the same species.

HOUSING

The design of mammal enclosures, like any other animal enclosure design, should accommodate the individual's impairment and species' natural history. Careful consideration and planning is needed to meet all of the individual's housing requirements. Double door construction is highly recommended for any mammal enclosure to prevent escapes.

Materials for the walls, ceiling, and floor will depend on the natural behavior and size of the animal. For example, an opossum may be adequately housed in a wood enclosure, but a beaver or other rodent would chew their way to freedom eventually. All surfaces should be checked for any sharp edges that could cause injury, and any projections should be eliminated. Fur, paws, and eyes are especially vulnerable to injury from sharp or pointed projections.

Enclosure design should include provisions for easy cleaning. Using a "shift area" or separate area to contain the mammal during daily cleaning or feeding may be the best option. Larger mammals should have access to the outdoors if possible. The enclosure could have direct access, or two different enclosures may be needed, like a shift from inside to outside. Access to the outdoors allows for exposure to normal photoperiods as well as providing enrichment for the individual.

As with any type of animal housing, mammal enclosures should be predator-proof and escape-proof. Chainlink fencing material is a good choice for enclosure construction, but carefully attach chainlink panels together, as this juncture is a favorite escape route. Another way to prevent escapes is having a double door system, as previously mentioned. All outdoor enclosures should have a reliable base constructed to prevent escapes (or entry by predators) by digging. If constructed of metal wire or chainlink, the base (floor) should be covered with dirt, sand, or other substrate, to protect the animal's feet from abrasion.

The area within the enclosure where the mammal eats or drinks requires careful planning. How the food and water are to be presented needs careful consideration as well. Food can be spread in an interesting way throughout the enclosure or placed in a clean bowl. No matter how it is presented, food must remain clean, and uneaten food removed to prevent spoiling and attracting other animals or insects. Drinking water must be presented safely; specifically so the animal can drink but cannot drown. Water and food dishes can be weighted to prevent tipping.

If the cage is outdoors, there must be some type of shelter or partially covered roof to provide protection from the weather. This shelter may have to be insulated and partially heated if the animal is outside during very cold temperatures. Provide a gradient of warmth so the animal can choose where they are most comfortable.

If the animal would naturally spend a lot of time in the water, a pool is needed inside the enclosure. To keep the water clean, use an overflow pipe or have the water running constantly by another method. Determine the proper depth for the pool by assessing the disability of the animal.

Cage furniture can be very important to an animal's comfort and security. Wire mesh hammocks covered in leaves and hung from a secure corner of the cage can be a resting or playing area for squirrels, raccoons, and opossums. A nest box hung on the side of the cage or from a large branch can be a shelter and resting place. Platforms of different widths and materials, placed at different levels in the enclosure, can allow the animal choice in its environment.

Toys can be considered additional furniture. Make sure that toys (or any other furniture) cannot hurt the animal. Remove any toy if it is chewed up, or if the animal could swallow or get caught in it. Toys can be as simple as paper towel tubes or phone books to more complicated "puzzle" toys. Some toys require the animal working (and thinking) to gain access to food treats hidden inside the toy.

Chapter 10 contains many ideas that can be easily configured to work with mammals. Stimulate your animal by providing toys and having the ability to change the platforms, nesting structures, and shelters within the enclosure. Other cage furniture is discussed in Table 22.

Chapter 7: Mammals

TABLE 21
MINIMUM HOUSING GUIDELINES FOR EDUCATION MAMMALS (MILLER 2000)

Family	Common Name	Minimum Cage Sizes (W x L x H)	Codes
Dasypodidae	Armadillo	6 x 8 x 4 ft. (1.83 x 2.5 x 1.2 m)	O
Didelphidae	Opossum	4 x 4 x 8 ft. (1.2 x 1.2 x 2.5 m)	H, D
Vespertilionidae	Foliage roosting bat	30 x 18 x 24 in. (76.2 x 45.7 x 61.0 cm) for one bat*	W, F
Molossidae, Vespertilionidae	Crevice dwelling bat	2 x 2 x 3 ft. (0.61 x 0.61 x 0.92 m) for one bat*	S, R, C
Procyonidae	Raccoon	6 x 8 x 8 ft. (1.83 x 2.5 x 2.5 m)	H, D, P, O, B
Coati		6 x 8 x 8 ft. (1.83 x 2.5 x 2.5 m)	H, D, P, B
Bassariscidae	Ringtail	6 x 8 x 8 ft. (1.83 x 2.5 x 2.5 m)	H, D, P, B
Canidae	Fox	6.5 x 6.5 x 5 ft. (1.98 x 1.98 x 1.52 m) for one or two animals	D, O, B, A, H
Sciuridae	Woodchuck	6 x 8 x 6 ft. (1.83 x 2.5 x 1.83 m)	M, O, B
	Tree squirrels	4 x 4 x 8 ft. (1.2 x 1.2 x 2.5 m)	H, M
Capromyidae	Nutria	8 x 12 x 6 ft. (2.5 x 3.66 x 1.83 m)	P, M, I
Muridae	Muskrat	8 x 8 x 6 ft. (2.5 x 2.5 x 1.83 m)	P, M
Castoridae	Beaver	8 x 12 x 6 ft. (2.5 x 3.66 x 1.83 m)	P, M
Erithizontidae	Porcupine	6 x 8 x 6 ft. (1.83 x 2.5 x 1.83 m)	H, M

KEY:

- **A** ~ Gray fox are arboreal, so if the animal is able to climb, height would be very important for the caging.
- **B** ~ Provide a den area made of a plastic drum, wooden box, or metal garbage can on its side. Fill with tree trimmings, shavings, natural dirt, and grass.
- **C** ~ Colonial roosting bats should not be housed alone.
- **D** ~ Special cage furniture includes: hammocks made of 1 in. (2.54 cm) square mesh, burlap sacks, or old firehose attached to the walls or the roof that are removable for cleaning, and plastic barrels, logs, or other things in which to hide; logs, tree limbs, and platforms at various heights to promote climbing if the animal is able to do so.
- **F** ~ The cage furniture should be branches with foliage (silk plants will do) attached to the ceiling of the cage and to upper sides. The substrate on the bottom should be soft, like sheepskin. Do not use shavings or similar material.
- **H** ~ The enclosure height may have to be modified depending on the disability.
- **I** ~ Nutria were introduced to the United States from South America.
- **M** ~ Enclosures must be made of material such as hardware cloth to prevent chewing and escaping. Dirt or sand floors should have hardware cloth buried along the interior sides of the cage, approximately 12 in. (30.48 cm) below ground or completely across the bottom of the cage under the flooring substrate. Any wood for the cage structure should have hardware cloth stapled at least on the interior surfaces. Non-toxic branches for gnawing should be available at all times in the cage. For arboreal animals such as squirrels, height is more important than length, so branches, nest boxes, and platforms should be provided for climbing.
- **O** ~ Animals that like to dig should be provided with sand or pesticide-free dirt in a three-foot deep box. Also "dig-proof" the cage (see "M" above).
- **P** ~ A pool should be provided. For an animal like a raccoon or coati, a wading pool applicable to the animal's size is appropriate. For a beaver, the water container must be large enough to swim and made of material that cannot be chewed apart (e.g. metal troughs, bathtubs, or concrete pool).
- **R** ~ Roosting places should be provided along the sides of the cage. All walls and flooring (in a plastic cage) should be covered with soft snag-resistant material such as tee-shirt or flannel material. Environmental enrichment and security can be in the form of roosting pouches, or ramps made from plastic mesh craft sheets.
- **S** ~ The sides of the cage should be a polyethylene mesh no larger or smaller than 0.25 in. (0.635 cm). On solid walls, grooves should be horizontally placed and 0.25 to 0.50 in. (0.635 to 1.27 cm) apart.
- **W** ~ Soft-sided cage made from soft fabric like polyester or nylon sheer, no more than 0.0625 in. (0.16 cm) mesh. Use 0.50 in. (1.27 cm) PVC pipe to form the frame of the cage.
- ***** ~ (Lollar and Schmidt-French 1998)

Editor's note: This publication addresses those animals used in on-site and off-site education programming. Any cage sizes noted are a minimum size to be used when animals are not in transport carriers. This publication does not address animals used in static displays, who have much different requirements for permanent caging.

FEEDING

The mammals discussed in this section require a large variety of food items. What type and what quantity of food to offer is best determined through research and consultation with experienced caregivers. The healthiest choice for these mammals is to replicate the natural diet as closely as practicable. The mammals should be fed at similar times as they would feed in the wild. For example, if the mammal feeds throughout the day normally, food should be offered throughout the day; or if the mammal feeds mostly in the morning or evening, then offer the food accordingly.

Placing the food in locations where the mammal would forage in the wild will encourage feeding. You will need to research natural history information on the species to determine if the mammal forages on the ground, low in the bushes, or higher in the trees. Place food dishes at specific locations within the enclosure to meet those preferences.

It is useful to record the amount and types of food fed and consumed. Weigh the mammal on a regular schedule and compare changes with your feeding records to determine if the individual is eating enough, too little—or too much! Uneaten moist items or food that may spoil quickly should not be left in the cage for more than three to four hours. If the weather is warm, then the uneaten food should be removed even more quickly to prevent spoilage and unwanted insects.

CLEANING

Cages should be cleaned at least once a day. You need to establish a schedule for completely cleaning and disinfecting the cage on a regular basis as well. All food and water dishes should be cleaned daily and bath water should be cleaned at least several times per week and more often if needed. Perches, logs, and branches should be regularly cleaned and replaced as necessary.

Handling and Transport

Some mammals may only work as education animals if they were injured as youngsters. Older animals may have a hard time adapting to being handled, especially in front of audiences. These animals may experience increased stress or become frightened or even aggressive. Some individuals may be more relaxed inside a portable display cage left in front of an audience and not being handled. A great idea is to use a video camera to project "live" images of animals in display carriers onto a large screen so everyone in the audience can see them (Lollar and Schmidt-French 1998).

Transport carriers should be appropriate in size and material, depending on the species. Properly sized ventilation holes are needed. You must ensure the holes are small enough that no foot or head can get through and protrude out of the carrier. The holes can be covered with screen material that would protect the animal and keep curious human eyes and fingers out. Commercial domestic pet carriers, homemade wooden boxes, or smaller plastic containers can be used as transport carriers. Properly trained mammals will accept and even enjoy being in the transport carrier.

You will need to determine a comfortable range of temperatures for transporting your education mammal. Do not transport the animal if the temperature is too warm or too cold. For example, transport between 21 and 89 degrees F may be acceptable. Always consider the humidity during warm weather, and do not assume your heater or air conditioner will work or be adequate during extremes in temperatures. Appropriate temperature ranges will vary between regions of the country.

Literature Cited

Burt, W. H., and R. P. Grossenheider. 1980. *Peterson Field Guides: Mammals*. 3rd Edition. New York, NY: Houghton Mifflin.

CDC Preliminary Report: Multistate Outbreak of Monkeypox in Persons exposed to Pet Prairie Dogs. June 9, 2003 from the Center for Disease Control (CDC). Web page: www.cdc.gov/ncidod/monkeypox/report060903.htm and

CDC Telebriefing Transcript. Update: Monkeypox Investigation in the U.S. June 11, 2003 from the CDC web page: www.cdc.gov/od/media/transcripts/t030611.htm).

Lollar, A., and B. Schmidt-French. 1998. *Captive Care and Medical Reference for the Rehabilitation of Insectivorous Bats*. Mineral Well, TX: Bat World Publication.

Miller, E. A., Ed. 2000. *Minimum Standards for Wildlife Rehabilitation, 3rd Ed*. St. Cloud, MN: National Wildlife Rehabilitators Association.

Wilson, D. E., and S. Ruff., eds. 1999. *The Smithsonian Book of North American Animals*. Washington, DC: Smithsonian Institution Press.

Additional Reading

Abate, A. 2000. *Thoughts for Food: A step by step manual for providing healthy, nutritious, and varied live food to insectivorous reptiles, amphibians, birds, mammals, and other creatures. San Diego, CA:* Chameleon Information Network.

Animal Keepers Forum 2001. Special Issue Bat Husbandry and Conservation. *The Journal of the American Association of Zookeepers*. 29(12)

Barnard, S. M. 1991. *The Maintenance of Bats in Captivity*. Atlanta, GA: Susan Barnard.

_____. 1992. Caring for Non-releasable Adult Bats. *Wildlife Rehabilitation Today*. 4(1):20-27.

Bauer, E. 1983. *Deer in Their World*. New York, NY: Outdoor Life Books.

Fenton, M. B. 1983. *Just Bats*. Toronto, ON: University of Toronto Press.

_____. 1992. *Bats*. New York, NY: Facts on File.

_____. 1998. *The Bat: Wings in the Night Sky*. Toronto, ON: Key Porter Books.

Fetter, B. 1992. Life of the Coyote (Canis latrans). *Wildlife Rehabilitation Today*. 3(3):53-54.

Gilbert, B. 1970. *The Weasels: A sensible look at a Family of Predators*. New York, NY: Pantheon Books.

Gurnell, J. 1987. *The Natural History of Squirrels*. New York, NY: Facts on File.

Henry, J. D. 1986. *Red Fox: The Catlike Canine*. Washington, DC: Smithsonian Institution Press.

Jones, J. K., Jr., and E. C. Birney. 1988. *Handbook of Mammals of the North-Central States*. Minneapolis, MN: University of Minnesota Press.

Kays, R. W,. and D. E. Wilson. 2002. *Princeton Field Guides: Mammals of North America*. Princeton, NJ: Princeton University Press.

Lawrence, R.D. 1977. *Paddy: The Classic Story of a Baby Beaver and the Naturalist Who Adopted Him*. New York, NY: The Lyons Press.

Marcum, D. 2002. Mammal Nutrition: Diets Part IV–Species-Specific Diets for Selected North American Wild Mammals. In *NWRA Principles of Wildlife Rehabilitation, 2nd ed*. A. Moore and S. Joosten, eds. St. Cloud, MN: National Wildlife Rehabilitators Association. Pp 8.65-8.82.

Moore, A. T. 1988. The Use of Coyotes in Rehabilitation/Education. *Wildlife Rehabilitation*. 7:201-209.

Nowak, R. M. 1994. *Walker's Bats of the World.* Baltimore, MD: Johns Hopkins University Press.

Riccardo, M. L. 1990. A Natural History of the Beaver (*Castor Canadensis*). *Wildlife Rehabilitation Today*. 1(4):30-31.

Roze, U. 1989. *The North American Porcupine*. Washington, DC: Smithsonian Institution Press.

Ryden, H. 1981. *Bobcat Year.* New York, NY: Lyons and Burford.

Santangelo, A. L. 1997. Using Live Bats for Education. *The NWRA Quarterly*. (15) 4:13.

Woodworking for Wildlife: Homes for Birds and Mammals, 2nd ed. 1992. St. Paul, MN: Department of Natural Resources, Nongame Program Section of Wildlife.

Tuttle, M. D. 1988. *America's Neighborhood Bats: Understanding and Learning to Live in Harmony with Them.* Austin, TX: University of Texas Press.

Wilson, D. E. 1997. *Bats in Question: The Smithsonian Answer Book*. Washington, DC: Smithsonian Institution Press.

Wishner, L. 1982. *Eastern Chipmunks: Secrets of Their Solitary Lives*. Washington, DC: Smithsonian Institution Press.

Whitaker, J. O., Jr. 1998. *National Audubon Society Field Guide to North American Mammals*. New York, NY: Knopf..

United States Department of Agriculture Animal and Plant Health Inspection Service (APHIS) Standards. www.aphis.usda.gov.

US Department of Agriculture: APHIS. *Animal Care Resource Guide, Research Facility Inspection Guide, and Husbandry: Marine Mammal Water Quality*. http://www.aphis.usda.gov/ac/researchmanual/12-7MMWA.PDF

_____. Licensing and Registration Under the Animal Welfare Act: Guidelines for Dealers, Exhibitors, Transporters and Researchers. http://www.aphis.usda.gov/ac/awl.creg.html.

Chapter 8

TRANSPORTATION

OVERVIEW

Whether your educational programs are on-site at your facility or off-site in classrooms or auditoriums, education animals will need to be transported. The transport carrier is a convenient way to move the animal and is useful to reduce stress. If the program venue is at your facility, you probably plan to move the animal out of its enclosure, bring it to the classroom to do your presentation, and then return the animal to its home enclosure. In most circumstances, however, it is beneficial to have a transport carrier for the animal, even for travel within your own facility. Animals in carriers should be supervised at all times, or placed in a secure area. Refer to the transportation sections in each chapter for detailed information pertaining to transportation of specific animal types.

The transport carrier should be large enough to comfortably accommodate the animal without being so large that the animal may get hurt if frightened or panicked in the carrier. For example, too tall a carrier could be dangerous if an excited bird were to fly up and hit the top of the carrier. A properly-sized carrier should provide the animal with head and tail clearance (especially birds), with enough room to comfortably turn around without touching the sides.

The carrier should have ventilation holes that allow for air circulation, but do not allow for a lot of light to enter. The holes should be covered with mesh. The mesh can be fiberglass window screen, metal window screening material, hardware cloth, or similar material. Attach the mesh over the holes so that all sharp edges are inaccessible to the animal. The mesh prevents smaller animals from escaping or becoming caught in the openings. The mesh also prevents curious human fingers and eyes from looking inside, and paws from investigating outside of the carrier.

Transport carriers should be light, strong, easily cleaned, and kind to feathers, feet, skin, and fur. Commercial domestic pet carriers available through mail order or pet stores work well for many species of mammals and birds. The door can be covered with plywood or 0.25 in. (0.635 cm) thick plastic. Side vents can easily be covered with mesh. Perches can be attached to the sides with screws. Newspaper or mat material can be slid in and out for cleaning. Most carriers are disassembled easily for cleaning and disinfecting. Cover the carrier with a light sheet or towel to reduce light.

An easily latched door is needed for any transport carrier. If the latch can be worked with one hand, the other hand can either place the animal inside the carrier or cue it to move inside. The latch should not come undone accidentally or be accessible to the animal inside the carrier. Clips or other snaps make good secondary latches to prevent escapes.

Animals that will not easily fit into a commercial carrier may need a custom carrier. Carriers can be made from plexiglass, plywood, or stainless steel. Amphibians and reptiles can be transported in plastic sweater boxes or shoeboxes. Be sure to provide proper ventilation and proper light levels when designing custom carriers.

When moving the transport carrier, keep it level for the comfort and balance of the animal. The person carrying the container should use good posture and the power and strength of their legs to pick up and move the carrier. Two people may be necessary to move the carrier depending on the weight of the animal or awkwardness of the crate.

Transport to most off-site programs will be by car. Animals should not be left unattended in a car for any length of time, especially in very hot or very cold weather. Use the air conditioner and heater as needed, and do not smoke while transporting an animal. Orient the carrier perpendicular (sideways) to the direction of travel, especially for birds on a perch. Animals can more easily balance with the motion of the vehicle with the carrier placed in this manner. Visualize standing on a bus and trying to balance. It is easier if you have one leg in front of the other and are standing parallel to the direction of travel than if you were facing forward with your feet next to one another. The carrier should not be in direct sunlight when in any automobile or classroom because the inside of the crate will heat up dramatically and become dangerously hot. Drive safely!

SPECIAL REQUIREMENTS

Airline travel requires the animal to be under someone else's care until arrival. Even if you are accompanying the animal, the airline will place the carrier into the cargo hold, not in the passenger cabin. Animals smaller than ten pounds (or so) may travel in the passenger cabin of some airlines, but the carrier must fit under the seat.

Each airline has unique and changing regulations about transporting animals, so be sure to research all requirements before traveling. Contact the airline well in advance of your travel date. Most airlines require specific containers be used for animals. Transport in extreme temperatures is not allowed by most airlines.

You will need to produce copies of all required health documents and permits. Airline personnel may ask you to open the carrier and take the animal out so that the container may be inspected at check-in. Be sure to use the appropriate "drop-off" area. The carrier door should be locked during transport, but do not lock the carrier until after inspection. You can quickly lock a plastic dog kennel by using cable ties through the door to the sides of the kennel. These ties can be easily cut upon arrival or in case of emergency.

Most airlines require that the transport carrier be marked with a label reading "Live Animal" on the top and on one side. Have "This Side Up" arrows on at least two sides as well. Attach copies of the following documents to the transport carrier:

- Health certificate
- Contact name, address, and phone number for both home and destination, and the name of the person traveling with the animal
- Origin and destination airports
- All permits (state and federal)
- Sign reading "Do not feed or water"

Travel tips
- Consider removing any wheels from the carrier during flight. Non-locking wheels on a carrier can allow it to move freely and possibly injure the animal.
- Use newsprint or other material to line the transport carrier to absorb fecal matter.
- Try to schedule a non-stop flight and avoid heavy travel times.
- Fly when temperatures are moderate (on both ends of the travel) when the weather is extreme. For example, in very hot weather, try to schedule the flight in early morning or late evening, when it is the coolest.
- It would be wise to contact the USFWS, even if your destination is in the same federal region.
- Refer to Appendix B for airline contact information.
- Travel between states, either flying or driving, requires permission and permits from origin and destination states.

Additional Reading

Airline Travel with your Bird. 1997-2004. Veterinary and Aquatic Services Department, Drs Foster and Smith, Inc. From http://www.peteducation.com/article.cfm?cls=15&cat=1794&articleid=2270

Guidelines for traveling with your pet. 1999. From http://www.takeyourpet.com/pages/air.htm

King, T. Have Parrot will Travel: Tips for Traveling with Your Feathered Friends. BirdTimes Magazine. www.birdtimes.com/articles/travel.shtml

Library Gateway, University of Illinois at Urbana-Champaign. Traveling with your Pet. gateway.library.uiuc.edu/vex/cpl/faq/travel.htm

Molenda, S. 2001. Traveling by Air with Birds in the Cabin After 9/11. Winged Wisdom Pet Bird Magazine Ezine, November. www.birdsnways.com/wisdom/ww62eii.htm

Pet friendly airlines and shipping information. http://www.bullwinkle.com/index.html?travel/shipping.htm~indexmain

The Safe Air Travel for Animals Act. 2003. [Electronic version] From http://www.hsus.org/ace/11848

Transporting Live Animals. [Electronic version] from the United States Department of Transportation web site: www.dot.gov/airconsumer/animals.htm

Traveling. United States Department of Agriculture (USDA) Agricultural Research Service National Agricultural Library. http://www.nal.usda.gov/awic/companimals/travel.htm

Traveling with your Pet. Champaign Public Library. From http://gateway.library.uiuc.edu/vex/cpl/faq/travel.htm

Traveling with your Pet. Misc. Publication No. 1536. (1997, August and 1998, October) [Electronic version]

From the USDA, Animal and Plant Health Inspection Service web site: http://www.aphis.usda.gov/oa/pubs/petravel.html

United States Department of Transportation. Transporting Live Animals. http://airconsumer.ost.dot.gov/publications/animals.htm

Wright, M. 2000. [Electronic Version]. *Traveling with Your Companion Bird.*

From http://www.lafeber.com/articles/wright/traveling.asp

Chapter 9

LEGALITIES AND LIABILITIES

PERMITS, ORDINANCES, AND COURTESIES

In the United States, to hold any native bird or mammal (sometimes reptiles/amphibians) in captivity for educational purposes, you will need to obtain the proper permits and permission from one to several agencies. All appropriate permits or permission must be obtained before the acquisition of an animal.

Different ordinances, rules, regulations, and laws may govern whether or not you are allowed to have a certain species of wildlife for educational purposes on your property. You may have to work with many groups from township, city, state, and federal offices. Listed below are the most common permits and or permission you will need to acquire education wildlife. These requirements are listed starting with the local level and moving through the federal level. This list may not be complete for your situation and you should check with local authorities as to what may be allowed in your area. See Appendix B for contact information for state and federal agencies to help address your questions regarding permits.

NEIGHBORS

Talk to your business or residential neighbors as a courtesy to them, and make them aware of your intended activities. You should be prepared to answer questions regarding safety, cleanliness, noises, and any other concerns they may have.

NEIGHBORHOOD/COMMUNITY BOARDS

If you live in a neighborhood that regulates what you can and cannot do on your own property, prepare a proposal for the community leaders that explains your plans to use education animals. You will need to address any concerns the community leaders may have including where the animals will be housed, any smells, what the facility will look like, noise levels, and public safety.

TOWNSHIP BOARDS AND CITY ORDINANCES

Check with any local boards and research city ordinances regarding the activities you would like to pursue. Obtain permission from the local authorities as required.

STATES

Rehabilitation permits do not cover educational programs using native species. Each state has a Department of Natural Resources or its equivalent that governs and protects that state's wildlife and other natural resources. Some wildlife species are not protected at the state level, and you will not need a state permit in order to obtain or use one for educational uses; however, you may need permission or permits from local or federal agencies for that particular species. Each state will have a list of species that are protected (or unprotected). State personnel will be able to help you find the person in charge of those lists and the permits. State regulations vary; be sure the person you are working with fully understands what you will be doing so they can give correct advice on the appropriate regulation and permits. In some states the use of rehabilitation animals or animals that are obviously handicapped (amputees, blind, etc.) is prohibited.

UNITED STATES FISH AND WILDLIFE SERVICE (USFWS)

"The United States Fish and Wildlife Service is the principal Federal Agency responsible for conserving, protecting and enhancing fish, wildlife and plants in their habitats for the continuing benefit of the American people" (USFWS website). To that end, to use any migratory bird species for educational purposes, you will need a Special Purpose Permit. This includes all birds except the English house sparrow (*Passer domesticus*), European starling (*Sturnus vulgaris*), rock dove, also known as feral pigeon (*Columba livea*), and upland game birds (families: Cracidae, Odontophoridae, Phasianidae). Obtain an application from your US Fish and Wildlife Regional Office. Make sure that an Application Supplement for Special Purpose Possession Education is included. A federal permit is not valid without a sustaining state permit, if required. For endangered species and eagles, you will require additional permits from the USFWS: Endangered Species Permit and Eagle Exhibition Permit. Refer to the General Permit Procedures under the rule 50 CFR 13, Migratory Bird Permits under rule 50 CFR 21.27, and Eagle permits under 50 CFR 22.21. Currently there are no unique migratory bird education permit regulations, but there is activity by government to create such regulations.

United States Department of Agriculture (USDA)

If you use mammals in educational programming or displays, you will need a permit from the United States Department of Agriculture, called a "Class C" license. Anyone seeking this license should apply on a form that will be furnished by the person in charge of the official work of the AAPHIS REAC Sector Supervisor in the state in which you intend to operate.

Many of these permit applications ask for similar information; name, address, organization address, your experience working with the animals you would like to use, species of animal with which you want to work, cage dimensions (and diagrams or pictures), cage furniture, where you will be getting food, the name of the veterinarian that will be helping you, the type of programs you will be doing, and other background information. Once a permit is granted, all minimum or standard conditions must be fulfilled. Accurate and complete records must be kept as required by permits and husbandry protocol. Yearly reports are also required.

Special consideration should be taken if you are planning live animal presentations outside your home state. Crossing state lines with wild animals requires written consent from the wildlife agency in the state where you are going, and from the state you are leaving. In the case of migratory birds, you will also need consent from your United States Fish and Wildlife Service office.

INSURANCE

Insurance is another component to consider when conducting educational programs. Liability insurance is recommended for any program utilizing education animals both for outreach/off-site and for on-site programming. The International Association of Avian Trainers and Educators (IAATE) recommends a one million dollar policy to cover any accidents.

Chapter 9: Legalities and Liabilities

Additional Reading

Airline Travel with your Bird. 1997-2004. Veterinary and Aquatic Services Department, Drs Foster and Smith, Inc. Retrieved January 16, 2004 from. http://www.peteducation.com

Bald Eagle Protection Act. 16 U.S.C. 668-668d, June 8, 1940, as amended 1959, 1962, 1972, and 1978. USFWS at www.fws.gov

Endangered and Threatened Wildlife and Plants; Final Rule to Reclassify the Bald Eagle from Endangered to Threatened in All of the Lower 48 States. Federal Register for Wednesday July 12, 1995, Volume 60, Number 133, pp 36000-36010. USFWS at www.fws.gov

Guidelines for traveling with your pet. 1999. Retrieved January 16, 2004 from: http://www.takeyourpet.com/pages/air.htm

Horton, M. 1995. Obtaining the Right Permits for Education Animals. *NWRA Quarterly.* 13(4):17.

King, T. 2000. Have Parrot will Travel: Tips for Traveling with Your Feathered Friends. [Electronic version] *BirdTimes Magazine.* Pet Publishing, Inc. Retrieved January 17, 2004, from http://www.petpublishing.com/birdtimes/articles/travel.shtml

Migratory Bird Treaty Act, 16 U.S.C. 703-712, July 3, 1918, as amended 1936,1960,1969,1974, 1978, 1986, and 1989. USFWS at www.fws.gov

Molenda, S. Traveling by Air with Birds in the Cabin After 9/11. (2001, November) *Winged Wisdom Pet Bird Magazine Ezine.* Retrieved January 17, 2004 from http://www.birdsnways.com/wisdom/ww62eii.htm

The Safe Air Travel for Animals Act. 2003. [Electronic version] Retrieved January 16, 2004 from http://www.hsus.org/ace/11848

Transporting Live Animals. [Electronic version] Retrieved January 16, 2004 from the United States Department of Transportation web site: www.dot.gov/airconsumer/animals.htm

Traveling. (2003, May 29) Retrieved January 16, 2004 from the United States Department of Agriculture Agricultural Research Service (USDA) National Agricultural Library web site: http://www.nal.usda.gov/awic/companimals/companimals/travel.htm

Traveling with your Pet. Champaign Public Library. Last updated June 19, 2001. Retrieved January 17, 2004 from http://gateway.library.uiuc.edu/vex/cpl/faq/travel.htm

Traveling with your Pet. Misc. Publication No. 1536. (1997, August and 1998, October) [Electronic version] Retrieved January 17, 2004 from the United States Department of Agriculture, Animal and Plant Health Inspection Service web site: http://www.aphis.usda.gov/oa/pubs/petravel.html

US Fish and Wildlife Service, Department of the Interior. http://www.fws.gov

Wild Bird Conservation Act of 1992. 16 U.S.C. 4901-4916, October 23, 1992. USFWS. www.fws.gov

Wright, M. 2000. [Electronic Version]. *Travel with Your Companion Bird.* Retrieved January 16, 2004 from http://www.lafeber.com/articles/wright/traveling.asp

Chapter 10

ANIMAL HEALTH

MENTAL HEALTH

Before the animal arrives, you must determine the best strategy for keeping the individual in optimal mental health. Optimum mental health means reducing "bad" stress in the environment and increasing enrichment opportunities. High or bad stress refers to stress that is mentally or physically detrimental to an animal's health.

Different animals will have different mental health needs. The best way to provide proper care is to fully understand the animal's natural history and behaviors. This understanding will allow you to identify potential negative stressors and what enrichment technique to try. Each species will have characteristic behaviors that will give you general guidelines, but individual animals, much like individual people, vary in normal behavior and tolerances. Understanding the individual's preferences and comfort zone is crucial to providing a healthy environment.

Enrichment can be an incredibly important component of a captive animal's life. Enrichment is defined as manipulating an animal's environment to provide mental stimulation. Enrichment can take many forms, including new perches, toys, treats hidden in the enclosure, different scents, outdoor enclosures, and training the animal with positive reinforcement.

The enclosure itself can offer enrichment. Mary Deroo (1993) believes foraging or food-searching is only a part of an animal's life, one that is often the sole focus of enrichment. She believes that more work needs to be done in rearranging the enclosure to create a more chaotic environment, similar to life in the wild. Of course, predation is eliminated, but exploratory behaviors should be encouraged and reinforced. The introduction of disposable and/or removable furniture, on a random schedule, will encourage and reinforce exploratory behavior and reduce boredom. Removable logs, rocks, portable trees or limbs, large potted plants, ramps, mud-holes, sand-piles, and other objects may encourage the animal to investigate its environment.

Different enrichment techniques will work with different animals. Understanding the natural history and behavior of the species will help determine what may be successful. Further in this chapter, you will find a few examples for enrichment for captive animals. The Oregon Zoo Discover Birds Show uses Enrichment Charts to help keep track of enrichment items and how they work for an individual animal (Appendix C). All enrichment items, scents, toys, or food items must be safe for the animal.

Sometimes anything new in the enclosure may actually cause a fear response, especially the first attempt. You may run the risk of scaring the animal, perplexing it to the point of confusion, or inducing displacement behavior, aggression, or stereotypic behaviors. Start slowly. The animal is being placed in a state of learning, so moving slowly will acclimate the animal to changes in routine, objects, and cage furniture (Poulsen 1994).

ENRICHMENT FOR ANIMALS IN CAPTIVITY

Below are examples of ways to stimulate permanently captive wild animals. Some of the examples can be used for species other than the ones listed. Any enrichment however should not harm the animal in any way, mentally or physically.

TABLE 22 – ENRICHMENT ACTIVITIES (Oregon Zoo Discover Birds Show 2003)

Enrichment	Type of Animal	Description
Grooming board for hoofed stock	Animals such as horses, deer antelope and goats.	This rough surface is used for scratching and to shed winter coats. Make a grooming board with a 2 x 3 ft. (0.61 x 0.92 m) section (or whatever size is appropriate) of 0.75 in. (1.905 cm) plywood. Drill holes about 1 to 2 in. (2.54 to 5.08 cm) apart through the plywood. The holes should be 0.50 in. (1.26 cm) deep and 0.25 in. (0.635 cm) in diameter. Cut a 0.25 in. (0.635 cm) wooden dowel rod into 1.5 in. (3.81 cm) lengths; enough to fill the holes on the board. Round each peg at one end with a wood file. Use wood glue inside the holes of the plywood board and pound the pegs into the holes, rounded end out. Affix the board securely to any vertical surface. Make sure that the board cannot injure an animal by swinging or falling, and animals cannot get caught in any chain or rope that might be used to hang the board. (Larimer 2001)
Monkey buckets	These were originally designed for rhesus monkeys *(Macaca mulatta)* but could be used for any climbing mammal and snakes or lizards with some modifications.	Remove the metal handle from a five-gallon bucket, and drill a 0.50 in. (1.26 cm) hole on opposite sides near the top of the bucket. Thread rope through the holes. Suspend the bucket so it swings and spins completely around the rope. Drill six holes, 1.5 in. (3.81 cm) in diameter into the bottom that allows waste and water to fall out. Try drilling the holes off center for a different action. Cut the bottom out of a bucket and suspend it sideways from the rope, forming a tube for yet another variation. Although more difficult to sit in, this tube can be an interesting play area. Alternates to rope include bungee cord material and latex tubing (Suarez 1994).
Pumpkins	Turkey vulture *(Carthartes aura)*, Caracara *(Caracara cheriway)*; also other birds such as jays or parrots, and some mammals.	Cut small triangular holes into whole pumpkins. Fill the holes with chicken necks and mealworms and place in enclosures with the birds. The birds will manipulate the pumpkins and tear at them to get the treats out. Use fruits or nuts for the jays, parrots, and mammals (Cleaver 1994).
Hiding food items, cricket dispensers	Otters, meerkats *(Suricata suricatta)*, and other similar animals	Otters enjoy having their food hidden in their enclosure; under logs and in rock piles. Minced meat can be placed in holes in logs. Simple dispensers can be made to slowly release crickets. The dispenser consists simply of a tube with holes cut intermittently along one side. Make the holes just large enough to allow a cricket to emerge and the insects should come out at irregular intervals, thus providing an "interest" food for the otters. A similar tube is used to dispense mealworms and works for animals like meerkats (Partridge 1992)
Object replacement	Reptiles	Regular replacement of objects in reptile exhibits, such as twigs, stones, and plants, stimulates exploratory behavior (Copenhagen Zoo 1992).

TABLE 22, Continued

Enrichment	Type of animal	Description
Fruit fly (Drosophila) generator	Insectivores	Take a 2.5 liter container, such as an ice cream carton, and fill it half way with fruit waste. Add fruit fly eggs. Slash the base of the carton four or five times for ventilation, and make a one centimeter hole at the top to allow the fruit flies to escape. The fermenting fruit provides warmth for hatching. Fruit flies will escape into the enclosure and provide a source of food and interest suitable for insectivorous birds, mammals, and reptiles. Vestigial (wingless) flies are available from laboratory suppliers and may be suitable for less active animals (Phipps 1993).
Christmas trees	Ravens *(Corvus corax)*, white-tail deer *(Odocoileus virginianus cousei)*, black bear *(Ursus americanus cinnamomum)*	Use donated trees that have not had fire retardant sprayed on them. Check carefully for tinsel or decorations. Ravens and other birds may use the trees for perching/hiding options. White-tail deer may enjoy nibbling the branches, and black bear may chew or carry the trees around (Acuna 1993).
"Popsicles"	Various animals	Put treats frozen inside all shapes and sizes into enclosures for animals to get at and eat.
Sounds	Various animals	Introduction of constant low level sounds, especially those derived from natural habitats, the subjective loudness of other sounds can be reduced—a phenomenon called "masking." Sometimes noises around the animal enclosures can be very loud, masking the noise can reduce stress for the animal. Sounds can also be introduced for enrichment purposes. Many, but not all species will orient to or search for certain types of sounds. These usually include sounds of conspecifics or prey species (Tromberg 1994).
Pine cone treats	Various birds	Collect open pinecones and place wire around the base so they can be tied to a tree. Treats such as seed, mealworms, and raisins can be dipped in honey and stuffed in the holes. The pinecones can be shredded by the birds after they are finished with the treats if left in the cage (Palm 1994).
Unusual browse	Herbivores	Offer new and different plants as browse for animals. You have to make sure that the plants offered are non-toxic to the animal.
Hammocks	Originally made for chimpanzees but should work for raccoons, squirrels, and other arboreal species.	The hammock is made from sail canvas, and the center is reinforced with a double thickness of 9 oz. canvas. The corners are reinforced with two inch webbing sewn inside two triangular thicknesses of canvas. The finished measurements are 56 x 70 in. (142.24 cm x 177.80 cm) long. Each corner strap measures 47 in. (119.38 cm) long. A 1 in. (2.54 cm) diameter grommet is hydraulically set into each corner. Four 7-in. (17.78 cm) webbed nylon straps, each containing seven 1-in. (2.54 cm) grommets, spaced 2 in. (5.08 cm) apart, are sewn to the corners through the 1 in. (2.54 cm) grommet. When hung, each strap is doubled over around what it will be hung from and the grommet can be matched up and secured with stainless steel shackles through the aligned grommets. Clean by hosing off or scrubbing with a cleaning solvent (Wolper 1995).
Suspended feeding "ball"	Various animals	Use a log with holes drilled in it, or a hollow log or a wire basket made to put hanging plants in, center is filled with treats (raisins, fruit, nuts, or other foodstuff). The rest of the "ball" is filled with hay, straw, or vegetation. This ball is then suspended above the ground so that it is reachable, but not so easy to get at. The animal is randomly reinforced when they are able to get a treat out. These "balls" are cleaned every day (Cartlidge 1995).

TABLE 22, Continued

Enrichment	Type of animal	Description
Scattering food	Reptiles	Scattering insects in unpredictable quantities and at irregular intervals creates a variety of foraging opportunities. Creating scent trails for larger lizards, using materials like rodent bedding or urine, may be beneficial by increasing foraging time. For herbivorous species, placing a variety of edible wild plants as whole branches may increase foraging interest (Skelton 1996).
Corn cobs	Various animals	Drill a small hole at the base of the corncob and string a wire through this and attach to the side of the cage. Birds enjoy eating the kernels off the corn and chew on the cob after the kernels are gone (Bergen County Zoo 1996).
Animal shower	Various animals	Create a shower that the animal can self activate. Mount a standard showerhead where you want it and run a hose between the showerhead and the water source. Mount a motion sensor near the showerhead. Install an electric solenoid valve at the water source. Use one that is normally closed when the power is off and open when the power is on. Run electrical power to the motion sensor. Use the two wires that would normally hook to the light fixture, and attach them to the electric solenoid valve. In other words, when the sensor senses motion, instead of turning on the lights it will open the valve and turn the water on to the showerhead. You could also set this up on a timer so that it goes on and off at desired intervals throughout the day. Hook the electric solenoid valve up to an electric timer, instead of the motion sensor (Krajniak 1997).
Various	Stork, barn owl, hawk, falcon	• Paper bag with holes torn in it stuffed with paper, food pieces inside. • Multiple feedings • Dirt bath with or without several mice on top • Small pieces of browse on the floor • Egg carton with part of diet in egg sections • Place food around mew • 1 to 2 ice cubes in mew • Red flying saucer toy with part of diet inside • Hand feed part of diet • Cardboard tube with mouse pieces visible from ends • Pinecone stuffed with bird of prey diet • Shed snake skin (Oregon Zoo Discover Birds Show 2003)
Various	Condor, vulture	• Place part of diet around mew • Phone book in mew (can put part of diet between pages) • Large paper bag filled with crumpled paper • Browse left on mew floor • Multiple feedings, part in the morning, part in the afternoon • Large cardboard tube with food visible from ends • Rolling drilled stump with food pieces placed in the drilled areas • Ice cube with mice frozen inside • Large open boxes • Multiple feedings • Browse on mew floor, food hidden among it • Large boomer ball with bird of prey diet smeared on top • Pig's ear chew toy • Small pieces fruit as treat • Shed snake skin (Oregon Zoo Discover Birds Show 2003)

TABLE 22, *Continued*

Enrichment	Type of animal	Description
Various	Ducks	• Ice cubes in pond • Small pieces sticks, grasses in cage • Dirt bath • Mist them • Large pinecones • Multiple feedings • Bath toy in water 　　　(Oregon Zoo Discover Birds Show 2003)
Various	Rats and small mammals	• Change boxes • Small paper bags • Paper towels in cage • Small pieces of fresh browse • Cardboard tubes • Shredded paper for nesting material • Lettuce/kale, etc. • Wooden toys to chew • Multiple feedings 　　　(Oregon Zoo Discover Birds Show 2003)
Various	Raven, crow	• Part of diet hung in a toy • Cardboard box stuffed with paper and part of diet • Egg cartons filled with "treats" • Phone book with part of diet between pages • Fish head in paper bag • Scatter food in cage • Pig's ear chew toy • Cardboard tube stuffed with paper and part of diet • Suet feeder with part of diet inside • Browse in cage • Pinecone with bird of prey diet inside • Dirt bath • 1 to 2 ice cubes in water bowl • Shed snake skin 　　　(Oregon Zoo Discover Birds Show 2003)

PHYSICAL HEALTH

Determine the physical health of your new education animal before its arrival. Have a veterinarian evaluate the animal and set up a care plan to follow before an animal is accepted. A full health history should be reviewed with the veterinarian before accepting any animal. Education animals should receive regular exams from a veterinarian (at least yearly) that include a fecal check and basic bloodwork. This practice provides an annual record of that animal's health and an opportunity to treat for any parasites.

Once the animal's history has been reviewed and the individual is determined to be in good health, place the animal into quarantine upon arrival. All new animals should be quarantined for a pre-determined length of time, especially if there are other animals at the facility. Normally, 30 to 90 days in quarantine is recommended, and the exact length of time should be determined in consultation with your veterinarian. The veterinarian should also do a thorough physical exam during quarantine. Quarantine time can allow the animal to become familiar with its surroundings and prevent disease transmission to other animals.

After the quarantine period, the animal can be moved to permanent housing and given an opportunity to become comfortable in its new environment. The amount of time needed will vary from animal to animal, but is usually 7 to 30 days. Only minimum disturbances should be made while the animal is becoming acclimated. Observe the animal's behavior to determine the animal's progress. Once the animal is comfortable, a cleaning and feeding routine can be established. Some basic training can begin, and should include moving willingly into another area, holding crate, or enclosure and being weighed.

Weighing an animal on a regular basis is an effective way to keep track of weekly, seasonal, and yearly changes. Animals can be weighed anywhere from twice per week to twice per month. Weight can be an indicator of health. If an animal is becoming ill, they will often start losing weight before any other symptoms develop. Weight can tell you if the animal is at a good weight range for the season or sex of the animal and if the animal is overweight or underweight. Knowing the natural history and talking to others that have worked with similar species will give you a baseline. Of course, many animals, especially raptors, are trained with food and are weighed often as part of their training regime.

Ascertaining the health of an animal requires an understanding of normal behavior, natural history, and time spent observing the animal. You should know what a wild healthy counterpart looks and acts like, and how the feathers, fur, or scales on a healthy specimen are supposed to look and feel. Know what normal fecal material looks like and how often they normally defecate. If you have a bird that casts pellets, you need to know what normal ones look like and how frequently the bird should produce a pellet. Other life history details you need to know include: when do they shed or molt; when is the animal active; when is the animal dormant; and if or when do they hibernate.

Keeping regular records on the animal's weight, food consumption, fecal output, and behavior will give you and your veterinarian an overall view of the animal's health and will help keep them healthy.

Literature Cited

Acuna, M. 1993. Christmas Trees For Environmental Enrichment. *The Shape of Enrichment.* 2(4):1-2.

Behavioral Enrichment – A Catalogue of Ideas. 1990. Frederickburg, Denmark: The Copenhagen Zoo.

Bergen County Zoo, Metro Washington Park Zoo, Oregon. 1996. *The Shape of Enrichment.* 5(2).

Cartlidge, D. 1995. Simple and Cheap Enrichment for Omnivores. *The Shape of Enrichment.* 4(4):1-2.

Cleaver, L. 1994. Pumpkins for Turkey Vultures and Caracaras. *The Shape of Enrichment.* 3(3):4.

Deroo, M. 1993. Enrichment through Vertical and Horizontal Spacing. *The Shape of Enrichment.* 2(3):9-10.

Krajniak, E. 1997. Animal Shower. *The Shape of Enrichment.* 6(2):14.

Larimer, T. 2001. Grooming Board for Hoofed Stock. *The Shape of Enrichment.* 10(3):20.

Oregon Zoo Discover Birds Show. 2003. Staff, Personal communication.

Palm, S. 1994. Pine Cone Treats for Birds. *The Shape of Enrichment.* 3(4):11.

Partridge, J. 1992. Little Things can Mean So Much. *International Zoo News.* Apr/May 1990.

Phipps, G. 1993. A Fruit Fly Generator for Insectivores. *The Shape of Enrichment.* 2(3):7.

Poulsen, E. 1994. Think Like a Bird: A Practical Guide to Enrichment. *The Shape of Enrichment.* 5(1):3-4.

Skelton, T. 1996. Can Reptiles be Enriched? *The Shape of Enrichment.* 5(1):3-4.

Suarez, S., and M. Smith. Monkey Buckets. *The Shape of Enrichment.* 3(3):3-4.

Tromberg, C. T. 1994. Shaping Sound Environments. *The Shape of Enrichment.* 3(4):7-9.

Wolper, C. 1995. A Hammock in the Rain Forest for Chimpanzees. *The Shape of Enrichment.* 4(3):1-2.

Additional Reading

Guide for the Care and Use of Laboratory Animals. 1985. US Department of Heath and Human Services. NIH Publication No. 85-23.

Heyn, S. 2002. Behavioral Enrichment for Mammals. In NWRA *Principles of Wildlife Rehabilitation.* 2nd ed. A. T. Moore and S. Joosten, eds. St. Cloud, MN: National Wildlife Rehabilitators Association. Pp 6.35-6.40.

Laule, G. 1992. Addressing Psychological Well-Being: Training as Enrichment. *The Shape of Enrichment.* 1(2):11-12.

Priest, G.1993. Reinforcement: The Key to Shaping Behavior. *The Shape of Enrichment.* 2(3):12-13.

Shepherdson, D. 1992. The Case for Enrichment. *The Shape of Enrichment.* 1(2):3-4.

Trivedi, B. P. 2002. Zoos use New Tricks to Stimulate Animals. *National Geographic News.* www.nationalgeographic.com

Williamson K., and M. Scarpuzzi. 1993. *The Shape of Enrichment.* 2(4):13-14.

Chapter 11

ANIMAL SELECTION

The most common mistake made by educators is to try to design a program around an animal previously acquired. Before selecting an animal, have your program design finalized. Know the goals of the program. For example, do you plan on placing emphasis on the plight of endangered species or local fauna? Are you focusing on birds or mammals? There are many ways to design education programs and you need to know what you are going to do before you acquire animals. The best plan is to have the program determine what animal is needed, rather than trying to fit an animal you already have into a program.

Most wild animals do not make good education animals for use in front of an audience, in a classroom, or in an auditorium setting. Even animals raised in captivity or permanently injured may not be comfortable in education program situations. The normal behavior, natural history, and temperament of the animal are only some of the components you need to understand in determining what individual will be a good education animal. You also should know what types of animals other educators successfully use in programs.

Consultation with zoo, bird show, and other types of animal program personnel is recommended. These professionals make it their job to understand and train animals for their programs. Nature centers and wildlife rehabilitation facilities that have education programs using live animals can also provide information. These places will often have permanently injured animals for their programs. Not only can you see what animals are being used, but also understand what disabilities are common to non-releasable animals regularly used for educational purposes.

The physical appearance of the animal is an important consideration. If the disability is obvious and visible, for example, part of a wing or leg missing, part of a beak missing, or an eye missing, will it detract from the message being conveyed? If the audience is only concerned about what happened to the individual animal, and miss the message (even if it is conservation), then the animal will not work.

If the program goal is to teach identification of certain animals using an education animal, a disfigured education animal may not be appropriate. If the program message focuses on injuries caused by human actions, and the disabilities were caused by human actions, that particular animal may be perfect. The physical appearance of the animal must be considered before acquiring an education animal.

Below are general criteria for selection of an education bird, mammal, or reptile; and for presenter qualifications.

Animal Criteria
- The animal's injury should not prevent it from normal daily activities such as eating, perching, and bathing.
- The disability should not cause undue stress or other health problems to the animal. For example, a hawk with only one leg will get bumblefoot in the remaining foot.
- Some injuries make it difficult for the handler or the bird to live comfortably in captivity.
- Full wing amputees have difficulty balancing and righting themselves if they lose their balance. Their respiratory system may be compromised as well since in most birds, a large air sac is contained in the humerus bone of the wing. A bird with a permanent injury of this sort should not be used for any type of education.
- Young animals may adapt faster to life in captivity and program use than adult animals. Older animals may still be suitable for program use, however their training time may be longer or require a more experienced trainer.

Animal criteria, continued
- Special permits may be required for certain species; endangered species, and eagles, for example.
- Federal regulations may restrict the use of education birds with certain injuries.
- Imprinted animals, especially birds, may be very tractable when they are young but may become aggressive and territorial when they are older.

HANDLER REQUIREMENTS
- The handler/trainer has either handled the species before, or has training to handle the species and has support if they need help (other people who have experience with the species).
- A veterinarian is willing to help with the education animal and has experience with the species, or has support.
- The relationship with a veterinarian is established before receiving any animal.
- Any vaccinations for the trainer (i.e. rabies vaccinations) are received before the animal arrives.
- All permits are acquired.
- Enclosures and caging areas are acquired and built for a specific animal.
- Food sources are established before acquiring the animal.
- A budget is set up for care of the animal year round.
- Equipment needed to handle the animal is in place.

Additional Reading

Arent, L., and M. Martell. 1996. *Care and Management of Captive Raptors.* St. Paul, MN: The Raptor Center, University of Minnesota.

Display Environments for Permanently Damaged Birds and Rehabilitation Facilities for Injured Birds of Prey. Woodstock, VT. Vermont Institute of Natural Science.

Holley, D. 1997. *Animals Alive! An Ecological Guide to Animal Activities.* Gillette, NJ: Bookends

Professional Standards for the Use of Live Animals in Environmental Education. Iowa Association of Naturalists. 15 pages. Conservation Education Center, RR1, Box 53, Guthrie Center, IA 51005.

Thorne-Bolduc, K. 2002. The Differences between Imprinting, Habituation, and Tameness. In *NWRA Principles of Wildlife Rehabilitation.* 2nd Edition. Eds. A. T. Moore and S. Joosten, eds. St. Cloud, MN: National Wildlife Rehabilitators Association. Pp 9.77-9.79.

Chapter 12

TRAINING

Training animals for education programs is a complex subject, involving a tremendous variety of animals and situations, and is beyond the scope of this text. Almost anyone can learn how to train an animal, but it does take time, practice, and study. A few basic precepts apply to training any animal, however. The most important and most basic step is learning as much as you can about the species' natural history and behaviors. A few obvious examples are; when the animal is normally active, if the animal is a predator or prey species, and what is the animal's normal defensive behavior.

Of course, you should read as much as possible about training techniques. The authors recommend learning about operant conditioning techniques and consulting experienced wild animal trainers, handlers, and rehabilitators. Operant conditioning can been a very rewarding activity for a captive animal. This interaction enhances the animal's experiences, and because they are more comfortable, they are healthier and make better ambassadors and teachers for the earth.

The act of training is often associated with animals doing "tricks" for human entertainment. Proper training does not involve the performance of tricks, but does engage the animal in a two-way communication with the trainer. An animal that is properly trained is more comfortable in its surroundings and suffers from less stress. Operant conditioning is a type of training that involves the "operator" (the animal, in this case) in determining the outcome of the training. This technique gives the animal control over its surroundings and develops a pattern that the animal can understand. Training is not being "superior" to the animal or forcing them to perform. Instead, training will enrich and enhance the animal's daily routines.

Knowing the normal behavior of each individual animal is a necessity for successful training. You need to know where the animal feels most comfortable in the enclosure, what time of day the animal is active, what behaviors or objects make the animal comfortable or uncomfortable, and what is the animal's favorite food. Understanding the animal's tolerance to stress and individual personality will help you be a better trainer. This is part of a relationship and a communication system between trainer and animal.

Have a training program planned in advance. Make the first goals simple ones, but result in learned behaviors with far-reaching benefits. For example, teaching the animal to step on a scale is a management tool that can be used throughout the animal's life to assess its health. This first small step in training is an important building block for the trainer and the animal. Animals that are used in education programming should be trained and conditioned to behaviors that are consistent with their natural history. Training is used to facilitate the daily management of the animal; weighing, shifting from one cage to another, transferring into a travel crate, trimming nails, and other husbandry tasks.

Most animals coming from a rehabilitation facility have had unpleasant experiences with people. These creatures are sometimes frightened because they have been restrained and examined by humans for incomprehensible (to them) reasons. Escape is the animal's natural reaction. Being placed in an education facility before a group of large, scary, and staring humans is a very bewildering and terrifying experience for the non-releasable animal. If the animal is exposed to operant conditioning training before use in education programs, and stress is reduced. When properly trained animals are in front of the group of "scary" humans, they are no longer frightened, but confident in these activities and surroundings.

Additional Reading

Arent, L., and M. Martell. 1996. *Care and Management of Captive Raptors.* St. Paul, MN: The Raptor Center, University of Minnesota.

A Manual for the Apprentice Falconer. Phoenix, AZ: Arizona Falconer's Association.

Barberis-Weisenmiller, L., and P. Blum. 2003. *Woody the Woodpecker: Training a Pileated Woodpecker for Animal Shows.* In Conference Proceedings. Portland, OR: International Association of Avian Trainers and Educators Portland Oregon.

Barth, C. 2003. *Stepping up the Training Process: The Benefits of Stationing an East African Crowned Crane and Marabou Storks.* In Conference Proceedings. Portland, OR: International Association of Avian Trainers and Educators.

Beebe, F. L., and H. M. Webster. 1994. *North American Falconry and Hunting Hawks.* Topeka, KS: Jostens Printing and Publishing.

Ford, E. 1992. *Falconry: Art and Practice.* London, UK: Blanford Books.

Fox, N. 1995. *Conditioned Learning. Understanding the Bird of Prey.* Blaine, WA: Hancock House.

Griffin, D. R. 1984. *Animal Thinking.* Cambridge, MA: Harvard University Press.

Horton, M. 1997. *Training is not a Bad Word.* The NWRA Quarterly. 15(3):4.

Kimsey, B., and J. Hodge. 1992. *Falconry Equipment.* Kimsey/Hodge Publications.

Martin, S. 1995. *Bird Training Guide.* Natural Encounters Inc., and *Thoughts on Training Birds,* a three-part series. In Newsletters. Portland, OR: International Association of Avian Trainers and Educators.

Neumann, K. *Educating with Raptors: A Resource Booklet.* Carroll, IA: Stone Printing.

Parry-Jones, J. 1994. *Training Birds of Prey.* Newton Abbot, UK: David and Charles Books

Priest, G. *Reinforcement: The Key to Shaping Behavior. The Shape of Enrichment.* 2(3):12-13.

Pryor, K. 1999. *Don't Shoot the Dog: The New Art of Teaching and Training, Revised.* New York, NY: Bantam Books.

Tardona, D. R. 2002. *Animal Behavioral Requirements and Wildlife rehabilitation: The need to use and Evaluate Enrichment programs in the Rehabilitation Process.* Wildlife Rehabilitation Bulletin. 21(1):26-29.

Upton, R. 1991. *Falconry: Principles and Practice.* London, UK: Adam and Charles Black.

Vincent, J. 2002. *Top Trainer, Top Dog, (Top Hog, Top Parrot...): The Building Blocks to Becoming a Well Rounded Trainer.* In Proceedings. Portland, OR: International Association of Avian Trainers and Educators.

Watson, J., and A. Spencer. 1995. *Operant Conditioning: Enhancing Daily Management, Health, and Well-being of Captive Animals.* Wildlife Rehabilitation. 13:215-223.

Williamson, K. and M. Scarpuzzi. 1993. *At Sea World, Pleasure is the Key to Enrichment. The Shape of Enrichment.* 2(4):13-14.

Woodford, M. H. 1967. *A Manual of Falconry.* London, UK: Adam and Charles Black.

Videotapes

African Lion Safari. *Birds of Prey: Their Care and Training.* Two Volume video and manual set. Full size gauntlet pattern and 17 jess patterns are included. 1995. Birds of Prey Training Video, African Lion Safari, R.R. 1, Cambridge, Ontario, Canada N1R 5S2.

Busch Entertainment Corporation. *Husbandry Training As a Tool For Marine Mammal Management Update.* 1994. BEC, One Busch Place, St. Louis, MO 63118-1952.

Martin, Steve. 1995. *The Positive Approach to Parrots as Pets* (Two tape video series). Part I is *"Understanding Bird Behavior"* and Part II is *"Training through Positive Reinforcement".*

Chapter 13

SAFETY

PHYSICAL SAFETY

Concerns for physical safety pertain not only to the education animal in your care, but also to handlers, bystanders, and audience members. There is a whole range of activities required to ensure the safety of all the people and animals involved in education programs. For example, you must carefully design, construct, and maintain the animal's permanent and transport enclosures. You must also provide safe conditions for training, handling, and transportation, provide adequate medical care, and properly conduct the actual programs. People handling the animals and attending the programs must be protected as well. This means preventing any disease transmission, having enough expertise to properly train and maintain control of the animal, and taking proper steps to protect yourself and others from any injuries. Obviously, safety is a complex process, but is well worth the time and effort required to "do right."

Safety, of course, starts at home. In this case, it is the animal's home. The enclosure that serves as the animal's home must be safe. The enclosure must provide safety from predators (if outside) and must be escape-proof. Inspect the enclosure for sharp edges, nails, wires, or other objects that may physically harm the animal. The enclosure must be kept in good condition and built with appropriate materials. All perches, hutches, and, of course, the enclosure itself must be maintained in good repair and safe condition. These factors should be considered in the construction and during regular inspections of the enclosure.

The animal needs to be kept safe during transport and when any handling or training activity takes place. The animal must be shielded from the prying eyes and hands of any curious, or even malicious, people. The cage and transport enclosures should be made to be locked or have another secure system so that bystanders cannot gain access to the animal. The animal needs to be kept safe from temperature extremes and have adequate ventilation when traveling. You must ensure the animal is not placed under undue stress or exposed to diseases from other animals.

Having training procedures in place concerning how to handle, transport, and present a program with an animal will help ensure handler safety. Understanding the animal's defenses and knowing how to respond to the animal's fear or aggression will reduce handler injury. Having a contingency plan for difficult situations, including having another trained handler nearby, is important and prudent.

Bystanders and audience members need to be kept safe because no one should get hurt while watching an education program (or any other program for that matter). In addition, the presenter's credibility is placed in doubt when an animal or person is injured. Lastly, there are certainly liability concerns if such an event occurs. One certain way to keep the audience safe is to have a well-prepared program with well-trained and prepared animals and a well-prepared and trained presenter. Keep audience members a safe distance from the animals in use and also away from the transport enclosures. Do not let audience members touch the animal that is being presented. Use pelts, skins, feathers, or other bio-facts for people to touch. This will keep the audience safe and the animal safe. The presenter will have a lower stress level if he or she does not need to keep a constant eye on the animal and bystanders.

ZOONOTIC DISEASE CONTROL

A zoonoses is an infection or infestation shared in nature by people and animals. The zoonotic disease can be passed from animal to human and vice versa. All handlers should consider obtaining vaccinations against zoonoses such as rabies and inoculation against tetanus. Keeping animal enclosures clean and human food and drink separate from any anima-related location reduces the risk of transmissible diseases.

Miller (2000) offers several ways to control animal diseases transmissible to humans.

- Clothing should be clean and changed as often as necessary.
- Shoes and boots should be kept clean of fecal matter, dirt, and cage litter.
- Disposable gloves and surgical masks must be available for such procedures as necropsies or cleaning contaminated animal quarters.
- Lavatory facilities should be accessible with hand washing sinks and suitable washing agents.
- Eating, drinking, and smoking should be restricted to designated areas free of animal waste materials.
- The supervisory staff must be given basic information on zoonoses. Personal hygiene rules should be established and the supervisory staff should set an example.
- All personnel and volunteers should be advised to seek the consent of their physicians before working at the facility. They should acquire any necessary vaccinations (especially tetanus). If working with mammals, they should inquire about the possibility of pre-exposure rabies vaccinations. Female workers who become pregnant should be asked to renew medical consent. People handling potential Rabies Vector Species (RVS), (most mammals) should have pre-exposure rabies vaccinations.
- There must be separate refrigeration facilities for food (animal food kept separate from human food) and for carcasses and postmortem specimens.

Additional things to think about when working with education animals

- Newly arrived education animals should be put into quarantine for a period of time determined by the veterinarian. All quarantine procedures set up with the veterinarian are strictly followed.
- Non-releasable wildlife should be screened for as many diseases as possible during the quarantine period when the animal first arrives. The animal should have an annual exam that includes fecal screening, bloodwork, and radiographs, if possible, and appropriate vaccinations.
- Any human injuries from working with an animal should be treated immediately. A physician should be consulted on how best to treat an animal-related injury before arriving at the physician's office and whether or not the injury needs a physician's care.
- A protocol should be in place for injuries sustained from an animal, caging, or anything else in the facility.
- Personnel and volunteers should be advised to tell their physicians that they are working with wildlife and to provide them with a list of possible zoonotic diseases.

Chapter 13: Safety

ZOONOTIC DISEASES

The following information is based on information from the Beginning Rehabilitation Education Workshop developed by the Minnesota Wildlife Assistance Cooperative.

A zoonoses is an infection or infestation shared in nature by people and animals. The zoonotic disease can be passed from animal to human and vice versa. There are hundreds of causative zoonotic agents. A causative agent is a bacterium, virus, fungus, parasite, or other organism that causes the disease.

VIRAL DISEASES

There are many potentially zoonotic viral diseases. Examples of these include rabies, Eastern and Western equine encephalitides and West Nile virus.

Rabies, a rhabdovirus, affects any warm-blooded vertebrate. It is especially prevalent in skunks, foxes, raccoons, and bats. Rodents are rarely involved, with woodchucks accounting for about 70 percent of all rodents testing positive for this virus. The Virginia opossum is one of the most resistant animals to the virus due to a lower metabolic rate and body temperature. Transmission of this virus is primarily via a bite or scratch and rarely from mucous membrane contact. It is also rarely transmitted vertically, or from mother to fetus.

Clinical signs in animal hosts include both a furious form and a dumb form. In the furious form the animal is restless, nervous, and aggressive, has no fear of humans, and bites at anything that draws attention. The animal is unable to swallow (hydrophobia), has excessive salivation, exaggerated responses to light and sound, is hyperesthestic, and shows neurologic abnormalities consistent with progressive encephalitis. Animals showing the dumb form of rabies exhibit depression, paralysis, and coma. Most victims succumb to the disease and the case fatality rate is almost 100 percent. However, a few animals may recover from infection and show severe, long-term neurologic abnormalities.

There is no treatment for this disease. Humans may receive a series of three pre-exposure vaccines. If then exposed to a rabies-positive animal, these individuals receive an additional two-dose course of vaccine. Obviously, control measures include having an index of suspicion for the disease, knowing proper handling and restraint techniques for each individual species, and taking measures to avoid being bitten.

Symptoms of human infection are similar to that found in wildlife. There is no reliable antemortem test available. Many positive animals do not show clinical signs at the time of bite or other exposure. If rabies is suspected, the animal must be euthanized and the brain tissue collected for testing. This is a reportable disease.

Eastern and **Western equine encephalitides** or "sleeping sickness" are alphaviruses with two types of hosts. Birds, especially Passeriformes, are the reservoir hosts for these viruses. Dead-end hosts include horses, humans, and, possibly, livestock. Transmission of the disease is via an insect bite, especially mosquitoes: *Aedes, Culex,* and *Anopheles* spp. There are few clinical signs in reservoir hosts. Both Eastern (EEE) and Western (WEE) equine encephalitis result in clinical signs in horses such as severe fever, depression, anorexia, and aimless walking, followed by paresis, and paralysis. Symptoms of human infection are flu-like and rapidly progress to severe central nervous system signs. The disease is seen when mosquitoes are prevalent, especially late summer into fall. Currently there is no treatment for either virus, though immune serum can be given after exposure. An inactivated vaccine is available for horses and birds. This is a reportable disease in humans.

Hantavirus species can cause hemorrhagic fever with renal syndrome and Hantavirus pulmonary syndrome in humans. These viruses are found worldwide in rodents, who act as the reservoir host. Infections are spread among the natural hosts by aerosol and bites. The virus is shed in rodent saliva, feces, and urine. Humans become incidental hosts when they come into contact with infected rodents or their excretions. Hantaviruses can also be transmitted through broken skin, the conjunctiva and other mucous membranes, by rodent bites, and possibly by ingestion. Hantavirus-associated diseases have not been reported in domestic animals.

West Nile virus (WNV) has a wide range of hosts including birds, mammals, and reptiles. The American crow and blue jay have been shown to be very sensitive to the strain of virus found in the United States, although the virus has been identified in over 160 species of birds at the time of this writing. Dead-end hosts include horses, humans, other mammals and reptiles. Transmission of the virus is via infected mosquitoes and other arthropods. Most host animals do not show any clinical signs, but, in some individuals, neurological signs such as ataxia, weakness of limbs, muscle spasms, listlessness, inability to stand, and uncoordinated movement are seen. The affected animals may also have a mild fever, visual abnormalities, and sudden death.

Horses infected with WNV appear lethargic, have hindquarter weakness, involuntary muscle spasms, incoordination, circling, convulsions, paralysis, and coma. Most humans infected with the disease do not get sick. If the illness does develop, people will usually have mild flu-like symptoms. Rarely does a severe illness develop, except in affected immunocompromised individuals; the disease is characterized by high fever, neck stiffness, muscle weakness, convulsions, and paralysis.

Treatment of host animals includes supportive care only, such as maintaining nutritional and fluid intake, and providing anti-inflammatory medications. An equine vaccine exists and has been used experimentally in many different avian species, with varying results. Avian-specific vaccines are currently under development. Suspected WNV cases should be housed individually from other birds. In horses, treatment is also supportive.

Control measures for WNV include using mosquito repellents and avoiding outdoor activities at dawn and dusk. Eliminating mosquito-breeding habitats will reduce the risk of WNV transmission by these vectors. These habitats are areas where water can collect and stagnate, such as old tires, birdbaths, and clogged rain gutters. This is a reportable disease in humans.

RICKETTSIAL DISEASES

Rocky Mountain spotted fever is a disease caused by the organism *Rickettsia rickettsii*. Wild rodents serve as the primary reservoir host. Transmission of this disease is via a tick bite, especially from the American dog tick *(Dermacentor variabilis)* and by the brown dog tick *(Rhipicephalus sanguineus)*. Reservoir hosts show few clinical signs. The disease in dogs causes a mild, febrile illness and is treated with tetracyclines and supportive care. People show a sudden onset of headache, fever, chills, muscle aches, and a flushed face, followed by a rash. Control measures focus on the use of tick repellents, insecticides, and careful tick removal.

Typhus Fever is caused by *Rickettsia prowazekii*. One strain of this bacterium is found only in humans and the other also occurs in flying squirrels in the United States. Transmission of typhus occurs by arthropod vectors, inhalation, or contact with the mucous membranes and eyes. Transmission can occur between flying squirrels by squirrel lice, particularly in the winter when populations are concentrated in nests. There is little known about the disease in flying squirrels. In humans, clinical signs include a sudden onset of headache, chills, fever, and muscle aches. A rash develops in about 50 percent of cases.

FUNGAL DISEASES

Aspergillosis *(Aspergillus fumigatus)* is a potentially zoonotic fungal infection. The fungal organism is ubiquitous in the environment. Immunocompromised bird and mammals are susceptible to this disease. Transmission of the disease is usually through inhalation of airborne spores. Clinical signs in the host include anorexia, weight loss, weakness, depression, and respiratory distress later in the course of the disease. Treatment entails the use of antifungal medications given over a long period of time. Control measures include housing animals in well ventilated areas, avoiding bedding material that can house fungal spores, and practicing good hygiene. It is important for immunocompromised individuals to avoid working with any animal suspected of having aspergillosis.

Dermatophytosis, or **ringworm**, *(Microsporum canis* or *Trichophyton mentagrophyte)* can affect both mammals and birds. Transmission can be via direct contact with the animal or indirect contact with spores on hair or sloughed skin of an infected animal. Clinical signs in the animal host include a typical circular lesion with a "bull's-eye" appearance, itchiness, hair loss, and scabbing. Treatment includes topical antifungal drugs such as lime sulfur dips or systemic drugs such as griseofulvin. Antibiotics are administered for secondary bacterial infections. The symptoms of human infection are similar and include reddened, circular, or "bull's-eye" skin lesions.

Chapter 13: Safety

BACTERIAL DISEASES

Anthrax *(Bacillus anthracis)* is endemic to several regions of North America. Free-ranging bison have been reported with this disease in central and western Canada and it occurs in cattle in several Southeastern and Midwestern US states. Outbreaks are also sporadically reported in sheep and white-tailed deer in western Texas and adjacent Mexico. In general, herbivores are susceptible, while carnivores are relatively resistant. The disease progression depends on the route of entry. Ingestion or inhalation of spores results in septicemia and rapid death characterized by fever, respiratory distress, convulsions, collapse, and bloody discharge from the bodies' openings. Cutaneous entry of the bacteria via contact with an infected animal or carcass is the most common form of transmission in humans. This results in itching of the skin followed by skin lesions that progress to a ring of fluid-filled vesicles. These ulcerate and develop into a depressed, black scab, surrounded by significant fluid swelling. Swelling of the face or neck may occlude airways. Penicillin is the treatment of choice for anthrax, though other antibiotics, such as tetracycline or erythromycin are also effective if started early. Antibiotics are only effective against the vegetative form of *B. anthracis*, not the spore form. This is a reportable disease, especially given the recent use of *B. anthracis* as an agent for bioterrorism.

Botulism is not an infection, it is a toxicosis, and as such, is not a zoonotic disease. People most commonly develop botulism from exposure to botulinum toxin in improperly home-canned foods.

Brucellosis *(Brucella sp.)* hosts include hoofed mammals, dogs, marine animals and rodents. Transmission is primarily via inhalation or ingestion. Clinical signs in animal hosts include reproductive tract infections and abortions. Treatment, which can consist of antibiotics and antipyretics, are not usually pursued due to the potential for zoonotic spread and the economic importance of maintaining Brucella-free cattle herds. Symptoms of human infection include septicemia and fever (mild to severe "undulant fever.") If left untreated, arthritis, endocarditis, and neurological symptoms may occur. The disease is well controlled in the United States, but is found in wild populations of elk, bison, and deer. Testing of suspected cases is required by many states, check with your local Department of Public Health.

Campylobacteriosis *(Campylobacter jejuni)* hosts include ruminants, horses, canids, and felids. Wild and domestic birds are regarded as major reservoirs of *Campylobacter*. Transmission is fecal-oral or can be in utero. Clinical signs in animal hosts are commonly fever, diarrhea, intermittent vomiting, and tenesmus. Treatment consists of antibiotics chosen on the basis of culture and sensitivity. Symptoms of human enteric infection are fever, abdominal pain, nausea, blood in feces, and diarrhea.

Chlamydiosis or **psittacosis** *(Chlamydophila psittaci)* is particularly common in psittacine birds. Birds may be asymptomatic carriers and shed the bacteria intermittently, particularly when stressed. Transmission is via inhalation or ingestion of dust and aerosols produced by feces, urine, feather dust, and carcasses. Fomites can also spread chlamydiosis and biting insects may be important in mechanical transmission. Clinical signs in animal hosts include anorexia, depression, nasal and ocular discharge, conjunctivitis, respiratory distress, and greenish diarrhea. Antibiotics, such as doxycycline, are effective in treating the symptoms of chlamydiosis. Symptoms of human infection are respiratory disease with atypical pneumonia, headaches, fever, and chills. In rare instances, a severe systemic illness may develop. Wear a mask if you suspect these bacteria in an animal. This is a reportable disease in some states, check with your state Department of Public Health.

Colibacillosis *(Escherichia coli spp.)* bacteria have many hosts, which include both birds and mammals. Transmission is fecal-oral. Clinical signs in animal hosts include reproductive abnormalities, fever, enteritis, diarrhea, respiratory disease, navel infections, and lameness. Treatment includes antibiotics chosen on the basis of culture and sensitivity and supportive care, such as fluid therapy. Symptoms of human infection include hemorrhagic colitis, blood disorders, and hemolytic uremic syndrome. Most cases can be prevented with good hygiene.

Erysipelas *(Erysipelothrix rhusiopathiae)* has hosts that include marine mammals, pigs (Suidae), birds, and reptiles. Transmission is via a wound infection or direct contact. Clinical signs in the animal host include a characteristic rhomboid (diamond) skin disease in swine, arthritis in sheep and swine, and cyanosis and widespread hemorrhages in adult turkeys. In reptiles, there is a high mortality with or without any signs. Treatment includes antibiotics and fluids. In humans, the disease is primarily occupational among those handling swine or poultry, e.g. slaughterhouse workers. Symptoms of human infection are scaly skin lesions that cause pain and severe itching. If generalized, clinical signs include fever, malaise, and headache.

Leptospirosis *(Leptospira interrogans)* is a bacterium that includes marine and hoofed animals, rodents, and carnivores as hosts. Although infection by *Leptospira* is common in a wide range of wild animals, clinical disease has rarely been reported in free-ranging wildlife. However, leptospirosis has occurred regularly in California sea lions with a high case fatality rate. Transmission is via inhalation or ingestion of infected urine or urine contaminated soil, water, or food. The organism can invade through wet or abraded skin. Clinical signs in animal hosts include anorexia, fever, hemorrhagic mucous membranes, icterus (jaundice), red urine, vomiting, and diarrhea. The leptospires are sensitive to a wide range of antimicrobial drugs. Symptoms of human infection are similar, including septicemia, fever, headaches, nausea, vomiting, diarrhea, constipation, petechial hemorrhages, and icterus. Control measures include wearing gloves and other protective clothing when appropriate, and practicing good hygiene.

Listeriosis *(Listeria monocytogenes)* is often present in the environment, but has also been found in rabbits, canids, birds, and ruminants, among many other species. *Listeria* is not transmissible from animal to animal but is acquired from the external environment. Clinical signs depend on the route of entry. Visceral entry through transepithelial invasion in the intestine is common in monogastrics (rabbits, canids, and humans.) Signs include septicemia and liver damage. A second route of transmission is possibly via damaged upper GI mucosa, teeth, or conjunctival mucosa leading eventually to neurologic signs. Symptoms of this neurologic, or "circling disease" of ruminants, include circling and facial paralysis. Avian listeriosis may be asymptomatic or show clinical signs associated with septicemia, liver damage, or encephalitis. Most common antibiotics except cephalosporins are active against *Listeria*. However, treatment of clinical cases is often unsuccessful, probably due to the intracellular location of the organism. Human infection may be subclinical but can also include febrile systemic, neurologic, or respiratory tract disease.

Lyme disease *(Borrelia burgdorferi)* is a tick-borne disease of people and domestic animals caused by spirochetal bacteria. Certain species of wild mammals and birds, including canids, rodents, and rabbits, act as reservoir hosts for the bacteria. *Cervids* (deer) act as major hosts for adults of important tick vectors for this disease. Transmission from reservoir host to people or domestic animals is through the bite of an infected deer tick *(Ixodes* spp.) Deer are innately poor hosts for *B. burgdorferi*. Clinical signs in infected animals include fever, swollen or painful joints, and muscle soreness, with occasional renal, neurologic, ocular, and cardiac abnormalities. Symptoms of human infection include a red radiating swelling around the bite site, arthritis, and flu-like symptoms (fever and muscle soreness). Symptoms can progress to neurological and cardiac abnormalities. Treatment is with appropriate antibiotics, such as amoxicillin and fluoroquinolones.

Pasteurellosis *(Pasteurella multocida)* is a bacterium whose hosts include mammals, especially rabbits (snuffles) and birds, especially waterfowl (avian cholera). Transmission is via bite or scratch wounds, inhalation, or ingestion. Clinical signs in mammal hosts include respiratory infection, discharge from nose and eyes, fever, difficult respiration, and emaciation. In birds, signs include bloody discharge from nostrils or beak, loose droppings, respiratory difficulty, and acute death. This bacterium is also commonly found in the mouth or throat of healthy dogs and cats, hence a common infection of prey species after a dog or cat attack. Treatment with amoxicillin or fluoroquinolones is often effective. Although pasteurellosis is uncommon in humans, symptoms of human infection include infected wounds, respiratory signs, and infrequent septicemia.

Plague *(Yersinia pestus)* is usually spread between rodents, the reservoir hosts, and humans by the bites of infected fleas, such as the rat flea *(Xenopsylla cheopis)*. In addition, the bacteria is present in the tissues and body fluids of infected animals and can be transmitted directly through mucous membranes and broken skin. Aerosols from people or animals with the pneumonic form are infectious. Most reservoir hosts remain asymptomatic or only show mild illness. Clinical signs in other animal hosts include fever, enlarged lymph nodes, abscesses in internal organs and sudden death. The pneumonic disease is rapid and acute, causing septicemia and pneumonia. Dogs, coyotes, raccoons, skunks, and other carnivores may seroconvert after exposure without symptoms. Humans show three major forms of plague: bubonic plague, septicemic plague, and pneumonic plague. Antibiotics are effective in treatment in the early stages of the disease. Control measures include flea control, proper handling and restraint of rodent hosts, and proper hygiene.

Salmonellosis *(Salmonella* spp) is a bacterium that affects most mammals, birds, and reptiles. Transmission is fecal-oral or through inhalation. Clinical signs in animals include diarrhea, "pasty vent" in birds, cyanosis, weakness, drowsiness, ruffled feathers, anemia, paresis, and fever. The main symptom of human infection is acute gastroenteritis.

Tuberculosis in animals is caused by an infection of *Mycobacteria* sp. Hosts of tuberculosis *(Mycobacterium bovis* and *M. avium)* include hoofed mammals and birds, respectively. Transmission is via inhalation or ingestion. This is a chronic, insidious disease and most clinical signs are seen in adult animals. Infected animals are often emaciated, weak, and lethargic, have an unthrifty appearance, and may show respiratory or gastrointestinal abnormalities. Treatment is long term with a multiple drug regimen and is difficult to effect in birds. Humans primarily show pulmonary signs though the organism can also produce disease in extrarespiratory locations. Tuberculosis is a particular problem in immunocompromised individuals. Enclosures are usually destroyed, as disinfection is not effective and the organism can live for long periods of time in the environment.

Tularemia *(Francisella tularensis)* is a bacterium whose hosts include rabbits, muskrats, beavers, small rodents, and other mammals and birds. The subspecies found in rabbits is highly virulent for humans and domestic rabbits. Transmission can be through ingestion, inhalation, arthropod-borne transfer, or direct contact through the skin and mucous membranes. Many cases in animals may be asymptomatic. Signs of septicemia, such as fever, lethargy, anorexia, coughing, diarrhea, and stiffness, may be seen in some mammals. Tularemia can be treated with various antibiotics but early and long term treatment may be necessary. There are six forms of tularemia in humans; typhoidal, ulceroglandular, glandular, oculoglandular, oropharyngeal, and pneumonic. The latter has a high mortality rate. About one percent of rabbits in the United States are infected with these bacteria. Cottontail rabbits account for approximately 70 percent of all human exposure.

PROTOZOA

Protozoa are one-celled organisms with multi-stage life cycles. Some protozoa, such as *Giardia* sp. and *Cryptosporidium* sp. may infect the gastrointestinal tract of susceptible hosts, leading to clinical signs of abdominal pain and diarrhea. Others, such as *Leishmania* sp. result in cutaneous infections. Many others, such as the species that cause malaria, invade the bloodstream. The following zoonotic diseases may be encountered by exposure to animals in rehabilitation.

Cryptosporidiosis *(Cryptosporidiu parvum,* other sp.) is a gastrointestinal disease seen in many species of mammals and a respiratory disease in some birds, such as poultry. Oocysts are readily transmitted via the fecal-oral route and large outbreaks have been associated with contamination of water supplies. Clinical signs in animal hosts, such as ruminants, include abdominal pain, diarrhea, dehydration, weight loss, anorexia, and depression. Young of the species are most commonly infected. Symptoms of human infection are similar to that of wildlife. Thirty to fifty percent of AIDS patients worldwide develop chronic cryptosporidiosis. As with any zoonotic disease, people should be especially careful if immunocompromised.

Giardiasis *(Giardia lamblia* and other sp) commonly results in gastrointestinal abnormalities in the host animal. Human infections usually originate from other humans but may result from contact with dogs, cats, rodents, beavers, or nonhuman primates. Approximately ten percent of beavers tested for this disease are infected. Transmission is via ingestion of cysts, especially in contaminated water supplies or on food, or direct fecal-oral transfer. Clinical signs in animal hosts, including humans, include abdominal bloating and pain, diarrhea, flatulence, fatigue, and weight loss. Cysts are resistant to treatments of bleach. They also survive in water as cold as 50 to 54 degrees C.

Sarcocystis sp. are found worldwide and can affect mammals, reptiles, and birds The most common species in North America is *S. rileyi*. Cysts develop in striated muscles of the intermediate hosts, such as waterfowl, and are then ingested by the definitive carnivore host. Oocysts are then shed in carnivore feces where they are in turn ingested by the intermediate host in contaminated food or water. Severe infections in the intermediate host can cause muscle loss, resulting in lameness, weakness, and, occasionally, paralysis. These animals may have fever, weight loss, nausea, and diarrhea. The case fatality rate is low. Humans generally acquire these protozoa from ingestion of cysts in raw or undercooked beef or pork or via fecal-oral contact.

Toxoplasma gondii is a facultative two-host organism. Wild and domestic felids are the definitive hosts. Most species of birds and mammals can serve as intermediate hosts. Oocysts are shed in cat feces. Intermediate hosts are infected by ingesting oocysts from soil or other substrates contaminated with cat feces, or ingesting bradyzoites in undercooked meat from other infected animals. Transplacental infection may also occur. Clinical signs in intermediate animal hosts include generalized multi-organ disease with depression, lethargy, fever, abnormal lymph nodes, and muscle pain. Symptoms of human infection are similar to that seen in animals, and the disease is especially a problem in immunocompromised people. Good personal hygiene should always be practiced to decrease the transmission risk of this disease.

Trypanosoma cruzi is found in the Western hemisphere in a variety of different mammalian reservoir hosts, including armadillos, opossums, rabbits, rodents, dogs, and cats. Most human cases are in children. Transmission is via contamination of the bite wound with feces from infected triatomid bugs of the family *Reduviidae* ("assassin bugs") during feeding. In addition, transmission via blood transfusion and transplacentally has been documented. The disease is subclinical in most wild animals but humans and domestic dogs may show inflammation at the site of the bite, fever, enlarged lymph nodes, enlarged liver and spleen, heart abnormalities and meningoencephalitis. The disease is most common in Central and South America, but has also been seen in the southern United States.

PARASITES

There are many parasitic infestations that are zoonotic. Included in this list are ectoparasites, nematodes (e.g. roundworms), cestodes (tapeworms), and trematodes (flukes).

ECTOPARASITES (EXTERNAL PARASITES)

Fleas ~ Ectoparasites include various species of fleas, some of which are host specific, though many will bite different hosts, including humans. Bites may lead to fleabite dermatitis due to a hypersensitivity to flea saliva. Fleas may act as vectors for diseases such as plague. These parasites may also serve as an intermediate host of tapeworms *(Dipylidium caninum)* and filarial worms *(Dipetalonema reconditum)*. There are numerous insecticides in many different forms available for use on animals and premises. Be sure to use those that are least distressful and toxic to the animal, such as pyrethrin products.

Lice infest most animals. They are very host specific and rarely infest animals other than the preferred host. A significant infestation of blood-sucking lice may lead to clinical signs of anemia.

Mites can infest various hosts with a few that can affect humans. *Cheyletiella parasitivorax* causes scaly dermatitis. *Sarcoptes scabei* causes sarcoptic mange or scabies. Inflamed crusty lesions with hair loss are seen, as well as severe pruritis leading to skin inflammation and secondary bacterial dermatitis. Scabies is commonly seen in many mammalian hosts, such as squirrels, foxes, and coyotes, and is transmitted to humans via direct contact with the affected animal.

Ticks ~ There are many different tick species that infest various hosts. Most ticks will bite humans. Ticks are the vectors of many diseases, including Lyme disease, tularemia, and Rocky Mountain spotted fever. Ticks in large numbers cause blood loss and anemia. There may be damage at the bite sites, causing susceptibility to myiasis or other infections. Soft-bodied ticks can be found on birds and bats. These ticks are periodic (day or night) feeders and may be found in bedding or housing at times when they are not feeding.

Warble *(Oestromyia* spp.) and **bot flies** *(Cuterebra* and rodent bots) are another type of ectoparasite. The hosts of these parasites include rodents, lagomorphs, cattle, and humans. Most species are host specific. Eggs are laid on the soil near burrows. The larvae enter natural openings and the skin when the animals enter or exit the burrow. Humans are infected by coming in contact with larvae on the soil around burrows or on infected animals. Clinical signs on animal hosts and human hosts include obvious "warbles" or lumps under the skin. When viewed closely, one may see the small breathing hole in the skin and the movement of the fly larvae residing inside.

Endoparasites (internal parasites)
Nematodes

Cutaneous larval migrans *(Ancylostoma* sp., *Uncinaria* sp., *Strongyloides stercoral,* other sp.) is a skin disease of humans that come in direct contact with filariform larvae in soil contaminated with feces from the animal host, most often domestic dogs and cats. The larvae enter the skin resulting in papules at the entry site and serpentine lesions. These lesions are often extremely pruritic, reddened, and secondarily infected with bacteria. Control measures include periodic de-wormings of domestic animals and wearing protective clothing when in contact with possibly infected environments.

Visceral and ocular larval migrans result from contact with the larvae of various species of roundworms. These include: *Toxocara canis* in cats, dogs, wolves, foxes, coyotes, and raccoons; *T. cati* in cats, mountain lions, lynx, and bobcat; and *Toxascaris leonine* in wild carnivores. There is also *Ascaris columnaris* in skunks, *Ascaris devosi* in ferrets and mink, and *Baylisascaris procyonis* in raccoons. The parasite living in the definitive host rarely produces disease and completes the life cycle in the gastrointestinal tract. In accidental hosts, after ingestion of embryonated eggs, the larvae of all these species migrate through various tissues, producing clinical signs. Diagnosis in humans and other accidental hosts cannot be made on the basis of fecal egg counts because larvae do not mature in these hosts. Clinical signs are similar in animals and in humans, including irritability, intermittent fever, anorexia, weight loss, hepatosplenomeglay, pneumonitis, and sometimes encephalitis and ocular lesions. Clinical disease and mortality have been observed in a broad range of mammals and birds. These include wild and domestic rabbits, mice, gray and fox squirrels, ground squirrels, woodchucks, nutria, beavers, prairie dogs, armadillos, porcupines, quail, chickens, partridges, turkeys, emus, cockatiels, and humans. Most infected humans are young children who are more likely to come into contact with contaminated soil and other substrates.

Cestodes

The **double-pored** or **flea tapeworm** *(Dipylidium caninum)* is a very common parasite seen in domestic and free ranging carnivores. The adult lives in the gastrointestinal tract of the host, and produces eggs, which are then shed in packets in the feces. These eggs are picked up by the intermediate hosts, which include fleas *(Ctenocephalus felis, C. canis, Pules irritans)* and occasionally the biting louse *(Trichodectes canis.)* The life cycle is completed when the definitive host ingests the intermediate host containing infective larvae. Humans can be infected when they accidentally ingest fleas containing cysticercoids (infective stage). The tapeworm infestation can lead to non-specific abdominal signs, including diarrhea and constipation, unthriftiness, weight loss, and anal itching.

Echinococcus sp. are hydatid tapeworms of carnivores, especially canids. The intermediate hosts are herbivores and omnivores in which larval "hydatid cysts" develop, especially in the liver and lungs. They are very small tapeworms and usually seen in large numbers. Humans can be infected when they accidentally ingest eggs, developing hydatid cysts in the liver, lungs, eye, brain, or kidneys. Clinical disease is rare in definitive hosts and non-human intermediate hosts. In humans the cysts can grow quite large and accidental rupture may produce fatal anaphylactic shock.

Trematodes

Fasciola sp. *(F. hepatica, F. gigantica)* are trematodes that are found worldwide. Reservoir hosts are cattle, sheep, and other herbivores. These hosts shed eggs which then develop into cercariae in snails. Transmission to humans is via ingestion of aquatic plants with incysted metacercariae. Most human infestations are asymptomatic but may result in abdominal pain, diarrhea, and icterus. In accidental animal hosts, infestation may lead to hepatic necrosis, weight loss, ascites, and death.

TRANSMISSIBLE SPONGIFORM ENCEPHALOPATHIES (TSE)

Eds. Note: Included here although this disease is not known to be a zoonosis.

TSEs include such diseases as **bovine spongiform encephalopathy (BSE), chronic wasting disease (CWD) and Creutzfeld-Jacob disease (CJD).** The disease agent is classified as a prion, an abnormally shaped protein that leads to characteristic spongiform changes in the brain of the host. CWD occurs in cervids; for example farmed and free ranging mule deer, white-tailed deer, black-tailed deer, and elk. Transmission between animals is likely by animal-to-animal contact or contamination of food or water sources with saliva, feces or urine from a diseased animal. Transmission to humans is not known to occur. The known prion diseases of humans and other domestic animals are different than CWD. Clinical signs in affected cervids include progressive weight loss, behavior changes (repetitive movement), becoming less fearful, salivation, drooping ears, decreased social interaction and listlessness. Tissues most affected include brain, spinal cord, eyes, lymph nodes, spleen, tonsil, colon, nerves ,and bone marrow. CWD is fatal to infected animals.

Literature Cited

Miller, E.A., 2000. *Minimum Standards for Wildlife Rehabilitation, 3rd edition, 2000.* St. Cloud, MN: National Wildlife Rehabilitators Association.

Minnesota Wildlife Rehabilitation Study Guide. 1999. Minnesota Department of Natural Resources. St. Paul, MN.

Additional Reading

Beginning Rehabilitation Education Workshop (BREW) developed by the Minnesota Wildlife Assistance Cooperative (MWAC), PO Box 130545, Roseville, MN 55113 email: info@mnwildlife.org website: http://www.mnwildlife.org/MWAC

Fox, A. S., K. R. Kazacos, N. S. Gould, P. T. Heydemann, and T. C. Boyer. 1985. *Fatal Eosinophilic Meningoencephalitis and Visceral Larva Migrans Caused by the Raccoon Ascarid Baylisascaris procyonis.* New England Journal of Medicine. 312:25.

Friend, M., and J. C. Franson. 1999. *Field Manual of Wildlife Diseases: General Field Procedures and Diseases of Birds.* US Department of the Interior, US Geological Survey, Biological Resources Division, Information and Technology Report 1999-001.

Hugh-Jones, M. E., W. T. Hubbert, and H. V. Hagstad. 2000. *Zoonoses: Recognition, Control, and Prevention.* Ames, IA: Iowa State University Press.

Williams, E. S., and I. K. Barker. 2001. *Infectious Diseases of Wild Mammals.* Ames, IA: Iowa State University Press.

Chapter 14

PRESENTATION THEORY AND DESIGN

One of the goals in environmental education, including the use of non-releasable wildlife, is promoting the conservation of our natural world. Presentations utilizing live animals can be an asset to this goal only if done properly. You must consider how to design a program that is both informative and educational while motivating people to take actions that preserve the environment

How do you decide on the message when designing an education program from start to finish? A good place to look is the mission statement of your facility. The mission statement will clearly state the focus of the facility and that can be the basis of your presentation. If no mission statement exists, try listing important educational goals. Examples of such goals include raptor conservation, habitat types, desert ecology, basic bird watching, raptor identification, or wildlife rehabilitation. Once the goal (or thesis) of the presentation is chosen, objectives need to be identified that move the presentation toward that goal.

Using the subject of Raptor Conservation as an example, some objectives may be:

What makes a raptor a raptor?
The habitats raptors use.
Different challenges raptors face, both natural and human-caused.
The importance of conserving raptors.
Actions that "we" take to help them.

These objectives make up the body of the presentation. Generally, a presentation should have three to five major points. Tim SanJule (1997) states "keep it simple and repeat it often in different ways." In other words, tell them what you are going to tell them, tell them, and then tell them what you told them.

You will need to flesh out the objectives. What is going to be said? What is going to be shown? How is it going to be presented? Using the examples above, here are some examples of what your program design might look like, using the model of Raptor Conservation.

What makes a raptor a raptor
You can start by defining the word raptor, and then show bio-facts for the different parts that make a raptor a raptor. Then you can talk briefly about each one – legs and talons, and a skull showing eyes and beak, for example. You can then show a trained raptor on the glove and point out the parts. Put the parts together by talking about adaptations that help raptors survive, and finish with an activity with a volunteer(s).

The habitats raptors use
Begin with a brief slideshow that demonstrates the types of habitat and have a few bio-facts on prey species in those habitats. Display nests or something tangible and/or present a raptor or prey (education animal) species. Explain why those habitats are important to humans, for example; tropical rainforests and how people use products made from the rainforests (chocolate, fruit, medicines, coffee, etc.). Show examples of the products when talking about them. Finish with an activity with the entire audience (or a volunteer).

Different challenges raptors face, both natural and human-caused
Start your program by describing the statistics regarding how many raptors make it to maturity. Display lead shot in a container, tangled fishing line, toy car, or, chemicals, etc., to show what some of the dangers are to raptors. Display a raptor and tell a brief story; for example, the DDT (Dichlorodiphenyltrichloroethane) story in conjunction with peregrine falcons. This example works well, because it has a successful ending. The birds became endangered because of the chemical use, people in the United States stopped using DDT, and now the peregrine is no longer an endangered species. Ingrain the message in the audience with an activity demonstrating your story.

The importance of conserving raptors.
Introduce your topic by talking about predator-prey relationships, and illustrate predation by using an owl eating a dead mouse. Incorporate an activity with volunteers or class. If the group is small enough, have owl pellets for the audience members to pull apart and examine, using proper safety precautions. Then continue by talking about and showing how all things are connected in nature, and explain that what affects wild animals will affect humans.

Actions that we can take to help them
Most experts recommend using "take-home" items, and this is a great place to distribute handouts on what people can do. Demonstrate to the listeners simple things that they can do now. Be sure you make these examples relevant to that particular audience.

Once the goal and objectives are determined, you are ready to write an introduction and a conclusion that relates the information together simply and clearly. The introduction includes brief information about who you are and your qualifications (the person giving the presentation) and what the presentation is about. This is when you "tell them what you are going to tell them." The introduction is the best place to let the audience know that there will be live animals involved in the presentation and what the "rules" are; for example, taking flash pictures, moving about, making loud noises, and when asking questions is allowed.

The conclusion must be carefully worded to "tell them what you told them," and to clearly state your take-home message. This is when you very succinctly reiterate to the audience the message you have been sharing with them throughout the presentation.

Most resources recommend that you write out the entire presentation, and then put it into outline form on note cards that are available for you to use during the presentation. Having a pre-determined format to follow is a good idea, but equally important is your ability to be flexible within that format in response to the audience. For example, the format may have to change because of the audience age, experience, or expertise. You may need to make last minute adjustments when facing an unexpectedly large (or small) audience.

Deciding on the length of your presentation in advance is another important part of a successful program. Hopefully, you have an excess of material allowing you to mix elements of a long program and create custom presentations for different age groups and different audiences. The attention span for audiences varies, but generally the younger the audience, the shorter the attention span. A presentation can be anywhere from ten minutes to one hour long, with a 30-minute program being the most commonly used time period. Most people find it hard to sit for more than one hour.

Deciding on the correct content and techniques to use in a presentation can be very vexing. What to put in and what to leave out? There is so much information to convey that you will find it difficult to make a concise, fun, and enlightening education program.

John Hendrickson (2003) states that when you are educating a child, not simply towards the retention of knowledge, but instead with the goal of fostering a person who is intrinsically motivated to conserve, care for, and even enhance our environment through both their decisions and actions; then your education must contain four essential, and for the most part sequential elements:

1. Experience, Awareness, Appreciation, Immersion (or bring it to them)
2. Knowledge—more importantly an enthusiasm for learning
3. Caring
4. Action and empowerment

This theory will work for any program. While you cannot always bring your audience into the natural world, you can bring some of the natural world to them through your education program. Allowing the audience to have direct experience is very important. Seeing the opossum up close, touching a bio-fact wing, or hearing the red tail hawk flap its wings or rustle its feathers is a memorable experience for many. Imparting some knowledge about the subject is important, but facts and figures are not nearly as compelling as your enthusiasm about your message. If you are excited and enthused and passionate about what you are teaching, that commitment helps to instill an enthusiasm for learning. From the knowledge and the immersion experience, springs caring. "We don't do what we know, we do what we care about" (Hendrickson 2003). When there is caring, there can be a desire to do action through empowerment.

If you are successful at establishing immersion, knowledge, and caring, then the fourth element, action, will follow naturally. It is important to have projects or a list of activities to share with your listeners. These suggestions must be doable activities, appropriate for the audience. For example, smaller children can build kestrel boxes (with an adult), put them up, and watch the kestrels nest there. This group can also put up bird feeders, start recycling, or design and put stickers on their windows to help birds see the glass. Older children can be given website addresses for more information, ideas for letters to write and to whom, or projects for which to volunteer, including building things, or helping with habitat restoration. Adults can be given those same ideas, and tasked with guiding others. The action project should be age appropriate, significant, and give some type of instant reinforcement such as birds coming to a bird feeder or kestrels nesting in a nest box (Hendrickson 2003).

SOME TECHNIQUES TO USE IN EDUCATIONAL PROGRAMS (SANJULE 1997)

- **Role modeling.** What words you choose and what you say to the audience is very important, and how you act in front of the audience is even more important. The old saying "a picture is worth a thousand words" is true. If you are not respectfully handling the animal or say things that are derogatory towards the animal, or the audience, your real message will be lost. Handling any wild animals in a presentation immediately gives the impression that the animal is "tame" and more like a domestic pet. At every opportunity presenters must strive to let the audience know that the animal is not a pet and is still a wild animal. The animal should never be touched, spoken to, or handled like a pet. This means no hugging, no kissing, and no baby talk.

- **Good teaching technique.** You must adapt on your feet and use whatever technique works for the person being taught. Presenters need to be flexible enough to change styles when presenting the same material to different audiences.

- **Content.** The emphasis should be on content and delivery (how it is taught) of the content. Students or audiences cannot be forced to learn something. If the information is presented in an interesting, entertaining, and captivating way, they will want to learn.

- **Tempo.** Keep the audience's attention and focus by regularly shifting or changing yours. Changing activities or changing styles frequently (every 10 minutes) will increase the audience's interest and attention span. Presenters can make things interesting just by changing their tone of voice. Move around the room (but do not pace), use hand gestures, make faces, tell stories, and use props. Again, keep it simple and repeat it often in different ways.

- **Be positive.** Avoid emphasizing catastrophes. By saying how bad the environment is and focusing on negative presentation, you will not empower anyone to take action to better the environment, including habitat today or in the future. Do not gloss over some of the problems, but do not dwell on them, either. The presentation can address problems that have been solved by using "success stories" and discuss problems today, while offering actionable solutions

- **Stimulation.** Presentations are a visual and auditory medium, so use imagery, mystery, challenges, and story telling to captivate the audience. Tell a story, use a few slides. Play dress up. Have the audience dress up the presenter, use puppets and other props, use humor, or do an experiment.

- **Focus on animals in the wild.** Using wild animals in a program can be very effective, but remember to focus not on the individual animal, but on its wild counterpart. Present your animal as an "ambassador" for its species and the habitat it lives in. "Teach not from sympathy, but from empathy" (Eckles 2003). You should tell the animal's story, but do not dwell on it or make the story the centerpiece of your presentation. The message is not about the captive animal, but about the wilderness it came from. Use the animal to connect the audience to the environment, and to instill a sense of empathy for wildlife in your audience.

- **Provide an example.** Again, examples are more powerful than words. Presenters should be "walking the walk." If presentations are aimed at improving the environment through recycling, habitat improvement, and similar actions; then presenters and their facilities should also be actively involved in the same activities. Do not be hypocritical. "You teach by doing."
- **Use volunteers.** Use demonstrations to illustrate your message and then discuss them with the audience. If silent flight is talked about, have two volunteers compare owl feathers with another type and then tell the rest of the audience what the differences are. Take that example one step further and have them swing straps around for the audience to hear and see, with one strap frayed to produce the quietness of an owl's flight. You could build a giant owl pellet and have a volunteer reach in and pull out what they find. Have the volunteer describe each item. Volunteers draw an audience in and focus their attention on the action taking place.

Presenter Etiquette

- **Be professional.** That means dressing neatly, knowing the subject matter, smiling, and answering all questions to the best of your ability. Do not lie or make up answers, "I don't know, but I can find out for you," is always the best choice if you are stumped.
- **Treat audience members with respect.** Answer questions heard many times like it is the first time, and be patient.
- **Treat the education animal with respect.** Know how to correctly handle any live animal being used in your program. Recognize if your animal has had enough, and know when to put any animal away. This can be as easy as covering the display or putting the animal into the transport crate if it is too stressed. Shared traits between the animal and the listeners, like being easily injured or feeling pain, can make a connection between the audience and the animal. Modeling respect by handling an animal correctly demonstrates caring and respect for the animal even if it is not verbally stated.
- **Show that the animal is wild.** Do not stroke the animal, treat it like a pet, or even handle it without an appropriate glove, even if that animal can be safely handled without gloves.
- **Know your audience.** The presenter should strive to know the audience before the presentation. How old are they (grade school, high school, families)? Where are they from (urban, rural, or foreign)? What experience level do they have (none, bird watching group, inner city, farm life)?
- **Be upbeat.** Have fun doing the program, and make it an enjoyable experience for everyone. Show your enthusiasm and passion!

> *Tell me, I forget. Show me, I remember.*
> *Involve me, I understand.*
> ~*Ancient proverb*

Chapter 14: Presentation Theory and Design

Literature Cited

Eckles, J. 2003. *The Plight of Parrots: Bad News and Good News.* Presentation at the 11th annual 2003 International Association of Avian Trainers and Educators Association (IAATE) conference, Portland, Oregon and personal communication. http://www.worldparrottrust.org/.

Hendrickson, J. 2003. *Kestrels Across America.* Presentation at the 11th annual 2003 International Association of Avian Trainers and Educators Association (IAATE) conference, Portland, Oregon and personal communication. http://www.kestrelsacrossamerica.org/start.html.

SanJule, T. 1997. *The Art of Teaching.* The NWRA Quarterly. 15(1):15-17.

Additional Reading

AZA Policy on the Use of Animals in Educational and Entertainment Venues. 2003. Silver Spring, MD: American Zoo and Aquarium Association.

Beck, S. 1992. *Conserving Wildlife: An interdisciplinary Middle School Curriculum.* Wildlife Rehabilitation Today. 3(4):54-57.

Caudell, J. N. 2002. *Assessing the Effectiveness of Using Live Animals in Environmental Education Programs.* Doctoral Thesis. Notre Dame, IN: University of Notre Dame, Department of Biological Science.

Crawford, W. 1996. *Wildlife Rehabilitators: Their Ecological Impact on the Future.* The NWRA Quarterly. 14(2):9-11.

Diehl, S., and C. Diehl. 2001. *Education: No Time? No Talent? No Problem!* Wildlife Rehabilitation. 19:161-167.

Educator's Activity Book About Bats. 1991. Austin, TX: Bat Conservation International

Guidelines for Live Bat Presentations. Bat World. 1991. Beneficial Animal Teaching Society (B.A.T.S.). Bat World, 217 North Oak Avenue, Mineral Wells, TX.

Horton, M. 1995. *I Can See You Naked!* The NWRA Quarterly. 13(4):16.

_____. 1995. *Obtaining the Right Permits for Education Animals.* The NWRA Quarterly. 13(4):17.

Howell, S., and S. Shepherd.1996. *Methods of Presenting Animals to the Public.* Wildlife Rehabilitation. 14:175-180.

Huckabee, J. 1996. *Education Animals—Why We Shouldn't Use Babies.* The NWRA Quarterly. 14(3):16-17.

Kosack Althouse, J. 1988. *Educate the Public: Change the Future by Using A Wildlife Education Program.* Wildlife Rehabilitation. 7:195-200.

Lewis, N. 2001. *Guidelines for Using Live Bats in Educational Programs: Recommendations by the American Zoo and Aquarium Association Taxon Advisory Group for Bats.* Animal Keepers' Forum: Special Issue Bat Husbandry and Conservation. The Journal of the American Association of Zookeepers. 28(12):440-443.

Neumann, K. *Educating with Raptors: A Resource Booklet. Carroll, IA:* Stone Printing

Nickerson, D. 1996. *Why Teach???* The NWRA Quarterly. 14(2): 7-8.

Peterson, S. I. 2001. *Wild Animals in Visitor Education: Education or Entertainment?* Wildlife Rehabilitation. National Wildlife Rehabilitators Association. 19:175-190.

Professional Standards for the Use of Live Animals in Environmental Education. 15 pages. Guthrie Center, IA: Iowa Association of Naturalists.

Santangelo, A. L. 1997. *Using Live Bats for Education.* The NWRA Quarterly. 15(4):13.

Sobel, D. 1996. *Beyond Ecophobia: Reclaiming the Heart in Nature Education.* Nature Literacy Series Number 1. Barrington, MA:Orion Society.

Thrune, E. 1993. *Wild Animals in Education.* NWRA Newsline. 11(3).

Warren-Ehresman, M. 1994. *Creation of a Desirable Presentation Experience: Topoi in my Bathtub.* Wildlife Rehabilitation. 12:249-257.

Westervelt, M. O. 1988. *Children's Opinions About Wildlife: Teaching Strategies for the Wildlife Rehabilitator.* Wildlife Rehabilitation. 7:187-194.

Wilkinson, B. 1997. *Multimedia Wildlife Education and Attitudes.* Northridge, DA: California State University.

Wolff, K. 1992. *The Positive Impact of Professional Education Programs.* Wildlife Rehabilitation Today. 3(3):42-43.

Zich, M. C., and B. Olds. 1995. *Participating in Wildlife Programs: Children with Special Needs.* Wildlife Rehabilitation. 13:205-213.

Chapter 15

DISPOSAL OF CARCASSES AND ANIMAL WASTE PRODUCTS

The following information is excerpted from the *Minimum Standards for Wildlife Rehabilitation, 3rd Edition* (Miller 2000). Obviously, this information was originally written for wildlife rehabilitators. Where appropriate, the words "rehabilitator" or "rehabilitation" were replaced with educator, education, or educational for the purposes of this text.

Each animal that dies or is euthanized while under the care of a wildlife educator should always be examined carefully to confirm that the animal really is dead (lack of pulse or heart beat). Carcasses should then be disposed of properly in accordance with local laws and parameters set forth in individual wildlife education permits (e.g., the educator may be required to transfer the carcasses of endangered species to a specified location). Unless otherwise directed, all bald and golden eagle carcasses and loose feathers must be sent to the National Eagle Repository.

If the educator plans to necropsy the carcass or transfer it to a diagnostic facility for the purpose of necropsy, the carcass should be wet with cold water, unless the animal is a victim of pesticide poisoning (water might remove pesticides contaminating the outside of the animal). The addition of a small amount of detergent to the water will help to penetrate the fur or feathers, speeding up the process of cooling the body. If the necropsy is not performed immediately, the wet carcass should be placed in a plastic bag, sealed, labeled, and refrigerated in an ice-chest or refrigerator which is not used for food storage. A necropsy performed shortly after death allows collection of more accurate information. This accuracy fades as more time passes due to postmortem changes, which can alter or mask signs. Gloves and surgical masks must be worn while conducting necropsies. Necropsies should be performed in a well-ventilated location, separate from live animals and food preparation. *Note: Endangered or threatened species and bald or golden eagles must not be necropsied without first obtaining permission from the USFWS.*

Carcasses that are not necropsied may be transferred to local natural history museums, universities or other institutions for study and/or addition to their collections. The wildlife educator should contact these institutions and arrange for proper handling of the carcasses so the institutions can gain the most benefit from them (e.g., the carcasses may need to be frozen, placed in formalin, etc.). Specific data may also need to be recorded by the educator such as date and location animal was found, live body weight, etc. In many cases, the information provided by the educator can be as valuable as the specimen itself.

If the wildlife educator desires to keep specific parts or portions of avian carcasses (e.g., skeletons or skins for educational purposes, etc.), special permits must first be obtained from the USFWS. Many state wildlife agencies also require special permits to possess wildlife parts. Special permits are not required for the educator to possess a limited number of feathers (excluding eagle feathers) for imping (feather repair) purposes.

All other carcasses and all animal waste products should be disposed of in accordance with acceptable practices as required by local ordinances as well as applicable state, provincial and federal regulations. Carcasses and organic waste suspected of disease contamination should be buried or incinerated. Where legal, burial of carcasses should be at a depth that will discourage scavenger species from unearthing them, and lime should be spread on top of the carcasses to assist in disease control. Incinerators are generally cost prohibitive to most educators and education facilities, and special permits are required to operate incinerators in most areas. Many local animal control shelters or laboratories have incinerators and the educator may be able to arrange for these facilities to incinerate carcasses. Carcasses may be frozen for a limited period of time (in non-food freezers) for storage prior to incineration or donation to pre-approved facilities (public institutions or individuals authorized to possess the specimens for educational purposes).

If an education animal dies, the state and federal (USFWS for birds) permit offices should be notified within 48 hours of the death. The federal offices also have a "Live/Dead worksheet" to fill out if there is a death of a bird at the facility. If the animal is an endangered species or an eagle, they will inform you regarding handling of the carcass.

Many educators seek out bio-facts (wings, legs, skins, skeletons, etc.) for use in educational programming. Bio-facts can be touched where the live animal cannot, and they can show things that the live animal cannot (skeleton, etc.). Salvage permits are required at the federal and state levels if bio-facts are desired for any educational programming. Natural history museums, zoos, nature centers, and some colleges and universities have people who are familiar with preparing bio-facts properly for the classroom. It is best to get some instruction on the proper methods and practice first before preparing the pieces desired for the program.

Literature Cited

Miller, E. A. 2000. *Minimum Standards for Wildlife Rehabilitation, 3rd ed. St. Cloud, MN:* National Wildlife Rehabilitators Association. Pp 13-14.

Additional Reading

Minnesota Wildlife Rehabilitation Study Guide. 1999. State of Minnesota Department of Natural Resources, Division of Fish and Wildlife, Section of Wildlife, Wildlife Population and Research Division. St. Paul, MN.

National Eagle and Wildlife Property Repository. Rocky Mountain Arsenal, Building 128, Commerce City, CO 80022, telephone 303-287-2110, email dennis_wiist@fws.gov.

Peterson, D., L. N. Irwin, and W. C. Crawford, Jr. 1993. *Composting Bird Wastes and Mortalities. Wildlife Rehabilitation.* 11:173-182.

Appendices

APPENDIX A ~ ASSOCIATION CONTACT INFORMATION

National Wildlife Rehabilitators Association (NWRA)
2625 Clearwater Road, Suite 110
St. Cloud, MN 56301-4539
Phone: 320-259-4086
Email: nwra@nwrawildlife.org   Website: www.nwrawildlife.org
The NWRA is dedicated to improving and promoting the profession of wildlife rehabilitation and its contributions to preserving natural ecosystems.

International Wildlife Rehabilitation Council (IWRC)
8080 Capwell Drive, Suite 240
Oakland, CA 94621
Phone: 510-383-9090 Fax: 510-383-9094
Email: office@iwrc-online.org   Website: www.iwrc-online.org
The IWRC is a nonprofit, international membership-sponsorship organization with a commitment to preserving our native wildlife.

International Association of Avian Trainers and Educators (IAATE)
350 St. Andrews Fairway
Memphis, TN 38112
Phone: 901- 685-9122
Fax: 901 685-7233
Email: secretary@iaate.org   Website: www.iaate.org

American Zoo and Aquarium Association (AZA)
8403 Colesville Road
Suite 710
Silver Spring, MD 20910-3314
Phone: 301-562-0777
Fax: 301-562-0888
Email: professional development: aweider@aza.org
Conservation education: ereinhard@aza.org
The American Zoo and Aquarium Association (AZA), is a nonprofit organization dedicated to the advancement of zoos and aquariums in the areas of conservation, education, science, and recreation. AZA's vision is to work cooperatively to save and protect the wonders of the living natural world.

Selected Naturalists Associations

Minnesota Naturalist Association
Kathy Dummer
Lowry Nature Center
PO Box 270
Victoria, MN 55386
Website: http://www.mtn.org/mna/

Federation of Nova Scotia Naturalists
FNSN Membership Secretary
6360 Young Street
Halifax, N.S. Canada B3L 2A1
Website:
www.chebucto.ns.ca/Environment/FNSN/hp-fnsn.html   (case sensitive)

Maryland Naturalist Organizations
Maryland DNR 1-800-8DNR
Website:http://www.dnr.state.md.us/wildlife/mno.html

**Coalition for Education in the Life Sciences
Center for Biology Education**
University of Wisconsin-Madison
1271 Genetics/Biotechnology Building
425 Henry Mall
Madison, WI 53706
Website: http://www.wisc.edu/cels/

National Association of Biology Teachers (NABT)
12030 Sunrise Valley Dr., Suite 110
Reston, VA 20191
Website: http://www.nabt.org

National Science Teachers Association (NSTA)
1840 Wilson Blvd.
Arlington, VA 22201-3000
Website: http://www.nsta.org

The Environmental Education and Training Partnership (EETAP)
University of Wisconsin-Stevens Point
College of Natural Resources
Stevens Point, WI 54481
Website: http://www.eetap.org/

The North American Association for Environmental Education (NAAEE)
1797 H Street NW, Suite 900
Washington, DC 20006
Website: http://naaee.org/

Environmental Education Web Resources
http://weblinks.schoolsgogreen.org/links/

Natural Encounters, Inc.
9014 Thompson Nursery Road
Lake Wales, FL 33859
Email: NatEncount@aol.com
Website: www.naturalencounters.com

World Bird Sanctuary
125 Bald Eagle Ridge Road
Valley Park, MO 63088
636-861-3225
Fax: 636-861-3240
Email: info@worldbirdsanctuary.org
Website: www.worldbirdsanctuary.org

Appendix A - Association Contact Information

US State Rehabilitation Associations

Listings are alphabetical by state.

California Council for Wildlife Rehabilitators (CCWR)
PO Box 434
Santa Rosa, CA 95402
415-541-5090
Email: info@ccwr.org
Website: www.ccwr.org

Colorado Council for Wildlife Rehabilitation (CCWR)
c/o Sigrid Ueblacker
RR 2 Box 659
Broomfield, CO 80020
303-665-5670

Connecticut Wildlife Rehabilitators Association, Inc. (CWRA)
PO Box 3556
Amity Station
New Haven, CT 06525
203-389-4411
Email: info@cwrawildlife.org
Website: www.cwrawildlife.org

Delaware Wildlife Rehabilitators Association (DWRA)
Robin Coventry, President
276 Cambridge Rd
Camden, DE 19934
302-698-1047
Email: coventrybird@aol.com

Florida Wildlife Rehabilitation Association (FWRA)
PO Box 1449
Anna Maria, FL 34216
941-778-6324
Website: www.fwra.org

Illinois Wildlife Rehabilitators Association (IWRA)
PO Box 28
Tremont, IL 61568
309-925-5321
309-925-3204 Fax
Email: wildan@dpc.net

Iowa Wildlife Rehabilitators Association (IWRA)
Beth Brown, Treasurer
Box 217
Osceola, IA 50213
641-342-2783

Kentucky Wildlife Rehabilitators Association (KWRA)
Kathy Hill, President
PO Box 554
Alexandria, KY 41001

Louisiana Wildlife Rehabilitators Association (LAWRA)
PO Box 90201
Lafayette, LA 70509
www.LAWRAonline.com

ReMaine Wild
PO Box 113
Newcastle, ME 04553
Lynne Flaccus, Co-Chair,
207-882-7323 (w), 207-549-3326 (h),
gshute@gwi.com
Kate Ziminsky, Co-Chair, 207-878-0034,
kziminsky@hotmail.com

Maryland Wildlife Rehabilitators Association (MWRA)
PO Box 296
Pasadena, MD 21122
410-255-4737
www.mwra.org

Wildlife Rehabilitators' Assn. of Massachusetts, Inc (WRAM)
25 Tami Court
Bridgewater, MA 02324-1236
508-279-3936

Minnesota Wildlife Assistance Cooperative (MWAC)
PO Box 130545
Roseville, MN 55113
info@mnwildlife.org

Wildlife Rehabilitators Association of New Hampshire (WRANH)
PO Box 1274
Lincoln, NH 03251
Ann McDermott, President 603-536-2592
admin@wranh.org
Christine Anderson, Secretary 603-745-9794
secretary@wranh.org

New Jersey Association of Wildlife Rehabilitators (NJAWR)
c/o Dave Purdy
24 Mountain Church Rd
Hopewell, NJ 08525

New York State Wildlife Rehabilitation Council (NYSWRC)
PO Box 515
Medina, NY 14103
www.nyswrc.org
Barb Cole, President 607-687-1584
brancher@clarityconnect.com

Julie Harjung, Vice President 518-891-7379
rangerncats1@juno.com

Amy Freiman, News Editor 518-582-3655
nisseq@aol.com

Cheri Adams, Membership 315-986-1043

Appendix A - Association Contact Information

Wildlife Rehabilitators of North Carolina (WRNC)
2542 Weymoth Rd
Winston-Salem, NC 27103

Ohio Wildlife Rehabilitators Association (OWRA)
c/o Betty Ross
1075 Rt 343
Yellow Springs, OH 45387-1895
937-767-7648
937-767-6655 Fax
bross@antioch-college.edu
www.owra.org

Pennsylvania Association of Wildlife Rehabilitators (PAWR)
Sue DeArment, President
221 Parker Dr
Pittsburgh, PA 15216
814-763-2574

Wild In Vermont
Nancy J. Carey, President
PO Box 163
Underhill Center, VT 05490
802-899-6810

Wildlife Rehabilitation Association of Virginia (WRAV)
Robin Eastham, President
Portaferry Farm
Batesville, VA 22924
540-456-8324
540-456-8788 Fax
robinjane@cstone.net

Washington Wildlife Rehabilitation Association (WWRA)
c/o PO Box 1037
Lynnwood, WA 98046
Kip Parker, President, 425-787-2500 x815, kparker@paws.org
Shelley McGuire, Secretary, 360-421-0914,
shelley.mcquire@att.net

Wisconsin Wildlife Rehabilitators Association (WWRA)
South 3091 Oak Knoll Rd
Fall Creek, WI 54742
262-662-1808
wwra_org@yahoo.com

Canadian Provincial Rehabilitation Associations

Listings are alphabetical by province.

Alberta Wildlife Rehabilitator's Association (AWRA)
Bill Tomlinson, President
PO Box 79113
70-1020 Sherwood Drive
Sherwood Park, AB T8A 2G4
CANADA
780-467-9411
a_w_r_a@hotmail.com

Wildlife Rehabilitators' Network of British Columbia (WRNBC)
1388 Cambridge Dr
Coquitlam, BC V3J 2P7
CANADA
604-939-9571
250-337-2021
www.wrn.bc.ca

Ontario Wildlife Rehabilitation and Education Network (OWREN)
40-1110 Finch Ave West, Suite 1071
Toronto, ON M3J 3M2
CANADA
905-735-9556
905-735-6885 fax
owren@email.com

APPENDIX B – FEDERAL, PROVINCIAL, STATE, AIRLINE AND OTHER CONTACT INFORMATION

United States Migratory Bird Permit Offices

The following list includes only the US Fish and Wildlife Service Migratory Bird Permit Offices.

REGION 1
CA, HI, ID, NV, OR, WA
Tami Tate-Hall, US Fish & Wildlife Service
Migratory Bird Permit Office
911 NE 11th Ave
Portland, OR 97232-4181
503-872-2715
tami_tatehall@fws.gov

REGION 2
AZ, NM, OK, TX
Kamile McKeever, US Fish & Wildlife Service
Migratory Bird Permit Office
PO Box 709
Albuquerque, NM 87103-0709
505-248-7882
kamile_mckeever@fws.gov

REGION 3
IL, IN, IA, MI, MN, MO, OH, WI
Robin Flaherty, US Fish & Wildlife Service
Migratory Bird Permit Office
1 Federal Dr
Fort Snelling, MN 55111
612-713-5449 direct office
612-713-5436 general line
612-713-5393 fax
robin_flaherty@fws.gov

REGION 4
AL, AR, FL, GA, KY, LA, MS, NC, SC, TN
Carmen Simonton, US Fish & Wildlife Service
Migratory Bird Permit Office
PO Box 49208
Atlanta, GA 30359
404-679-4130
404-679-7285 fax
carmen_simonton@fws.gov

REGION 5
CT, DE, ME, MD, MA, NH, NJ, NY, PA, RI, VT, VA, WV
David Dobias
Migratory Bird Permit Office
PO Box 779
Hadley, MA 01035-0779
413-253-8643
david_dobias@fws.gov

REGION 6
CO, KS, MT, NE, ND, SD, UT, WY
Janell Suazo, US Fish & Wildlife Service
Migratory Bird Permit Office
PO Box 25486 DFC 60154
Denver, CO 80225-0486
303-236-8171 x630
303-236-8017 fax
janell_suazo@fws.gov

REGION 7
AK
Meg Laws, US Fish & Wildlife Service
Migratory Bird Permit Office
1011 E Tudor Rd
Anchorage, AK 99503
907-786-3459
meg_laws@fws.gov

ANIMAL CARE REGIONAL OFFICES
UNITED STATES DEPARTMENT OF AGRICULTURE

Eastern Region
Alabama, Connecticut, Delaware, District of Columbia, Florida, Georgia, Illinois, Indiana, Kentucky, Maine, Maryland, Massachusetts, Michigan, Minnesota, Mississippi, New Hampshire, New Jersey, New York, North Carolina, Ohio, Pennsylvania, Puerto Rico, Rhode Island, South Carolina, Tennessee, Vermont, Virginia, West Virginia, Wisconsin

USDA, APHIS, AC
Regional Director
920 Main Campus Drive, Suite 200
Raleigh, NC 27606-5210
Telephone: 919-716-5532
Fax: 919-716-5696

Central Region
Arkansas, Iowa, Kansas, Louisiana, Missouri, Nebraska, North Dakota, Oklahoma, South Dakota, Texas

USDA, APHIS, AC
Regional Director
501 Felix Street, Bldg. #11
PO Box 6258
Fort Worth, TX 76115-6258
Telephone: 817-885-6923
Fax: 817-885-6917

Western Region
Alaska, Arizona, California, Colorado, Hawaii, Idaho, Montana, Nevada, New Mexico, Oregon, Utah, Washington, Wyoming

USDA, APHIS, AC
Regional Director
9580 Micron Avenue, Suite J
Sacramento, CA 95827-2623
Telephone: 916-857-6205
Fax: 916-857-6212

Appendix B - Federal, Provincial, State, Airline and Other Contact Information

CANADIAN PROVINCIAL AGENCIES

Listings are alphabetical by province.

The Honorable Lorne Taylor
Minister of Environment
#423, 10800-97 Ave
Edmonton, AB T5K 2B6

Wildlife Permit Officer
Ministry of Sustainable Resources
PO Box 9352 Stn Prougut
Victoria, BC V8W 9M2

Dr. James Duncan, Wildlife Branch
Manitoba Conservation
Box 24, 200 Saulteaux Crescent
Winnipeg, MB R3J 3W3
204-945-7465
204-945-3077 fax
jduncan@gov.mb.ca

Gerard MacLellen
Environmental Monitoring and Compliance
PO Box 697
5151 Terminal Rd, 5th Floor
Halifax, NS B3J 2T8
902-424-2547

Tamara Gomer
Wildlife in Captivity Specialist
Ministry of Natural Resources
Fish and Wildlife Branch
PO Box 7000, 300 Water Street 5th Fl N
Peterborough, ON K9J 8M5
705-755-1999
tamara.gomer@mnr.gov.on.ca

Delbert Miller
Ministry of Natural Resources, Aylmer District
353 Talbot St W
Aylmer, ON N5H 2S8

Mr. John Sullivan
Canadian Wildlife Service
465 Gideon Dr
PO Box 490 Lambeth Stn
London, ON N6P 1R1
519-472-5750
519-472-3062 fax

Edifice Marie-Guyart
Wildlife & Parks Quebec
675 Blvd Rene Leveque E, 10th Floor
Quebec, PQ G1R 5V7
418-521-3850

Mr. Phillip W Haughian
SE & RM - Fish & Wildlife Branch
436-3211 Albert Street
Regina, SK S4S 5W6
306-787-3017

STATE AND US TERRITORY WILDLIFE PERMIT OFFICES

Listings are alphabetical by state or US Territory.

Chief of Law Enforcement
Div of Wildlife / Freshwater Fisheries
PO Box 301456
Montgomery, AL 36130-1456
334-242-3467
ghouston@dcnr.state.al.us

Director of Wildlife Conservation
Dept of Fish & Game
PO Box 25526
Juneau, AK 99802-5526
907-465-4148

Wildlife Building Coordinator
Arizona Game & Fish Dept
2221 W Greenway Rd
Phoenix, AZ 85023-4312
602-789-3370
602-256-7627 fax

Karen Rowe, Wildlife Permit Officer
AR Game & Fish Commission
31 Halowell Lane
Humphrey, AR 72073
870-873-4302
krowe@agfc.state.ar.us

CA Dept of Fish & Game
PO Box 944209
1416 Ninth St
Sacramento, CA 95814-2090

Kathy Konishi
CDOW/Special Licensing
PO Box 49128
Colorado Springs, CO 80919
719-268-0143
kathy.konishi@state.co.us
www.wildlife.state.co.us/special_licensing

Wildlife Permit Officer
Dept of Env Protection
Wildlife Division
79 Elm St
Hartford, CT 06106-5127
860-424-3011
laurie.fortin@po.state.ct.us

Kenneth Reynolds, Program Manager
Div of Fish & Wildlife
4876 Hay Point Landing Rd
Smyrna, DE 19997
302-653-2883
kenneth.reynolds@state.de.us

Wildlife Permit Officer
Florida Fish & Wildlife Conservation Commission
620 S Meridian St
Tallahassee, FL 32399-1600
850-488-6253

Wildlife Permit Officer
Georgia DNR
Special Permit Unit
2109 US Hwy 278 S E
Social Circle, GA 30025
770-761-3044
marykay_blalock@mail.dnr.state.ga.us
www.gohuntgeorgia.com

Carol J Terry, PhD
Nongame Wildlife Biologist
HI Division of Forestry & Wildlife
1151 Punchbowl St
Honolulu, HI 96813
808-587-4184
carol_j_terry@exec.state.hi.us

Wayne Melquist
Dept of Fish & Game
600 S Walnut
Boise, ID 83707-0025
208-334-2920

Permit Officer
Dept of Natural Resources
1 Natural Resources Way
Springfield, IL 62702-1271
217-782-6431
bclark1@dnrmail.state.il.us

Linnea Petercheff
Wildlife Permit Officer
IN DNR
402 W Washington St #W273
Indianapolis, IN 46204-2781
317-233-6527
317-232-8150 fax

Daryl Howell
IA DNR
Wallace State Office Bldg
502 E 9th St
Des Moines, IA 50319-0034
515-281-8524
daryl.howell@dnr.state.ia.us

Appendix B - Federal, Provincial, State, Airline and Other Contact Information

Wildlife Permit Officer
KS Dept of Wildlife & Parks
512 SE 25th Ave
Pratt, KS 67124-8174
620-672-5911
kenb@wp.state.ks.us

Wildlife Permit Officer
KY Dept of Fish & Wildlife Resources
#1 Game Farm Rd
Frankfort, KY 40601
502-564-3400

Nongame Biologist
LA Dept of Wildlife & Fisheries
Natural Heritage Program
PO Box 98000
Baton Rouge, LA 70898-9000
225-765-2976
higginbotham_ne@wlf.state.la.us

Beth Turcotte
Dept of Inland Fish & Wildlife
284 State St, Station #41
Augusta, ME 04333-0041
207-287-5240

Mary Goldie
DNR 580 Taylor Ave
Tawes State Office Bldg E-1
Annapolis, MD 21401
410-260-8540
410-260-8596 fax

Wildlife Permit Officer
Division of Fisheries & Wildlife
251 Causeway St
Suite 400
Boston, MA 02114-2104
617-727-3151 ext327

Deb Christianson
DNR
Box 30031
Lansing, MI 48909-7531
517-373-2665

Nancy Huonder
WL Rehab Program Coordinator
DNR Non-game Wildlife Program
500 Lafayette Rd Box 25
St Paul, MN 55155-4025
651-297-8040
nancy.huonder@dnr.state.mn.us

Richard G Rummel
Dept of Wildlife, Fish & Parks/
MS Museum of Nat Science
2148 Riverside Dr
Jackson, MS 39202-1353
601-354-6367 x109
richardr@mmns.state.ms.us

Lynn Totten
Department of Conservation
PO Box 180
Jefferson City, MO 65102-0180
573-751-4115 ex3322
573-751-4864 fax
lynntotten@mdc.mo.gov

MT Fish, Wildlife & Parks
1420 E Sixth Ave, PO Box 200701
Helena, MT 59620-0701
406-449-1312
camacher@state.mt.us

Dana Miller, Wildlife Permit Officer
Game & Parks Commission
105 W 2nd Suite #201
Valentine, NE 69201
402-376-3116
dkmiller@ngpc.state.ne.us

License Office- special licenses
NV Div of Wildlife
4600 Kietzke Ln D-135
Reno, NV 89502
775-688-1500

Attn: Sgt Bruce Bonenfant
NH Fish & Game Dept
11 Hazen Dr
Concord, NH 03301
603-271-2501

Amy Wells
NJ Div of Fish, Game & Wildlife
PO Box 400
Trenton, NJ 08625-0400
609-292-2965
amy.wells@dep.state.nj.us

NM Department of Game & Fish
Special Use Permits Program
Law Enforcement Division
PO Box 25112
Santa Fe, NM 87507
505-476-8064

Patrick P Martin
NYS Dept Env Con
625 Broadway
Albany, NY 12233-4752
518-402-8985
pxmartin@qw.dec.state.ny.us

Wildlife Permit Officer
1724 Mail Service Center
Raleigh, NC 27699-1724
919-661-4872
919-662-4379 fax

Sandra Hagen
ND Game & Fish Dept
100 N Bismarck Expressway
Bismarck, ND 58501
701-328-6382
shagen@state.nd.us

Carolyn Caldwell, Asst Administrator Wildlife Management & Research
Division of Wildlife
1840 Belcher Dr
Columbus, OH 43224
614-254-6300
carolyn.caldwell@dnr.state.oh.us

Law Enforcement Division
OK Dept of Wildlife Conservation
PO Box 53465
Oklahoma City, OK 73152-3465
405-521-3719
405-522-3486 fax

Joel Hurtado
Oregon Dept of Fish & Wildlife
3406 Cherry Ave NE
Salem, OR 97303-4924
503-947-6318
joel.a.hurtado@state.or.us

Wildlife Permit Officer
Game Commission
2001 Elmerton Ave
Harrisburg, PA 17110-9797
717-783-8164

Wildlife Permit Officer
Division of Fish & Wildlife
Box 218
West Kingston, RI 02892
401-789-0281
401-783-7490 fax
lgibson@netsense.net

Wildlife Permit Coordinator
Sandhills Research & Educ Center
PO Box 23205
Columbia, SC 29224-3205
803-419-9645

Wildlife Permit Officer
Game, Fish & Parks Dept
Div of Wildlife
412 West Missouri, Suite 4
Pierre, SD 57501
605-773-4191

Captive Wildlife Coordinator
TWRA/Law Enforcement Division
PO Box 40747, Ellington Ag Center
Nashville, TN 37204
615-781-6647

Jennifer Blecha, Permit officer
Nongame Permits Specialist
4200 Smith School Rd
Austin, TX 78744-3291
512-389-4481
jennifer.blecha@tpwd.state.tx.us

DNR Div of Wildlife Resources
1594 W North Temple, Suite 2110
PO Box 146301
Salt Lake City, UT 84114-6301
801-538-4701

Law Enforcement Assistant
Agency of Natural Resources
Fish & Wildlife Dept
103 S Main St, 10 South
Waterbury, VT 05671-0501
802-241-3727
mallen@fwd.anr.state.vt.us

Diane Davis
VA Dept of Game & Inland Fisheries
PO Box 11104
Richmond, VA 23230-1104
804-367-1146
804-367-0488 fax

Judy Pierce
Division of Fish & Wildlife
6291 Estate Nazareth 101
St. Thomas, VI 00802-1104
340-775-6762
sula@vitelcom.net

Appendix B - Federal, Provincial, State, Airline and Other Contact Information

Peggy Crain
Dept of Fish & Wildlife
600 Capitol Way N
Olympia, WA 98501-1091
360-902-2513
crainpsc@dfw.wa.gov

Wildlife Permit Officer
Div of Natural Resources
Wildlife Resources
1900 Kanawha Blvd, Bldg 3, Rm 816
Charleston, WV 25305
304-558-2771

Wildlife Veterinarian-J Langenberg
DNR Bureau of Wildlife Management
Box 7921, 101 S Webster St
Madison, WI 53707-7921
608-266-3143
608-267-7857 fax
julia.langenberg@dnr.state.wi.us

Law Enforcement Coordinator
Game & Fish Dept
5400 Bishop Blvd
Cheyenne, WY 82006
307-777-4579

Airline Websites for Shipping Animals ~ Airlines that Ship Pets

Alaskan Airlines
www2.alaskaair.com/cargo/AS_QX_SpecialHandling.asp#Animals
Customer Service (cargo) 1-800-225-2752

All Nippon Airways (Japanese)
http://www.fly-ana.com/services/special_needs/travel_pets.php
1-800-2FLY-ANA

Aloha Air
http://www.alohaairlines.com/aq/CargoSpecialServices.shtml
Cargo Customer Service (Toll-Free) (888) 94ALOHA

Air Canada
http://www.aircanada.com/services/luggage/pets.html
1-888-689-2247

Air France
Air France frequently asked questions about traveling with pets. http://www.airfrance.com

Air New Zealand
http://www.airnz.co.nz/travelinfo/travelsupport/traveltips/baggage.htm
Domestic pets up to 32kgs (animal and cage total) may be carried as checked baggage on all domestic services. 64-9-357-3000

AirTrans Airways
http://www.airtran.com/info/faq/index.jsp
The weight of the pet plus enclosure cannot exceed 15 pounds.
1-800-AIR-TRAN

America West Airlines
http://www.americawest.com/services/travelpolicies/sv_pets.htm
1-800-2FLY-AWA

American Airlines
www.aacargo.com/shipping/instructions/animals.htm
1-800-334-5299

American Trans Air
http://www.ata.com/flifo/beforeyoufly.html#animals
1-800-435-9282

British Airways
http://www.britishairways.com/travel/pet/public/en_
1-800-403-0882

Continental Airlines
http://www.cocargo.com/cocargo/CargoPages/liveanim.asp
1-800-421-2456

Delta
www.delta.com/travel/trav_serv/pet_travel/index.jsp
Delta Pet First - 800-DL-CARGO (800-352-2746)

Frontier Airlines
http://www.frontierairlines.com/faq/index.asp#PP
1-800-432-1859

Hawaiian Airlines
http://www.hawaiianair.com/cargo/pets/
1-800-882-8811

Japan Airlines
http://www.japanair.com/e/travelplan/special_pets.php
1-800-JAL-FONE (525-3663)

Korean Air
http://www.koreanair.com/Miscellaneous/btmn_faq.html#14
1-866-782-2746

Lufthansa
http://cms.lufthansa.com/za/fly/en/gnf/0,3278,0-0-567780,00.html
1-800-645-3880

Northwest Airlines
www.nwa.com/services/shipping/cargo/products/ppet.shtml
1-800-800-1504

Singapore Airlines
http://www.singaporeair.com/saa/app/saa
1-800-742-8474

Spirit Airlines
http://www.spiritair.com/general.cfm#PETS
1-800-772-7117

United Airlines
www.ual.com/page/middlepage/0,1454,1047,00.html
1-800-864-8331

US Airways
US Airways accepts live animals for unattended cargo shipment.
1-800-943-5436

APPENDIX C ~ FORMS

This Appendix has a variety of forms that may help in recordkeeping of various aspects of housing, management, training, and medical treatment of educational animals.

Medications form was reprinted with permission from Wolf Ridge Environmental Learning Center, Finland, MN and modified from the Minnesota Zoological Gardens, Apple Valley, MN.

Daily cleaning and "major" cleaning/disinfection schedules are reprinted with permission from the Minnesota Zoological Gardens, World of Birds Show, Apple Valley, MN.

Checklists for training new handlers for the education animals were reprinted with permission from The Minnesota Zoological Gardens, World of Birds Show, Apple Valley, MN, Wolf Ridge Environmental Learning Center, and modified from The Minnesota Zoological Gardens, World of Birds Show, Apple Valley, MN.

Receiving or the disposition of an animal to another facility reprinted with permission from Wolf Ridge Environmental Learning Center, Finland, MN.

Daily record charts reprinted with permission from Wolf Ridge Environmental Learning Center and modified from the Minnesota Zoological Gardens, Apple Valley, MN.

Educational programs for state and federal educational permits reprinted with permission from the Minnesota Zoological Gardens, World of Birds Show, Apple Valley, MN.

Volunteer training checklists reprinted with permission from The Raptor Center, University of Minnesota.

MEDICATION FORM

Animal _____

Start and end dates: _____

Medication and its concentration (if known) _____

Dosage to give _____

How often to give: ☐ once/day ☐ twice/day ☐ three times/day ☐ refer to instructions

How to give: ☐ orally ☐ IM (intramuscular injection) ☐ Force-feed ☐ Other _____

Instructions: _____
_____

_____

Date	TX 1	TX 2	TX 3	Date	TX 1	TX 2	TX 3

Appendix C: Forms

CLEANING GENERAL BIRDS

DAILY CLEANING

1. Change water for each bird
2. Hose and scrub* floor and squeegee dry
3. Wash clean cage bottoms with hose (if bird is not frightened)
4. Empty drains
5. Fill out charts for each bird
6. Make any necessary repairs on perches or cages
7. Prepare diets
8. Wash dishes
9. Fill any supplies that you empty (food, soap, towels, etc.)

MAJOR (ONCE/WEEK)

1. Do everything from Daily Cleaning list plus:
2. Clean cage grates – remove if you can and scrub.
3. Hose, scrub* clean and disinfect (disinfectant must be left on for 10 minutes) floors, rinse and squeegee dry
4. Pull drain covers and clean
5. Empty and clean drains
6. Wipe down counters/clean sinks
7. Fill soap, paper towel, newspaper, soap, disinfectant, water containers, and seed containers
8. Give baths (Fall/Winter/Spring) on Thursdays
9. Change toys
10. Check supplies and refill as needed (seeds, soap, towels, etc.)
11. Wipe down all counters (vinegar works well)

> *** Important notes: You have a few choices when you are scrubbing the floor clean and/or disinfecting. You can:**
> 1. Use water, scrub brush and elbow grease to clean floor
> 2. Use Acid Detergent® or Simple Green® to scrub the floor clean. If you use a cleaner, follow label instructions. More is NOT better!
> 3. Disinfectant is NOT a cleaner. Area that needs disinfecting needs to be cleaned of organic matter—fecal material, food, etc.—for disinfectant to be effective. Know how to use disinfectant. Again, using MORE is NOT better! For Unicide you need to leave on the surface to be disinfected for 10 minutes for disinfectant to be most effective.

RAPTOR ROOM CLEANING

DAILY CLEANING

1. Clean water pans in room if necessary
2. Clean center aisle way if necessary
3. Make any necessary repairs on perches if necessary
4. Empty de-humidifier (in summer)
5. Prepare diets
6. Pick up any molted feathers and castings
7. Fill in charts
8. Bring bird outside to weather if temp/weather appropriate

MAJOR CLEANING (TWICE/WEEK)

1. Everything from above list, plus:
2. All birds should be weighed and feet/beak/feathers and equipment checked – this should be written in chart
3. All birds should be crated or weathered outside
4. All mats should be pulled from room
5. All water pans cleaned and disinfected, rinsed and filled
6. Perches hand–cleaned if necessary but not soaked with water or disinfectant
7. Floors and each cubicle should be washed, cleaned, disinfected (disinfectant left on for 10 minutes), washed clean of disinfectant and squeegee dry
8. Put clean Dri-Dek (on bottom cubes), and mats in all cubicles
9. Fill any disinfectant or cleaner that needs to be refilled

Note: twice/week during summer water pans/perches in the Weathering Area need to be cleaned and moved. Do this first before moving/weighing birds

* **Important notes: You have a few choices when you are scrubbing the floor clean and/or disinfecting. You can:**
1. Use water, scrub brush and elbow grease to clean floor
2. Use Acid Detergent or Simple Green to scrub the floor clean. If you use a cleaner, follow label instructions. More is NOT better!
3. Disinfectant is NOT a cleaner. Area that needs disinfecting needs to be cleaned of organic matter—fecal material, food, etc.—for disinfectant to be effective. Know how to use disinfectant. Again, using MORE is NOT better! For Unicide you need to leave on the surface to be disinfected for 10 minutes for disinfectant to be most effective.

Appendix C: Forms

SMALL MAMMAL ROOM CLEANING

DAILY CLEANING

1. Hallway should be cleaned of debris (picking up or washing down floor and squeegee)
2. Toys changed out for different ones if time
3. Mammal cages paper changed
4. Mammal waters filled if less than half full
5. Mammal hide boxes changed if dirty/torn or no longer inhabitable
6. Fill in charts

MAJOR CLEANING

1. Mammals should be weighed, remarked and in put in travel crates
2. Mammal cages need to be pulled apart, scrubbed, rinsed and disinfected. (Disinfectant needs to stay on for 10 minutes) then dry with a towel
3. Put mammal cages back together including labels, paper lining, and boxes
4. Give mammals fresh water
5. Compost wood shavings in travel crates
6. Clean, rinse, disinfect, rinse and dry travel crates
7. Refill travel crates with new shavings

> *** Important notes: You have a few choices when you are scrubbing the floor clean and/or disinfecting. You can:**
> 1. Use water, scrub brush and elbow grease to clean floor
> 2. Use Acid Detergent or Simple Green to scrub the floor clean. If you use a cleaner, follow label instructions. More is NOT better!
> 3. Disinfectant is NOT a cleaner. Area that needs disinfecting needs to be cleaned of organic matter—fecal material, food, etc.—for disinfectant to be effective. Know how to use disinfectant. Again, using MORE is NOT better! For Unicide you need to leave on the surface to be disinfected for 10 minutes for disinfectant to be most effective.

BIG BIRD ROOM CLEANING

DAILY CLEANING

1. Crate or shift animal
2. Power wash or wash with hose entire floor of cage and any perches that are dirty
3. Replace/repair any part of the cage/perches as necessary
4. Squeegee floors inside or outside
5. Change waters if necessary
6. Fill in daily charts
7. Bring bird outside if temperature/weather allows

MAJOR CLEANING

1. Do everything in Daily Cleaning list plus:
2. After you have washed floors/walls/perches, disinfect floor (disinfectant needs to stay on for 10 minutes) and any Dri-Dek™ that may be there
3. Pull any mats that may be on the floor, and when finished cleaning and disinfecting, replace mats with clean ones
4. Scrub/disinfect water pans and rinse VERY well and fill with clean water
5. Change toys if bird has any

> *** Important notes: You have a few choices when you are scrubbing the floor clean and/or disinfecting. You can:**
> 1. Use water, scrub brush and elbow grease to clean floor
> 2. Use Acid Detergent or Simple Green to scrub the floor clean. If you use a cleaner, follow label instructions. More is NOT better!
> 3. Disinfectant is NOT a cleaner. Area that needs disinfecting needs to be cleaned of organic matter—fecal material, food, etc.—for disinfectant to be effective. Know how to use disinfectant. Again, using MORE is NOT better! For Unicide you need to leave on the surface to be disinfected for 10 minutes for disinfectant to be most effective.

Appendix C: Forms

ANIMAL MANAGEMENT GOALS/ACCOMPLISHMENTS

Date indicates step is done

Checkmark indicates all steps are done

Responsibility	Intro	w/Assist	Unassisted	Integrated	Comments
RAPTORS					
Minor clean					
Major clean					
Diets					
MAT WASHING					
EQUIPMENT					
Leather jesses					
Leather bracelets					
Nylon jesses					
Nylon leashes					
TRAINING					
EDUCATION					
Scouts					
Summer camp					
SHOW					
AM setup					
Releases					
Cues					
Videocam					
Music					
Gates					
Catch/Release					
Set up					
Take down					
THE CART					

WILDLIFE IN EDUCATION: *A Guide for the Care and Use of Program Animals*

ANIMAL MANAGEMENT GOALS/ACCOMPLISHMENTS

Name_____ Start date_____ Date completed_____

Date indicates when step was started.   Initials indicate instructor.   Checkmark indicates all steps are finished.

Responsibility	Intro	w/Assist	Unassisted	Integrated	Comments
Cleaning mews					
Winter					
Summer					
Cleaning					
Mats					
Perches					
Pans					
Preparing food					
Reading food chart					
Deciding on food amounts					
Pulling food					
Opening in AM					
Closing in PM					
Writing in log					
Writing in daily charts					
Making equipment					
Paracord jesses					
Leather jesses					
Extenders					
Leashes					
Eagle size					
Owl size					
Merlin size					
Giving baths					
Casting a bird					

Appendix C: Forms

ANIMAL HANDLING GOALS/ACCOMPLISHMENTS

Name_____ Start date_____ Date completed_____

Date indicates when step was started.   Initials indicate instructor.   Checkmark indicates all steps are finished.

Bird/step	Intro	W/Assist	Unassisted	Integrated	Comments
Falconer's knot					
Bird equipment					
Intro to training					
Handler safety					
Bird safety					
Proper handling techniques					
Proper tethering techniques					
Intro bating					
Bird 1 Handle					
Weigh					
Crate					
Bate					
Present					
Feeding					
Check feet					
Bird 2 Handle					
Weigh					
Crate					
Bate					
Present					
Feeding					
Check feet					
Bird 3 Handle					
Weigh					
Crate					
Bate					
Present					
Feeding					
Check feet					
Bird 4 Handle					
Weigh					
Crate					
Bate					
Present					
Feeding					

WILDLIFE IN EDUCATION: *A Guide for the Care and Use of Program Animals*

RAPTOR INFORMATION TRANSFER

Federal education permit numbers: _____

State education permit number: _____

Date: _____
Bird: _____
Bird name/identification: _____

Band #: _____
DOB/age: _____

Transferring to (include address/phone and contact person):
_____
_____
_____
_____

Federal permit number(s): _____
State permit numbers: _____

Transfer reason: _____
_____
_____

History: _____
_____
_____

Medical history past and present: _____
_____
_____
_____

Weights and food amounts: _____
Contacted (date): ❑ USFWS _____ ❑ DNR _____ ❑ Other _____
Comments:

Appendix C: Forms

RAPTOR ADMISSION AND RESOLUTION FORM

Federal education permit numbers:_____
State education permit number: _____

ADMISSION TO PROGRAM

Date of arrival: _____   Contacted (date): ☐USFWS_____   ☐DNR_____   ☐Other_____

Species common name: _____
Scientific name: _____
Call name/identification: _____

Acquired from: _____address/phone:_____

Band # _____   DOB_____   Age _____

Good weight(s): _____
_____

History:_____
_____

Medical issues upon arrival:_____
_____

Training previous to arrival:_____
_____

RESOLUTION FOR BIRD AND PROGRAM

Date:_____
Bird:_____

_____Died   1. Contacted (date): ☐USFWS_____   ☐DNR_____   ☐Other_____
             2. Necropsied Y N   If Yes, where and results: _____
             3. Disposal method _____
_____Transferred
             1. To whom: _____
             2. Their Federal permit number(s) _____ and State _____
             3. Why? _____
_____Lost
Comments:

WILDLIFE IN EDUCATION

WILDLIFE IN EDUCATION: *A Guide for the Care and Use of Program Animals*

RAPTOR DAILY RECORD CHART

	cast	beak	feet	talons	equip	bath	comments	initial
1								
2								
3								
4								
5								
6								
7								
8								
9								
10								
11								
12								
13								
14								
15								
16								
17								
18								
19								
20								
21								
22								
23								
24								
25								
26								
27								
28								
29								
30								
31								

Bird _____ **Month/Year** _____

Page _____ **of Page** _____

Appendix C: Forms

RAPTOR PROGRAMS

Permit number(s): State_____ **Federal**_____

Date	Program	Time	# Adults	#Kids	#1	#2	#3	#4	#5	Comments	Initials
	Totals this page										

Columns #1–#5 are grouped under the header "Check bird(s) used".

TRAINING PLAN PART A – ANNUAL RECORD

Accession number: Animal's Name:

Original Date/initial: Species:

Revision Date/initial: Hatch Date:

Revision Date/initial: Sex:

Revision Date/initial:

HUSBANDRY INFORMATION

qualitative diet: _____

"winter" holding: _____

"summer" holding: _____

cleaning parameters: _____

weathering parameters: _____

toys: _____

medical notes: _____

other: _____

Appendix C: Forms

TRAINING HISTORY

WEIGHT HISTORY (M = Maintenance, W = Working Weight, T = Training Weight)

Date (m/d/y)_____ Weight_____ M / W / T Comments_____

Date   Time to get to weight   Amount fed per day
_____
_____
_____
_____

BEHAVIOR HISTORY

Date   Description of behavior   Time to train   Comments
_____
_____
_____
_____

BIRD SHOW TRAINING LOG

Accession number: Animal's Name:

Sex:

Species: Original Date/initial:

Hatch Date: Revision Date/initial:

GOAL BEHAVIOR:

Date   Weight   Diet   Comments
_____
_____
_____
_____
_____
_____
_____
_____

RAPTOR WEIGHT/DIET SHEET

Day_____ Date_____ Wrote Diets_____

Sprinkle Vitahawk on each raptor's food daily

R = Rat, WR = weanling rat, Q = Quail, M = Mice,
Sck = Day Old Chick, Ck = Chicken,
T = Tablespoon, H = harrison's pelleted diet

Name	Target weight	Weight (grams)	Casts	Diet (grams)	Food consumed	Comments	Fed

Appendix C: Forms

CLINIC VOLUNTEER TRAINING CHECKLIST

NAME: _____ START DATE: _____

CREW LEADER: _____ M T W Th F Sa Su   AM PM

Each new clinic volunteer will complete the tasks listed below. The crew leader will date and initial the tasks as they are completed competently (i.e. the volunteer does not need supervision to do the task). When the tasks have been completed, this sheet will be given to the volunteer coordinator.

DATE FORMAL CLASS TRAINING COMPLETED: _____
This is usually completed before the new volunteer begins on the clinic crew.

Part I. Basics   (approximately 4 weeks)
Orientation/Administrative
_____ Has reviewed and understands the rules, legal and non-legal regulations pertaining to raptors, feathers, and the Raptor Center
_____ Understands the importance of communication with crew members and staff (alerting them to lack of or damaged equipment; a distressed or injured bird; changes in a bird's appearance, weight, or behavior)
_____ Is familiar with:
    _____Volunteer hours sheets   _____Feeding/Treatment Sheet

Food Preparation and Feeding
_____ Knows where to find frozen food and how much to thaw
_____ Knows how to thaw food
_____ Able to prepare each kind of food (gutting, rinsing, weighing)
_____ Demonstrates competency in feeding patient raptors in their cages
_____ Demonstrates competency in feeding patient raptors in flight rooms and outside areas
_____ Demonstrates competency in ability to safely control head when feeding a restrained bird
_____ Demonstrate proper handling of feeding forceps and snips (disinfect and hang to dry)

Cleaning
_____ Able to clean cages (including latches and doors) and change pads in cages
_____ Able to change perches
_____ Able to do laundry
_____ Able to clean the cardboard pads from under the cages
_____ Able to clean patient room floors including disinfecting
_____ Able to clean floor drains
_____ Able to clean hallway and food prep room floors, surfaces, door handles and windows, and light switches

CLINIC VOLUNTEER TRAINING CHECKLIST, PAGE 2

Treatment
Familiar with how to interpret Feeding/Treatment sheet
_____ Understand how to interpret the instructions for each bird
_____ Knows what each four-letter code represents, i.e. GHOW is great horned owl
_____ Understands the terms "clean meat", skinned, etc.
_____ Understands the terms "HF" (hand feed) and "FF" (force feed)

Familiar with medicating birds
_____ Knows where the medications are located
_____ Knows how to prepare and distribute them per bird
_____ Observes a crew member "pilling" a bird
_____ Able to pill raptor in a cage
_____ Able to pill raptor being held
_____ Knows how to administer various liquid medications

Part II. Bird Handling (after approximately 4 weeks or as determined by the crew leader)

____ Observes several experienced people grabbing, weighing, and holding birds for examination by clinic staff
____ Demonstrates ability to grab GHOWs from their cages
____ Demonstrates ability to weigh a bird
____ Demonstrates ability to hold a bird for examination
____ Demonstrates above skills for:
    ____ Small birds
    ____ Owls
    ____ Buteos
    ____ Accipiters
    ____ Peregrines

After the volunteer has completed these tasks, other skills can be developed such as grabbing more difficult raptors and grabbing birds from flight rooms and outdoor pens.

A person who is trained to grab eagles:
- Has been an active, consistent clinic crew member for a minimum of one year
- Demonstrates good handling techniques with more difficult raptors
- Meets clinic staff approval.

Appendix C: Forms

FLIGHT VOLUNTEER TRAINING CHECKLIST

NAME: _____ START DATE: _____
CREW LEADER: _____ M T W Th F Sa Su   AM PM

Each new flight volunteer will complete the tasks listed below. The crew leader will date and initial the tasks as they are completed competently (i.e. the volunteer does not need supervision to do the task). When the tasks have been completed, this sheet will be given to the volunteer coordinator.

DATE FORMAL CLASS TRAINING COMPLETED: _____
This is usually completed before the new volunteer begins on the flight crew.

Part I. Basics (approximately 2 weeks)
Orientation/Administrative
_____Has reviewed and understands the rules, legal and non-legal regulations pertaining to raptors, feathers, and the Raptor Center
_____Understands the importance of communication with crew members and staff (alerting them to lack of or damaged equipment; a distressed or injured bird; changes in a bird's appearance, weight, or behavior)
_____Is familiar with various forms:
　　　____Volunteer hours sheets　　　____Bird Observation forms　　　____Shift report
_____Has reviewed emergency procedures:
　　　____Bird becomes loose in the laundry room　　____Bird is injured
　　　____Bird gets in trouble in the field　　____Volunteer is injured
_____Is familiar with equipment and their use:
　　　____Jess　　____Extender/creance　　____Hoods　　____Water bottle
_____Demonstrates competent use of safety equipment (glasses, goggles, gloves, vests)
_____Has observed other crew members performing various functions:
　　　____Weighing birds　　____Feather checks　　____Capturing birds　　____Flying birds
　　　____Cleaning pens　　____Returning birds to flight rooms/pens
Cleaning (outdoor cages in suitable weather)
_____Able to remove old food and change water
_____Able to brush and hose pens

Part II. Bird Handling (approximately 4-6 weeks)
Participation with Supervision
_____Jess up bird for flight
_____Conduct feather check
_____Check crop
_____Clean outdoor flight pens including picking up old food (if weather is suitable)
_____Cool down a bird
_____Weigh a bird
_____Restrain bird on table for flight preparation or staff treatment
_____Correctly release a bird into a flight room/outdoor flight pen
_____Capture a bird from indoor flight room
_____Capture a bird from outdoor flight pen
_____Participate in flying a bird (handling the bird and the line)
_____Perform proper technique for checking feet

After the volunteer has completed these tasks, other skills can be developed.
A person who is trained for Eagle Flight Crew:
• Has been an active, consistent flight crew member for a minimum of one year

ENRICHMENT FORM EXAMPLE

Day of the Week	Item Used	Not Done	Done	Rating	Comments
	Place food around mew				Please do not put food on the floor, use perches or platforms
	Take out on zoo grounds				
	Pine cone with bird of prey diet				Use 5 g or less
	Cardboard tube with mouse visible from ends				Make sure food has been eaten before leaving for the day
	Miscellaneous enrichment				Choose one: feed on glove or man on glove
	1 ice cube on platform				
	Red flying saucer toy with mice halves in openings				
	Small piece of browse				Try to find browse with just a few leaves; remove from mew if the animal is eating the leaves
	No enrichment today				
	Large, open box with 1 to 2 mice clearly visible				Put box securely on platform so the animal will not fall off when it lands
	Feed on glove				
	Perch in hall while cleaning				
	No enrichment today				
	Multiple feedings – part of diet in am, part in pm				

Rating Scale: 0 = avoidance; 1 = little or no interest; 2 = some interest; 3 = very interested

APPENDIX D – MANUFACTURER'S INFORMATION

Adams®	Glaxosmithkline, Research Triangle Park, NC	Dexamethazone (Azium®)	Schering-Plough Animal Health Corp., Union, NJ
Adaptic®	Johnson & Johnson Medical, Division of Ethicon, Inc., Arlington, TX	Diff-Quik®	American Scientific Products, McGraw Park, IL
		Dri-Dek®	Kendall Products, Naples, FL
Ampicillin (Ployflex®)	Fort Dodge Laboratories, Overland Park, KS	Duoderm®	Convatec, Skillman, NJ
Augmentin® (Amoxicillin + Clavulonic acid)	Glaxosmithkline, Research Triangle Park, NC	Elastikon®	Johnson & Johnson, Arlington, TX
		Emeraid	Lafeber Company, Cornell, IL
Avi-Era®	Lefeber Co., Cornell, IL	Energel®	PetAg, Hampshire, IL
Baytril® (Enrofloxacin)	Bayer Corportion, Shawnee Mission, KS	Enfalyte™	Mead Johnson & Co., Evansville, IL
Beechnut Baby Food®	Beech-nut Nutrition Corp., St. Louis, MO	Enrofloxacin (Baytril®)	Bayer Corp, Shawnee Mission, KS
Bene Bac®	PetAg, Hampshire, IL	Ensure	Ross Pharmaceuticals, Columbus, OH
Betadine®	Purdue Fredrick Company, Norwalk, CT		
Bioclusive®	Johnson & Johnson Medical, Division of Ethicon, Inc., Arlington, TX	Eukanuba®	The Iams Co., Dayton, OH
		Furacin®	Boehringer Ingelheim GmbH, Germany
Cara-Klenz™	Carrington Labs, Irving, TX	Furazolidone (synthetic Nitrofuran derivative)	Vet Products Laboratories, Phoenix, AZ
Carbaryl	generic name of Sevin®		
Catac Nipples	Catac Products, Ltd., Bedford, England		
		Gator Aid®	Stokeley-Van Camp, Chicago, IL
Centrum®	Wyeth Consumer Health, Madison, NJ	Isotone SA	VetaMix, Shenandoah, IA
Clavamox®	Pfizer Animal Health, New York, NY	Isocal®	MeadJohnson, Evansville, IL
		Karo®	ACH Food Companies, Memphis, TN
Co-Flex®	Wheaten Brace Co., Carol Stream, IL	Kaopectate®	Pharmacia Corp., Peapack, NJ
CVMD® (foam and dressing) NOTE: these products are now called:		KMR®	PetAg, Hampshire, IL
CaraFoam™	Carington Veterinary Medical Division, Irving, TX	Knox® Blox	Gelita North America, Sioux City, IA
CarraWash™	Carington Veterinary Medical Division, Irving, TX	K-Y Jelly ®	Johnson & Johnson Medical, Division of Ethicon, Inc., Arlington, TX

LabDiet®	Purina Mills International, Brentwood, MO	Purina ProPlan®	Purina Mills, Inc., St. Louis, MO
Lactated Ringers®	Abbott Laboratories, Libertyville, IL	Ricelyte® No longer made under this name – now Enfalyte™	Rubbermaid, Inc. Wooster, OH
Mazuri®	Purina Mills, St. Louis, MO		
Methylene Blue (multiple manufacturers:	Volu–Sol, Inc., Salt Lake City, UT;	Science Diet®	Hill's Pet Nutrition, Topeka, KS
	ASP, McGraw Park, IL;	Seatabs®	Pacific Research Labs, CA
	Fisher Scientific Col., Pittsburgh, PA,	Sevin®	Aventis Environmental Science, Raleigh, NC
	and others)	Silvadene®	Monarch Pharmaceuticals,
Multisol-R®	DHL Laboratories, Union, SC	(Silver sulfadiazine)	Bristol, TN
Nolvasan® (Chlorhexidine)	Fort Dodge Animal Health, Overland Park, KS	Sovereign® (syringes)	Monojet Div., Sherwood Davis & Geck, St. Louis, MO
Normosol®	Johnson & Johnson Medical, Division of Ethicon, Inc., Arlington, TX	Stomaheal® Stomahesive	Bristol-Myers Squib, New York, NY
		Sundown® (vitamins)	Rexall Sundown, Boca Raton, FL
Nutri-cal®	EVSCO Pharmaceuticals, Buena, NJ	Tek-Trol	Agri Labs, St. Joseph, MO
Osmolite®	Ross Pharmaceuticals, Columbus, OH	Tegaderm™	3M Healthcare, St. Paul, MN
Ovitrol®	Vet-Kem, Schaumberg, IL	Velcro®	Velcro USA Inc., Manchester, NH
Panacure®	Hoechst, Roussel, Agri-Vet Co., Kansas City, MO	Vetrap™	3M Healthcare, St. Paul, MN
Pedialyte®	Abbott Laboratories, Libertyville, IL	Vionate®	ARC Laboratories, Atlanta, GA
Pepto Bismol®	Proctor & Gamble, Cincinnati, OH	Vitahawk®	D.B. Scientific, Oakley, CA
Pharmaseal® (syringe)	American Hospital Supply, Silver Spring, MD	Wet-pruf®	The Kendall Company, Mansfield, MA
Piperacillin	Wyeth-Ayerst/Lederle Laboratories, Inc., Peach River, NY	Wright's-Geimsa®	(multiple manufacturers: Volu-Sol, Inc., Salt Lake City, UT; ASP, McGraw Park, IL; Fisher Scientific Co., Pittsburgh, PA, and others)
Playtex Nurser®	Playtex, Westport, CT		
Ployflex®	Fort Dodge Laboratories, Overland Park, KS		
		Zoologic®	PetAg, Hampshire, IL

APPENDIX E – EXAMPLE OF EDUCATION ANIMAL RECORD SET
(Academy of Natural Sciences, Philadelphia, PA)

Life History
Brown Rats (aka Norway Rats)
(Family: Muridae Scientific: *Rattus norvegicus*)

Distribution: Nearly worldwide, having been introduced to many continents and islands via ships and other means of transport.

Habitat: Highly adaptable, living in fields, barns, houses, sewers, among rocky outcrops, and wherever food and shelter are plentiful

Description: Length: 14 to18 inches; tail nearly as long as the body. Males (bucks) can be almost three times the size of females (does), weighing 1 to 1.5 lbs. Brown rats are typically a dark brown; however, black and albino rats are found occasionally in the wild. In captivity, there are numerous variations due to selective breeding, including albinos, hoodeds, silvers, agoutis, rexes, and more. The brown rat has a rather blunt muzzle, small fuzzy ears, and a naked tail.

Reproduction: Very prolific. Gestation (pregnancy) lasts 21 to 23 days and some does can have up to 5 litters per year. Number of offspring per litter varies from 1 to 20 (ave. 8). Rat babies are called "pups" or "kittens." They are born blind, deaf, and naked. Females nurse the pups for 3 to 4 weeks, after which the young are eating solid food and foraging on their own. (In large litters, young may suckle for six weeks.) Reach sexual maturity by eight weeks!

Longevity: 1 to 4 years. Albino rats typically live only 1 to 1.5 years, whereas "fancy" rats can live longer. Average age is 2 to 2.5 years. Females tend to live longer.

Diet in wild: Omnivores. Corn, wheat, other cereal crops (in field and stored), bird and reptile eggs, insects, fruit, vegetables, grass seeds, tubers, carrion, and human refuse. Rats will kill nestling birds, small frogs, small snakes, and other easily captured prey when available.

Natural History Facts:
- Brown rats were "domesticated" sometime in the 1800s presumably for both their benefits as laboratory specimens and as unusual pets. Some of the color mutations of the fancy rats were created at this time.
- The term "fancy rat" implies a rat of domestic origin which has been bred for a certain color pattern; they are the same species as their wild cousins, but have undergone breeding selection.
- Rats have a well-defined colony structure and generally forage in packs, although some will live/forage alone. They communicate by a series of ultrasonic squeaks and low grunts, inaudible to the human ear.
- Rats have "pecking orders" which are maintained through body posturing and stances. Fighting is generally avoided, but dominant rats will fight challengers (occasionally killing them). Males also leave small scent traces of urine wherever they go to mark territory.
- Rats are members of the order Rodentia. It is the most ancient mammalian order to inhabit this planet, originating some 70 million years ago towards the end of the Cretaceous period (during the time of dinosaurs). This order accounts for around 40 percent of all mammalian species. Over 1700 species have been classified to date.
- All rodents are characterized by their chisel-like incisor teeth, which are used to gnaw. The name "rodent" is derived from the latin verb rodere, "to gnaw." The incisors are ever-growing, and in captivity must be worn down by chewing on wood and other hard objects. Most rodents are herbivores or omnivores, with robust skulls and quite massive jaw muscles.
- Brown rats originated in Asia (not Norway) and travelled over land and by ship to many parts of the world. Early scholars believed that rats came back to England with the Crusaders (on their ships); however, more recent findings indicate that rats were already well-established in England by this time. In fact, it may have been the Romans that helped them spread initially.
- Wild rats sometimes carry fleas which can be infected with the bacterium which causes bubonic plague.
- Name means: *Rattus* = rat; *norvegicus* = of Norway

GENERAL CARE

General Rat Housing and Husbandry

Housing for Rats:
A store bought cage is acceptable. The entire cage should be as large as you can get it. A good cage is at least 1 x 2 ft. (0.305 x 0.61 m) per animal, minimum. The larger the house, the happier and healthier your rat will be. Be sure it is either an aquarium type enclosure or of material that the rat cannot chew through. Bottom should be solid. There should be ample bedding on the bottom at least 2 to 3 in. (5.08 to 7.62 cm) deep. Pine and aspen shavings and recycled paper are acceptable bedding. Cedar shavings should never be used. Inside the enclosure there should be room enough for a water dish, feeding area, a wheel for exercise, a hide box, several chew toys, and any other fun furniture that you see fit. Changing the "furniture" in the enclosure will keep the rats stimulated and happy. Be sure anything you place in the enclosure is safe to chew. If keeping multiple rats, be aware that "intact" males will fight and male/female combinations will produce many rats in a very short amount of time. Males can easily be altered.

Rat diet (Johnson-Delaney 1996)

Rodent chow (seed based diets are inadequate to meet a rat's nutritional requirements)	2 to 4 "blocks" per rat Crude protein 20 to 27 percent
Apple slice – 0.5 x 0.5 in. (1.26 x 1.26 cm) chunk	Pectin aids bowel function; Fructose (fruit-sugar) is easily digestible to rats.
Carrot slice – 0.5 in. (1.26 cm) chunk	Vitamin A source; tooth wear
1 Tbsp of Treats – dried fruits, seeds, nuts, other fruits and vegetables	Provide a variety of trace minerals and vitamins, as well as enrichment

- Fresh vegetables and fruits are a welcome addition to any diet plan. They provide dietary water, fiber, vitamins, and minerals, plus satisfy hunger and the urge to chew and forage without adding excess calories.

- Rats have a tendency towards obesity, so keep the high-calorie foods, such as seeds and nuts, to a minimum. Moreover, excess protein has been associated with some types of tumors in rats.

- Put treats in a treat ball that dispenses food when rolled around for a great enrichment idea. Suitably-sized treat balls are sold for ferrets and cats.

Appendix E – Example of Education Animal Record Set

GENERAL CLEANING

GENERAL CLEANING AND SANITATION PROTOCOLS

- Separate cleaning supplies should be designated for different groups of animals (i.e., reptiles, mammals, birds, etc.)

- Sponges should be replaced at minimum once a month.

- Scrub brushes should be replaced at minimum once every six months.

- ONLY paper towels should be used to clean the enclosures of sick or newly acquired animals. Rags and sponges can transmit disease and parasites to other animals.

- Only disinfectants approved may be used in animal enclosures.
    1. Nolvasan™ (blue) – use for reptiles, amphibians, fish, and invertebrate enclosures
    2. Roccal-D™ (green) – use for bird and mammal enclosures
    3. Dishwashing liquid – use to clean food and water bowls
    4. Chlorine bleach – use to disinfect enclosure accessories, food and water bowls, holding cages, etc. (Items MUST be thoroughly rinsed and allowed to dry for at least 24 hours before re-using.)
    5. Vinegar – use to remove mineral deposits and urine stains and to clean fingerprints off glass tanks

- Any NEW cleaning products to be used should be reviewed by full-time staff in charge of animal collection. (Many commercially available, general-type cleaning products can be toxic to certain types of animals!)

- Any utensils, counter tops, and sinks used for animal food preparation should be cleaned thoroughly after each use.

- Enclosures and carriers for animals should be cleaned after each use.

- Water bottles used in rat enclosures should be cleaned a minimum of once a week with a bottle brush and sanitized with a dilute chlorine bleach solution at least once/month (soak for at least 30 minutes, then rinse very thoroughly, let dry 24 hours before reuse.)

SPECIFIC CLEANING

Cleaning Education Rat Enclosures

Equipment Needed:

Dustpan or scoop
Bucket with warm water
Cleaning rag or sponge
Disinfectant
Hand broom
Aspen, Pine or paper bedding

Procedure for SPOT CLEAN: every day that you do not complete clean

1. Place rats into appropriate carrier, lined with black-and-white newspaper only.

2. Empty water bowl/bottle.

3. Scrub water bowl/bottle with dishwashing liquid and designated scrubber. Refill with cold water.

4. Using either a dustpan or scoop, remove wet, soiled bedding and fecal "pellets." (HINT: Dry fecals can often be scraped off the top layer of bedding.)

5. "Fluff" remaining bedding and spread out to fill in areas where bedding was removed. Add fresh bedding if needed to cover bottom of cage.

6. Return water bowl to enclosure.

7. Sweep off the front and sides of enclosure. Wipe off metal if needed.

Procedure for COMPLETE CLEAN: 2 to 3 times per week

1. Place rats into appropriate carrier, lined with black-and-white newspaper only.

2. Empty water bowl/bottle in sink.

3. Scrub water bowl with dishwashing liquid and designated scrubber. Refill with cold water.

4. Remove all hideboxes, wooden chew blocks, and other enrichment items (toys) from enclosure.

5. Discard wet or soiled cardboard.

6. Wash plastic toys and hideboxes with dishwashing liquid and scrubber.

7. Rinse or hose off metal wheel.

8. Using large dustpan, remove all bedding from bottom of tank.

9. Using small dust broom or scraper, remove all stuck-on pine shavings or feces.

10. Spray entire cage thoroughly with Roccal-D™ disinfectant (green disinfectant).

11. Using wet sponge or cloth, wipe cage inside and out. Rinse your sponge or rag in bucket, and go over trays again until clean.

12. Refill tray with fresh bedding to about 2 to 3 in. (5.08 to 7.62 cm) depth.

13. Return all hideboxes and toys (except those you discarded or put into laundry). You can also add shredded black-and-white newspaper.

14. Give fresh water.

15. Return rats to enclosure.

Appendix E – Example of Education Animal Record Set

HANDLING

SPECIES-SPECIFIC ANIMAL HANDLING INSTRUCTIONS:

Domestic rats:
1. Rats are very curious and agile creatures. They will be more interested in checking out their handler than staying still.

2. Most rats that have been handled will readily climb into the handlers hands. Be sure they do not jump or fall out of your hands.

3. Always wear protective gloves.

4. If the rat needs to be picked up, put one hand under the belly and with the other grasp the base of the tail. Gently lift the rat out of the enclosure. Always grasp the base of the tail and never support the rat's full weight by the tail, as this will cause injury.

5. Rest the rat across one hand and forearm.

6. If the rat turns toward the guests, use this opportunity to show the face.

7. Give the rat a couple of minutes to check out its handler before a program.

8. Wash hands.

SIGNS OF ILLNESS, INJURY, AND/OR STRESS IN ANIMALS

HINT #1: Become familiar with individual animals and their histories. You will have an easier time identifying abnormal behavior if you know the animal's normal behavior.

HINT #2: Become familiar with a species' natural history. What does it eat? How does it express "pleasure"? How does it play? What is normal posture?

MAMMALS – general signs and symptoms

- Bleeding from any part of the body

- Black or red urine (rabbit urine can be very dark orange or reddish due to foods in diet)

- Loose stools (watery, discolored, or "mushy" stools that cake around the bottom)
    – rabbits have both hard, round stools and softer, "grape-like" clusters called cecals;
    – guinea pigs and rats have soft, oblong stools that harden as they dry

- Discharge from the eyes, ears, nose or mouth
    – rats sometimes have a reddish-brown discharge from the eyes and nose which is normal, especially in older rats

- "Hunched" appearance, especially with biting or kicking at abdomen, grinding teeth, and lack of interest in "treats"

- Limbs held at odd angles (especially if animal fell)

- Loud, intense squealing or vocalizing

- Withdrawn, sluggish disposition

- Any other behavior you have never seen (spasms, seizures, difficulty breathing, etc.)

STRESS in MAMMALS – watch for these signs

- Shivering or shaking

- Loose stools

- Biting or scratching

- Unusual vocalizing

- Excessive running, retreating, or struggling while being held, touched, or picked up.

- Heavy, rapid breathing

- Dilated pupils (especially if accompanied by above)

Appendix E – Example of Education Animal Record Set

MEDICAL CARE

VETERINARY CARE OF RATS

How to find a veterinarian for your rat
- Call local or state veterinary association and ask for list of veterinarians who treat small exotic animals

- Look through phone directory for veterinarians who specialize in exotic pets

Questions to ask prospective veterinarians
- How many rat clients does he/she currently treat?

- How does he/she feel about a rat that gets sick? Is it worth treating?

- Is there someone else who is available if he/she is away or unavailable?

First visit or annual examination should include
- Physical exam including oral

- Fecal flotation/smear (to check for parasites)

- Other tests to discuss with veterinarian:
    1. CBC and chemistries (blood counts can show infections and other health problems)
    2. Urinalysis

- No vaccinations needed

Common problems and diseases
- Various types of tumors

- Over growth of teeth or dental malocclusion

Quick Facts:
- Life span — 2 to 4 years
- Rectal temperature — 35.9 to 37.5 degrees C (99.5 to 100.6 degrees F)
- Food consumption — 10g/100g/day
- Water consumption — 10 to 12ml/100g/day
- GI transit time — 12 to 24 hours
- Respiratory rate — 70 to 115/minute
- Heart rate — 250 to 450/min
- Able to reproduce — male 65 to 110 days
  female 65 to 110 days

Literature Cited
Johnson-Delaney, C. 1996. *Exotic Companion Medicine Handbook.* Lake Worth, FL: Wingers Publishing.

Additional Reading
Critters USA, *Guide to Buying and Caring for Exotic Mammals 2001 Annual.* Irvine, CA: Fancy Publications.

Fowler, M. 1995. *Restraint and Handling of Wild and Domestic Animals.* Ames, IA: Iowa State University Press.

MacDonald, D. 2001. *The Encyclopedia of Mammals,* Oxfordshire, UK: Andromeda Oxford Limited.

Mays, N. 1993. *The Proper Care of Fancy Rats,* Neptune, NJ: T.F.H. Publications.

Nowak, R. M. 1991. *Walker's Mammals of the World, 5th Ed.,* Baltimore, MD: Johns Hopkins University Press.

Appendix F: Zoonoses

APPENDIX F ~ ZOONOSES

The following is copied from the Beginning Rehabilitation Education Workshop, and was developed by The Minnesota Wildlife Assistance Cooperative in 1999.

1. Viral Diseases
a. Rabies (*Rhabdovirus*)
i. Hosts: any warm-blooded vertebrates
1. Especially prevalent in skunks, foxes, raccoons, and bats
2. Rodents rarely involved but woodchucks account for about 70 percent of rodents testing positive

ii. Transmission is primarily via bite or scratch wounds; rarely from mucous membrane contact or vertically (mother to fetus)

b. Eastern and Western Equine Encephalitides or Sleeping Sickness (*Alphavirus*)
i. Hosts are of two types:
1. Reservoir host is mainly passerine birds
2. Dead-end hosts include horses, humans, and possibly livestock

ii. Transmission is via insect bites (especially mosquitoes: *Aedes, Culex,* and *Anopheles,* spp)

c. West Nile Encephalitis (West Nile Virus—WNV)
i. Range of hosts including birds, mammals and reptiles. The American crow and blue jay have been shown to be very sensitive to the strain of virus found in the United States although the virus has been identified in at least 160 species of birds as of 2003.
1. Dead end hosts include: horses, humans, other mammals, and reptiles.

ii. Transmission is via infected mosquitoes and other arthropods.

2. Rickettsial Diseases
a. Rocky Mountain spotted fever (*Rickettsia rickettsii*)
i. Wild rodents are the primary reservoir host
ii. Transmission is via tick bite (especially *Dermacentor variabilis* – American dog tick and *Rhipicephalus sanguineus* – brown dog tick)

b. Typhus Fever (*R. porwazekii*)
i. transmission by arthropod vectors, notable host is flying squirrel

3. Fungal Diseases (Mycoses)
a. Aspergillosis (*Aspergillus fumigatus*)
i. Hosts usually birds and small mammals
ii. Transmission is via inhalation or ingestion of airborne particles

b. Dermatophytosis ~ "Ringworm" (*Microsporum canis* or *Trichophyton mentagrophyte*)
i. Hosts include mammals and birds
ii. Transmission is via direct contact or indirect contact with hair or sloughed skin (wear gloves)

4. Bacterial Diseases
a. Anthrax (*Bacillus anthracis*) ~ NOT common, but be aware of it
i. Hosts: herbivores are susceptible, carnivores relatively resistant
ii. Infection depends on route of entry:
1. Ingestion/inhalation of spores: septicemia, rapid death characterized by respiratory distress, convulsions, collapse, bloody discharge from body openings.

4. Bacterial Diseases, continued

      2. Cutaneous (entry through skin via direct contact): swelling of lymph nodes, throat

  b. Brucellosis (*Brucella abortus*)
      i. Hosts include hoofed mammals, dogs, marine mammals, and rodents
      ii. Transmission is primarily via direct contact or ingestion

  c. Campylobacteriosis (*Campylobacter jejuni*)
      i. Hosts include ruminants, horses, canids, and felids, but wild and domestic birds are regarded as major reservoirs
      ii. Transmission is fecal-oral or in utero.

  d. Chlamydioses or Psittacosis (*Chlamydophyila psittaci*)
      i. Common in psittacine birds, but found in birds and also mammals
      ii. Transmission is via inhalation or ingestion of dust/aerosols produced by feces, urine, feather dust, carcasses
      iii. Formites can spread chlamydioses and biting insects may be important as mechanical transmission

  e. Colibacillosis (*Escherichia coli*)
      i. Hosts include mammals and birds
      ii. Transmission is fecal-oral

  f. Erysipelosis (*Erysipelothrix rhusiopathiae*)
      i. Hosts include marine mammals, suids, birds, reptiles
      ii. Transmission is via wound infection or direct contact

  g. Leptospirosis (*Leptospira interrogans*)
      i. Hosts include marine and hoofed mammals, rodents and carnivores
        1. Especially foxes, squirrels, raccoons
        2. Clinical disease rarely reported in free-ranging wildife
      ii. Transmission is via inhalation/ingestion of infected urine or urine contaminated soil, water, food; possibly crosses skin

  h. Listeriosis (*Listeria monocytogenes*)
      i. Found in rabbits, canids, birds, and ruminants, among other species
      ii. Not transmissible from animal to animal but is acquired from external environment

  i. Lyme Disease (*Borrelia burgdorferi*)
      i. Wild mammals and birds, including canids, rodents, and rabbits are reservoirs
      ii. Transmission is via tick bites (*Ixodes scapularis* – deer tick)

  j. Pasteurellosis (*Pasteurella multocida*)
      i. Hosts include mammals (especially rabbits – snuffles) and birds (especially waterfowl – avian cholera)
      ii. Transmission is via bite wounds, inhalation, or ingestion

  k. Plague (*Yersinia pestis*)
      i. Primary host is rodents, but other animals can be affected
      ii. Transmission is via bite of infected Oriental rat flea (*Xenopsylla cheopis*), or infected rodent

  l. Samonellosis (*Salmonella* spp)
      i. Hosts include most mammals, birds, reptiles
      ii. Transmission is fecal-oral or through inhalation

Appendix F: Zoonoses

4. Bacterial Diseases, continued
m. Tuberculosis *(Mycobacterium* spp)
i. Hosts are hoofed mammals and birds
ii. Transmission is via inhalation or ingestion

5. Protozoal Diseases
a. Chagas' Disease ~ American Trypanosomiasis
i. Hosts include opossum, armadillo, dogs, cats, humans
ii. Transmission is via the bite of intermediate host cone-nosed bug.

b. Cryptosporidiosis *(Cryptosporidium parvum)*
i. Host include all mammals (not very host specific); other species in birds
ii. Transmission of oocysts via fecal-oral route

c. Giardiasis *(Giardia lamblia,* possibly others)
i. Many mammals can act as hosts, especially beavers; some species of birds (probably other *Giardia* species)
ii. Transmission is via ingestion of cysts, especially in contaminated water

d. Toxoplasmosis *(Toxoplasma gondii)*
i. Facultative two-host organism
  1. Definitive host: wild and domestic felines
  2. Intermediate host: mammals, birds
ii. Transmission via ingestion of oocysts in fecal materials or tissue cysts in infected intermediate hosts

6. Parasitic Diseases
a. Ectoparasites
i. Fleas (various species on various hosts)—many will bite humans
  1. Flea bite dermatitis: hypersensitivity to flea saliva
  2. Vector disease like plague
  3. Intermediate hosts of *Dipylidium caninum* (tapeworm) and *Dipetalonema reconditum* (filarial worm)
ii. Lice—infest most animals
  1. lice are very host specific and rarely infest animals other than the preferred host
  2. Pyrethroids now most favored treatment for biting lice (wide heads)
  3. systemic Ivermectin™ works for sucking lice (narrow heads)
iii. Mites (various species on various hosts) – a few will infest humans
  1. *Cheyletiella parasitivorax*—causes scaly dermatitis, no treatment registered
  2. *Sarcoptes scabei*—causes sarcoptic mange or "scabies," inflamed crusty lesions with hair loss; systemic Ivermectin™
iv. Ticks (various species on various hosts)—most will bite humans
  1. vector many diseases (see Lyme disease, Tularemia, Rocky Mountain spotted fever)
  2. In large numbers cause blood loss, anemia
  3. damage at bite sites, susceptibility to myiasis (see *Cuterebra* below)
  4. soft-bodied ticks can be found on birds, bats—these ticks are periodic (day or night) feeders, may find in bedding or housing at other times.

b. Tapeworms
i. *Dipylidium caninum* "Double-pored tape" or flea tape—very common in free ranging carnivores
  1. intermediate hosts include fleas (*Ctenocephalus felis, C. canis, Pulex irritans*) and occasionally the biting louse *Trichodectes canis*
ii. *Echinococcus granulosus* Hydatid tapes of carnivores (esp. canids)
  1. intermediate hosts are herbivores and omnivores in which larval 'hydatid cysts' develop – especially in liver and lungs
  2. very small tapes, usually seen in large numbers

6. Parasitic Diseases, continued

c. Visceral (and Ocular) Larval Migrans (various roundworms)
  i. Several species:
   1. *Toxocara canis* in cats, dogs, wolves, foxes, coyotes, raccoons
   2. *T. cati* in cats, mountain lions, lynx, bobcats
   3. *Toxascaris leonine* in wild carnivores
   4. *Ascaris columnaris* in skunks
   5. *A. devosi* in ferrets and mink
   6. *Baylisascaris procyonis* in raccoons
  ii. In both primary and accidental hosts, the larvae of all these species migrate through various tissues, producing clinical signs; diagnosis in humans cannot be made on the basis of fecal egg counts because larvae do not mature in humans

d. Warble Flies (*Cuterebra*, Rodent bots)
  i. Hosts are rodents, lagomorphs, cattle, people (most species are host specific)
  ii. Eggs are laid on soil near burrows, larvae enter natural openings and skin when animals enter/exit burrow

7. Transmissible Spongiformes Encephalitis

a. Chronic Wasting Disease (CWD)–classified as a transmissible spongiform encephalophy or "prion" disease.
  i. Hosts: farmed and free-ranging mule deer, white-tailed deer, black-tailed deer and elk.
  ii. Transmission between animals is likely by animal-to-animal contact or contamination of food or water sources with saliva, feces, or urine from a diseased animal. Transmission to humans is not known to occur. The known prion diseases of humans and domestic animals are different than CWD.